# Marketing and Design Management

# Marketing and Design Management

Margaret Bruce
*Professor of Design Management and Marketing*
*Department of Textiles, UMIST*
and
Rachel Cooper
*Professor of Design Management*
*Research Institute for Design, Manufacturing and*
*Marketing, University of Salford*

INTERNATIONAL THOMSON BUSINESS PRESS
I ⓣ P® An International Thomson Publishing Company

London • Bonn • Boston • Johannesburg • Madrid • Melbourne • Mexico City • New York • Paris
Singapore • Tokyo • Toronto • Albany, NY • Belmont, CA • Cincinnati, OH • Detroit, MI

**Marketing and Design Management**

**Copyright ©1997 Margaret Bruce and Rachel Cooper**

First published by International Thomson Business Press

I(T)P   A division of International Thomson Publishing Inc.
        The ITP logo is a trademark under licence

*British Library Cataloguing-in-Publication Data*
A catalogue record for this book is available from the British Library

**First edition 1997**

Typeset by J & L Composition Ltd, Filey, North Yorkshire
Printed in the UK by TJ International, Cornwall

**ISBN 1-86152-173-1**

International Thomson Business Press      International Thomson Business Press
Berkshire House                          20 Park Plaza
168–173 High Holborn                     13th Floor
London WC1V 7AA                          Boston MA 02116
UK                                       USA

**http://www.itbp.com**

*For Steve Glennon, Cary, Laura and Sarah Cooper.*

# Contents

# List of figures

# List of tables

# Preface

As long ago as 1984, Kotler and Rath advocated that marketing took account of design. This is succinctly expressed in their statement that design 'creates corporate distinctiveness in an otherwise product and image surfeited marketplace. It can create a personality . . . so it stands out . . . It communicates value to the customer, makes selection easier, informs and entertains (Kotler and Rath 1984: 17).' Design is a valuable marketing tool devoted to visual problem-solving. Design can differentiate products and services, can add value and create a unique selling proposition and stimulate desire and interest. Design can be used by manufacturing, retail and service organizations of all sizes, in all sectors, and by public and private entities. Design covers all aspects of corporate communications, such as branding, advertising, corporate identity, leaflets, packs, annual reports, product development and the retail environment.

Manchester City Council is a public organization that commissioned the design of a corporate identity for its Commonwealth Games bid of 1992. This had to appeal across the globe and the logo had to work across various media, including TV, posters, T-shirts and enamel badges. Levi jeans are a global brand that has a strong heritage, quality image and a youthful appeal. Kit-Kat has the largest market share for countline chocolate bars in the UK and has only once changed its distinctive red and silver packaging. This was in the Second World War when chocolate was extremely scarce and dark instead of milk choclate coating was used, and the wrapper was blue, not red. Karrimor is a specialist supplier of sports clothes and rucksacks that exploits a hard-wearing fabric for its products. Considerable attention is paid to the detail of each product to ensure safety and comfort for the wearer, for example brightly coloured strips to enhance the visibility of the walker at dusk and nightfall.

Marketing often interfaces with design to ensure that the product or service is appropriate for the target market. Frequently design and marketing share the same objectives, namely to develop the 'right product, for the right market, at the right price'. But they have different skills and ways of working to achieve these objectives. Indeed, managing design is increasingly becoming part of marketing's activities. Marketing strategies are implemented through myriad elements: products, packs, corporate identity, advertising and retail environments, all of which entail the use of design expertise. However, the scope of design in business, the different design disciplines and the skills entailed in managing design are not as well understood by marketing professionals as perhaps they could be. Design professionals can be resistant to management where they regard this as inhibiting their creativity. Designers are focused on 'doing' and 'visualizing' and so often do not record or reflect on their management practices or skills. As design has an increasingly important role to play in business – manufacturing, service and retail – it is timely to consider the processes of design management, and especially the interface between design and other disciplines. Marketing professionals utilize design skills, especially in service, retail and fast-moving consumer goods (FMCG) companies on an everyday basis, and so managing design is a key element of marketing. This book is about the interface between marketing and design and is focused on how to optimize and direct the design effort to achieve marketing's goals. This book focuses on the role of design in manufacturing and service organizations and is concerned with the issues of how marketing professionals can manage design effectively. Design management practices that are covered include design audits, sourcing design expertise, preparing design briefs, project management and design evaluation.

The book is divided into three parts. Part I is split into three chapters. Chapter 1 discusses the nature and scope of design in business, the different types of design disciplines and the evidence for investment in design. A model of design management is presented at the end of Chapter 1 (Figure 1.9). The model is not a prescriptive model, but serves as a checklist of the activities entailed in design management that a marketing professional needs to be aware of. Chapter 2 explores the interface between design and marketing. In particular, issues concerned with the outsourcing of design expertise and the management of a 'virtual project team' are discussed here. The final chapter of Part I explains the design management model presented in Chapter 1 and demonstrates the 'do's' and 'don'ts' of design management by working through various 'real-life' examples. This chapter provides insights into the problems that can arise at various phases of the design process, and the misunderstandings and conflicts that can exist between design and marketing.

Four cases are presented in Part II of the book, and these illustrate design management issues faced by different organizations. Irgo-Pic is about the development of a radical new product in the construction tools market. A new market opportunity arose with changes in European health and safety legislation and Ingersoll-Rand was one of the first manufacturers to take account of this. The small, multidisciplinary product development team had three in-house staff and one industrial designer who was a partner of design consultancy. The team produced the product under budget and in eighteen months, instead of the company norm of four years. Within a year of launch it had achieved its payback period, won a number of design awards and had opened up a new market for a range of construction tools. Royal Mail is a public-service organization that has a dedicated team of design managers to manage the company's corporate identity. This centralized organization of design management is unusual. The work of the design managers is described, together with their management practices. Stirling Cooper is a fashion retailer which underwent a repositioning and accompanying design change to communicate this change to the market. The case shows the importance of preparing a detailed design brief and shows the comprehensive range of information that a brief needs to cover, including indication of the target market, competitor analysis, costings, timescales and specific design details.

The final part of the book, Part III, reproduces a number of seminal papers that have influenced the area of design management. Design management is a discipline that is at an embryonic stage. Consequently, the seminal papers in the field, which are heavily quoted, are often promulgating a message of 'good design', or are putting forward exploratory ideas about design and its management. Kotler and Rath's (1984) paper is a classic and cogently expresses the importance of design for marketers. They note that consumers are influenced in their purchase behaviour by design factors and that these need to be carefully considered, rather than being left to chance. Gorb and Dumas (1987) argue that design is an activity that companies engage in but often in an unplanned and ad-hoc way. They suggest that design-competent firms have a clear sense of how design affects their business, so that design becomes infused into the norms and practices of the company. 'Silent design' is the phrase they use to describe this situation. The relationship and interface between marketing and

R & D in product development is the theme of Souder's (1989) paper. The kinds of problems that exist in the interaction between these two functions are similar to those that can occur between marketing and design. Souder produces a checklist of factors that it is particularly important to resolve. Sceptics of design suggest that design is an expensive 'fad' that is an 'add-on' luxury. This viewpoint is challenged by Roy and Potter (1993). Recently they have conducted an extensive survey of small and medium-sized UK enterprises and developed a methodology to evaluate the costs and benefits of design investment for a vast range of design projects. Their research findings demonstrate that investment in design is a sound investment which is relatively low cost and yet can yield substantial commercial benefit.

It is expected that after reading this book the marketing professional will be better equipped to:

- understand the role of design in business;
- appreciate the range of design disciplines and skills of design;
- gain insights into the nature of design to help to foster a creative and effective working relationship between marketing and design;
- be able to provide market information in a form that supports design;
- reflect on the design management skills and expertise that marketing professionals require.

## REFERENCES

Gorb, P. and Dumas, A. (1987) 'Silent design', *Design Studies* 8(3).

Kotler, P. and Rath, G. A. (1984) 'Design: a powerful but neglected strategic tool', *Journal of Business Strategy*, 5(2): 16–21.

Roy, R. and Potter, S. (1993) 'The commercial impacts of investment in design', *Design Studies* 14(2) (April): 171–95.

Souder, W. E. (1989) 'Managing relations between R&D and marketing in new product development projects', *Journal of Product Innovation Management*, 5: 6–19.

# Acknowledgements

The authors wish to acknowledge the assistance of the following people:

- Hans Billman, Network Development Manager, Co-operative Bank;
- Bob Buxton, Partner, Buxton, Wall, McPeake;
- Karen Freeze, Consultant, Design Management Institute, US;
- Steve Glennon, Managing Director, Tin Drum Associates;
- David Griffiths, Team Leader, Design Management Consultancy, Royal Mail;
- Anne Laudage, Marketing Manager, Fox's Biscuits;
- Charmaine Lovatt, Design Manager, Royal Mail;
- Earl Powell, President, Design Management Institute, US;
- David Quigley, David Quigley Architects;
- John Schofield, Marketing Manager, Ingersoll-Rand (UK).

In addition, the authors wish to thank Dale Littler, Professor of Marketing, Manchester School of Management, UMIST, for his support and helpful comments.

# PART I
## *Design and marketing*

# 1 *Design and the organization*

*Margaret Bruce and Rachel Cooper*

## INTRODUCTION

Managing design is increasingly becoming part of marketing's activities. Marketing strategies are implemented through a myriad elements: products, packs, corporate identity, advertising and retail environments, all of which entail the use of design expertise. Design includes the work of people from a wide range of disciplines – graphics, interiors, industrial and engineering – and is a creative and visual resource that generates ideas for new products and services. Design can help to create corporate distinctiveness and to devise a physical form that may have immediate charm and appeal for the consumer. Little is understood about the management of design activities, from a marketing perspective, about how to produce a given result, whether this is working with graphic specialists to produce a new letterhead or in the development of a new brand of chocolate or a different kind of car. Marketing practitioners – whether they are based in a service, retail or manufacturing companies – spend a significant proportion of their time working with design. In order for them to manage design effectively, it is essential that they understand the nature of 'design' in a business context and how design can contribute to achieving their marketing goals.

In this chapter, design is considered briefly in different contexts – product and manufacture, service and retail – and for different purposes: product design and corporate communications. Links with marketing are made, essentially by examining how design affects elements of the marketing mix. Finally, evidence is presented to support the argument that design makes a positive contribution to business performance. In other words, design investment affects the bottom line, but only if design is integrated into the business process and managed well. The chapter concludes with a general model of design management (Figure 1.9). This model is not intended to be prescriptive but to provide a checklist of the range of activities and information that is required to manage design effectively. The practical implications of the design management model are discussed fully in Chapter 3.

## MARKETING AND DESIGN

The connections between marketing and design are illustrated by different examples from manufacturing and service companies.

---

### FAST-MOVING CONSUMER GOODS(FMCG)

Sales of Fox's biscuits had been falling steadily. Despite price cuts and special promotions, the decline in sales ·continued. More drastic action was needed to revitalize the brand of biscuits. In 1996 the marketing staff commissioned market research to discover people's perceptions and attitudes of the brand to identify its main strengths and weaknesses. The market research showed that consumers were satisfied with the taste of the product but found the packaging was unappealing and the brand identity weak. The next step was to reposition the brand by creating a strong brand identity and personality. Previously, Anne Laudage, the Marketing Manager, had worked with a design company that specialized in branding and she decided to use this agency for the repositioning. A team consisting of the Marketing Manager, the market research company and the design agency was set up to identify the salient features of the brand, to devise a mission statement for the brand and to create a personality for this, as well as to agree on a name and visual identity. Within six weeks, the work had been completed and the product was ready for its market launch. A month later, sales had grown rapidly, with the expectation that the brand 'Rocky' would be able to achieve its target of increasing in value from £35 million to £60 million within eighteen months. Because no other aspect of the product had changed, the rise in sales may be attributed to the name, pack design and point-of-sales promotion material.

---

## PRODUCT INNOVATION

The Dual Cyclone system is the first breakthrough in technology since the invention of the vacuum cleaner in 1901. In 1995 the Dyson DC01 upright vacuum cleaner became the best-selling upright cleaner on the market, with 20,000 units being sold per month. James Dyson, the inventor and designer, had previously designed a new kind of wheelbarrow, the 'Ballbarrow'. Whilst manufacturing this Ballbarrow, Dyson noticed how the air filter in the Ballbarrow spray-finishing room was constantly clogging with powder particles (just like a vacuum cleaner bag clogs with dust), so to overcome this problem he designed and built an industrial cyclone tower, which removed the powder particles by centrifugal force, spinning the extracted air at the speed of sound. Dyson applied this principle to a vacuum cleaner, and 5,127 prototypes later the world's first bagless vacuum cleaner was developed, which had a totally radical styling. It would seem that innovative design does sell even at a premium price – the product was priced at three times that of competing products.
Source: Dyson Appliances Limited.

## FINANCIAL SERVICES

A few years ago, the CEO of the Co-operative Bank decided to invest in a new corporate identity to strengthen the bank's position and to extend its distribution network to reach new customers and to enhance service provision. Market research showed that people had a positive attitude to the heritage of the bank but regarded it as old-fashioned. The new identity was designed to build on the ethical heritage and to emphasize its innovative and progressive nature, in terms of types of customers, use of technology and range of services. 'Ship in and shape up' was the slogan underpinning the approach to distribution. The distribution team exploited the latest technology, including video conferencing, to provide 24-hour banking. The new branches were placed in specially designed kiosks that could be located in high streets, shopping malls, leisure centres, etc., or in rented retail outlets. Existing branches were overhauled and installed with new technology. The corporate identity has been extremely successful in repositioning the bank and attracting new

> customers, as well as encouraging a higher level of use by existing customers.

These examples illustrate the ways in which design is used by manufacturers and service companies to meet various requirements and they demonstrate the business role that design may take. Design expertise is an essential part of the creation and manufacture of new product ideas and consequently is associated with manufacture – product designers translate ideas into manufactured goods. Manufacturers have a tradition of having an in-house R&D or design department, usually specializing in product and engineering design and connected to engineering; whereas service and retail companies have bought in external design – graphic, interior, pack and corporate – expertise and, typically, it is marketing professionals in service and retail companies who interact with designers.

Design can generate ideas and solutions to address marketing's concern to provide effective products, at the right time, place and price. This relationship between design and marketing is succinctly expressed in the following comment:

> Around the globe, CEOs are depending more and more on product designers to make greater headway in the marketplace. That makes sense. The designer is the one who conceives what form the original product should take, the one who renews an ageing product line. Without designers, neither engineers nor marketers can do their magic. So, in the end, it is the American, European or Japanese designer whose creations define what a corporation is – what image it will have among the people who buy its products.
>
> (*Business Week* 1990: 171)

Design and marketing are interconnected. A change in the marketing plan often serves as a 'trigger' for design, and the following examples explore this interplay between marketing and design. A confectionery producer devises a novelty chocolate product for Christmas and engages graphic designers specializing in pack design to create the visual appeal of the product – imagery, colour, shape and branding – as well as ensuring that the pack can be manufactured cost-effectively. A TV manufacturer developing a new TV console draws on the skills of mechanical and electronics designers/engineers, as well as industrial designers with ergonomics expertise, to produce a product that is functional, easy to use and economical to make in mass volumes. A retailer uses interior design and graphic design skills to create 'atmospherics' that make a pleasant and attractive shopping environment that encourages shoppers to buy goods. The decor, layout, shop and pack signage should reinforce the identity of the retailer and be consistent with its overall image. The Visitors' Centre of a City Council employs designers to produce brochures, posters and leaflets about the city's attractions and any special events to capture attention and to draw visitors to the city. Design interfaces with different parts of the organization, but with marketing and manufacturing/operations in particular, to gain an understanding of the target market and method of manufacture or operations, which will have implications for the design (for example, the leaflets for a loan scheme will contain different visual statements for a student market than for an older age group). Gorb and Dumas (1987; see Chapter 8) have coined the term 'silent design' to refer to those non-design professionals in an organization who are none the less involved in making decisions that may affect the design process (e.g. market research indicating the target market). Marketing professionals are often 'silent designers', and as such they need to be aware of how their decisions may impact upon the design process. Hence, marketing professionals need to be aware of the different design disciplines and the expertise they can bring to a given project, and the range of marketing information that is required to get the optimum results from the design process.

*Figure 1.1* The organization's need for design

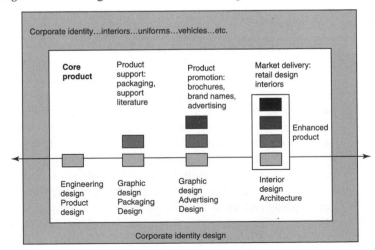

At any one time, it is likely that larger organizations will engage design expertise to address different issues: for example, engineering and industrial design to develop a new product or to modify an existing product; graphic design to produce the technical literature and point-of-sales material, interior designers to create the atmospherics of the salesrooms and corporate identity specialists. Designers need to know what the target market is for the design and to have some insights into the factors influencing consumers' buying decisions, as well as the competitor analysis and the organization's objectives for the project. Figure 1.1 depicts the ways in which design interfaces with different parts of an organization to help to produce the 'right product, at the right place and price, at the right time'.

## DESIGN DISCIPLINES AND DESIGN EXPERTISE

In Britain, design has had a long association with arts and crafts, and the designer William Morris, working a hundred years ago, was known for his design of wallpaper, houses, furniture, tapestries and books (McCarthy 1994). Nowadays design professionals specialize in graphics, product, interiors, fashion, and within these areas further specialize in pack design, corporate identity, furniture design, automotive design and so on (see Figure 1.2). A graphic designer will have a good sense of two-dimensional form, of space and colour, whilst an engineering designer will have an orientation towards scientific and mathematical problem-solving.

### Definitions

The word 'design' has various meanings and associations. Design can refer to the outcome of an activity – 'a design', meaning an idea or a plan from which an object can be made. Design has been described as intrinsically linked with innovation and treated as at 'the very core of innovation, the moment when a new object is imagined, devised and shaped in prototype form' (OECD 1982). It can refer to the form, structure, function and appearance of the artefact itself. The term has become synonymous with style, fad, quality and status: 'designer jeans'. 'Designing' means the process that starts with an idea described in a brief and ends with a product or visual material for manufacture or implementation.

All design activities involve the creative visualization of concepts, plans and ideas and the production of sketches, models and other representations of those ideas, aimed at providing the instructions for making something that did not exist before, or which did not exist in quite that form – which might be a building,

*Figure 1.2* Design disciplines

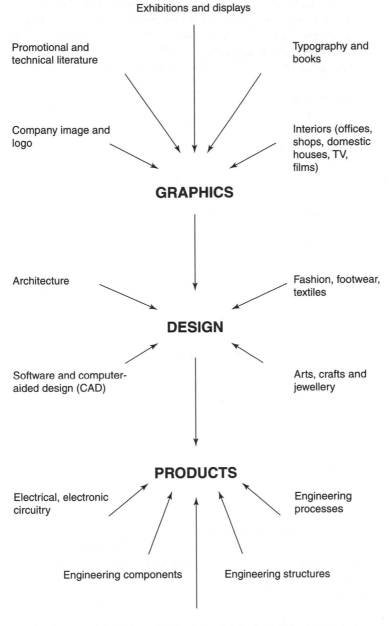

a machine, a logo or a chair. Similarly, product designers create the concept and the technical drawings for the product, and graphic designers send their concept, as artwork or disk file, to the printer for production. Where design is craft-based, the conceptual process is intrinsically linked to the making of the artefact, such as in the work of a silversmith or potter.

## Design techniques

Designers of all disciplines have a specific set of skills, both practical and cognitive, that they can bring to the aid of marketing and which they use to develop their design ideas. Such skills and activities include:

- *Creativity*. Creative problem-solving is a natural process for designers and constitutes a major aspect of a design method. Techniques such as brainstorming, lateral thinking and morphological analysis are used to develop concepts and create solutions to problems.
- *Visualizing*. To bring a concept or ideas into a recognizable form, designers will use drawings and diagrams; for example, a graphic designer will visualize a brochure by drawing on paper and/or computer.
- *Model-making*. Designers often have to make their ideas into a three-dimensional form to enable them to present their ideas to others, for instance a sketch model or a scale model to give shape, form and size to their design and to check if the idea is working. Such models are frequently used to test usability at an early stage in the design process.
- *Simulating/testing*. Designers often use test models and simulations to ensure that the item meets the operational criteria, for example performance and usability requirements.
- *Technical drawing and diagrams*. Detailed drawings will be produced to move from the concept to implementation. These have to be precise and give technical information to ensure that the article can be produced. Computer-aided design is now used in most design disciplines to develop the precise details necessary. In product design it is tooling and manufacturing drawings; in graphics it is desktop-based artwork; in architecture it is structural details.

A simple approach to categorizing design areas is that of Potter (1969), who refers to product design (things); environmental design (places); and communications design (messages). These categories are elaborated by reference to examples of three design specialisms: product design, interior design and graphic design.

## Product/industrial design

The range of products that an industrial/product designer can become involved with varies enormously, from sunglasses to cars to a hospital scanner. Chapter 4 describes product design. Product design training equips designers with an understanding of three-dimensional form and space, colour, texture and materials, together with an appreciation of the perceptual and psychological impact that these elements can have on the end-user. They are concerned with ergonomics and the human interaction with product form and function. In addition, product designers have to be conscious of manufacturing processes to ensure that their concepts can be made, and for a given cost. Product designers are not engineering designers, although the two disciplines overlap. A crude historical explanation of the differences is that product designers are concerned with the external form, function, appearance and usability of the design, whereas engineering designers focus on the internal aspects of the product and its manufacture. However, most product or industrial designers are conversant with the technology and functionality which need to be designed into a product and consequently work closely with engineering designers. The process a product designer follows depends on the complexity of the product and its manufacturing process, but four stages are usually undertaken. These are:

1   *Contracting*: preparation of design brief and specification, research to understand more about the company's needs and the issues faced by the end-user, etc.
2   *Preliminary design*: concept generation, producing visuals and perhaps models for further examination and discussion, consumer testing.
3   *Detailed design*: detailed drawings and feasibility tests and specification for manufacture.
4   *Production*: small-batch production and testing followed by full manufacture.

## Interior design

Interior designers are skilled in the use of space, light, colour, texture and scale, and the psychological aspects of built environments. Retail designers demand an understanding of customer flow, lighting, display systems and materials. Creating an atmosphere through the use of colour, texture, lighting, pattern and space is crucial for designers in the service or leisure industry. Chapter 6 shows the role of interior design for a high-street fashion chain. The design process can be split into four broad stages:

1  *Contracting*: defining the brief, research to gain insights into user and business needs.
2  *Preliminary design*: concept generation, visuals, sourcing materials and presenting proposals.
3  *Detailed design*: design refinement, production of three-dimensional elevations, plans and sections and appearance model, selection of fabrics, fittings and furnishings.
4  *Implementation*: supervision of construction.

## Graphic design

Graphic designers specialize in the development of two-dimensional images and are trained to be sensitive to word, image, colour, layout and texture. Chapter 5 refers to the work of graphic designers. They are sensitive to the mood a typeface can create, for instance, and how letter forms relate to illustrations. They work with different media, from computers – designing for the Internet, for example – to cloth, ceramics and paper. Graphic designers may be specialists in pack design or corporate identity, or may focus on advertising, TV or literature. Increasingly, graphic designers are working with three-dimensional images such as pack design, and they may also be involved in environmental design – for example to ensure that the corporate identity they have created for a bank is carried over into the bank branches – and the computer systems graphic designers use to generate and implement their designs are similar to those used by product designers. Graphic designers have an understanding of the psychological and perceptual qualities of communication. The graphic design process can be divided into three core elements, as follows:

1  *Contracting*: preparing the brief, carrying out research to understand the corporate and user need for the proposed design, working out production costs.
2  *Design research and preliminary proposals*: sourcing images and typefaces, and commissioning photographers, illustrators and multimedia specialists, idea generation, visuals and mock-ups for design review.

3   *Design detailing*: design development and specifications for production, monitoring production (e.g. checking proofs and quality).

## Ways of working/thinking

When designers approach problems, they question every aspect continuously, they push ideas laterally and have the continual desire to take risks with solutions. This, however, can cause problems when they are working with other, perhaps more conservative, functions, although if used appropriately it is an invaluable aspect of business. Designers' expertise resides in their area of professional competence, such as graphics, product design, etc. They do not just work on an intellectual or abstract 'know-how' level, but work intuitively, visually and sensually to 'know what' is required (Cross et al. 1991).

Designers use a combination of intuition, understanding and current knowledge to develop a design solution (see Figure 1.3). In addition, Glegg (1995) suggests that there is nothing automatic about creative design. Whether the designer is conscious of it or not, her or his mind has three realms of activity: the inventive, the artistic and the logical or rational. In the inventive the designer is

*Figure 1.3* Inputs into the design process (designer's head)

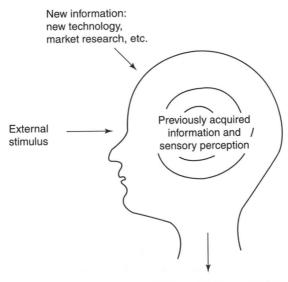

*Source*: Cooper and Press (1995)

using the subconscious to develop solutions to problems, as described above. The artistic is more difficult to define and is more to do with a sense of style and sensitivity. The rational realm is the designer's ability to analyse the inventive and artistic and make decisions.

Thus, all aspects of the personality and character of the designer go into the creation of a design solution. Effective design management needs to be sensitive to this aspect of the way a designer works because a fundamental element of the client–design relationship is the personal chemistry that exists between the designer and marketing professionals. The personal chemistry is part of the creativity of the design process (Bruce and Docherty 1993). The marketing-design interface is discussed in Chapter 2.


## DESIGN'S BUSINESS VALUE

### The designer's role

Each year 7,000 design graduates leave UK universities, and UK-trained designers are to be found working throughout the world for leading companies across all industrial sectors. It has been well documented that UK companies have been slow to adopt design, despite successive government campaigns targeted at companies to create awareness of design's commercial role (Farr 1955; Heskett 1980; Sparke 1986). Given the competing demands for resources, design is often treated as an activity that can be bought as and when required in an 'on–off' way and may be regarded as a dispensable luxury. Firms may view their projects as a one-off investment rather than as a way of incorporating design investment into their long-term strategy. James Dyson's (designer/manufacturer) view is that 'Manufacturers should not think of design as a bolt on thing. It's the total product – how it's used, how it is made, how reliable it is that all shine out' (*Design* 1995: 38–9).

None the less, ample evidence exists to suggest that design investment has a positive commercial benefit (Pilditch 1987; Service et al. 1989; Potter et al. 1991). Over the past few years, major studies have been conducted to measure the returns on investment of investment in design expertise. Chapter 9 reports on a survey of over 200 UK small and medium-sized enterprises where the costs of design investment were assessed at a project level. The results supported the case that investment in design has commercial value. Key results were:

■ 90 per cent of projects that were implemented in the market were profitable;

■ there was a 40 per cent increase in sales of redesigned projects, compared with the projected sales figures if no design work had taken place;

■ there was a 13 per cent increase in exports;

■ there were other benefits, including reduced manufacturing costs, stock savings, enhanced company image.

The results of this study provide a very good case for investing in design projects. The degree of risk varied across different types of design projects. Graphic design projects appear to involve little technical uncertainty or financial risk. Yet in product or engineering design a relatively high risk of failure exists at the start of a project; once a project has been implemented, the prospect of a rapid return on the investment becomes very good. The risk of financial loss is low for all types of design.

However, what is of particular interest in this study is the variety of design management skills that were evident and the 'hit-and-miss' approach often taken to design management, so that the main cause of project failure was not the result of a poor idea but the inability to budget fully for the design work and its market implementation, the failure to provide the designer with adequate information about the target market, the distribution channels and the manufacturing procedures available to the company. Attitudes to design did change; for example, the CEO of a firm that used an industrial design consultancy to help redesign its crash helmets previously felt that design was 'a waste of money'. Now he admits that 'the whole management team is aware of the contribution of visual design and packaging to sales'.

The more successful projects in the Roy and Potter (1993) study gave insights into effective design management practices, some of which have been echoed by other studies, notably Service et al. (1989). The key factors were:

■ clear project objectives;

■ comprehensive design briefs that included information about the target market;

■ regular communication with design;

■ top-level commitment;

■ sourcing of appropriate design skills;

■ integration of design with other corporate activities.

Each of these factors will be considered in greater detail in Chapter 3.

## The marketing–design relationship

Marketing and design are interrelated activities. Product planning, market research, competitor analysis and control of budgets are the realm of marketing professionals and these marketing issues affect design. Typically, marketing is a 'trigger' for a design change; for example, a decline in market share may stimulate a review of the product portfolio and lead to a design modification or a promotional activity to stimulate sales. Table 1.1 shows how market changes can 'trigger' different types of design.

Design can be viewed as a marketing resource that deals with the choices and decisions that determine the value and quality of the product. Whether technical performance, style, reliability, safety, ease of use or some combination of attributes is emphasized, the design of the product can offer quality and value for money in the eyes of the consumer. Consumers' perceptions and their willingness to buy are influenced by the design configuration of the product and its ability to convey 'value for money' in comparison with competing offerings. In addition, a unique design can create a desire in the consumer to purchase (Alessi's kitchen

*Table 1.1* Market triggers of design

| *Market objective* | *Design outcome* |
| --- | --- |
| Company seeking to launch the product on the market for the first time. | Industrial design of casing for innovative cheque-writing machine. |
| Company seeking to increase market share. | Graphic/styling design work for a range of garden tools. |
| Company seeking to regain lost market share. | Engineering design for a new design of bus shelter. |
| Company seeking to diversify into a new product market for the company. | Packaging design for new product – chilled cooked meats. |
| Company seeking to diversify into a new product market for the company. | Engineering design of a wire-joining device. |
| Company responding to customer request. | Design of a computerized control mechanism for a pottery-kiln booster. |

utensils) and so contribute to the competitiveness and business success of the company.

Design can be used as a market positioning tool; for example, Braun offers classical design in the consumer goods market as a ploy to maintain a position as a premium supplier. Failure to keep pace with market trends and to design attractive products may well threaten survival, as was the case with the UK toy company Airfix, which supplied model-making kits targeted at boys and which could not survive the onslaught of cheaper and more appealing products from the Far East.

## Marketing decisions affect design

In the study conducted by Roy and Potter (1993), which is reproduced in Chapter 9, it is clear that marketing decisions can have grave implications for the project outcome. Projects could be suddenly aborted because of changing market circumstances (e.g. a competitor launched a better design), and in other cases the projects may not be implemented because the promotional costs may not have been built into the estimates for the project. The success of a project does not rely solely on design, but on broader market considerations, such as identification of a target market, effective budgeting, market research that is conveyed in a meaningful way to design, and so on.

The main areas of design management skills for marketing professionals, which will be discussed in much greater detail in Chapter 3, revolve around:

- awareness of the need for design;
- sourcing of appropriate design skills;
- preparation of a clear and detailed brief;
- monitoring design and design budgets and schedules;
- evaluation of the design outcome.

## Design and the marketing mix

Design has a connection with each of the elements of the marketing mix, as follows:

- *Product*: design influences quality, function, usability and appearance. It contributes to product features, which add value to the product for the consumer. Design affects all of the differentiating features of products, such as performance, reliability, style, etc. Compare, for instance, a pair of shoes and a telephone; each must be functional, ergonomically and aesthetically appropriate. The designer contributes to each of these elements to varying degrees, depending on the nature of the product.

For service companies, insurance companies, for instance, use design to provide the information and evidence of the service, from policy document and chequebooks to the sales literature. Design is used for image differentiation by the provision of memorable corporate identities that are implemented on packs, logo, stationery, uniforms, environments and that create a visual harmony for the organization.

■ *Price*: products can be devised that are economical in terms of materials, energy and manufacture. Product enhancement, by adding a feature such as embroidery on towels and linen, or a call memory facility on a telephone, can affect the perceived value of the product, allowing it to be sold at a higher price.

■ *Place*: distribution considerations may affect the design, so that a product's pack may have a shape that facilitates storage and display. Shelf appeal is critical for FMCG goods – hence the importance of design elements such as colour, illustrations and shape. For example, Fisons spent considerable time developing the bottles which dominate the shelf display for Tomerite Fertiliser.

■ *Promotion*: most promotional activities rely on their visual qualities to convey the company's message. Packaging, promotional and sales literature, all forms of media advertising, point-of-sale displays and the retail environment all involve the skills of designers.

Design for service and retail areas is considered briefly here, before moving on to consider product design and corporate communications in more detail.

## Design and service

Service offerings are inherently intangible, for example the experiences encountered during a visit to a leisure park or restaurant, etc. According to Berry and Seiders (1992), customers see:

> various intangibles associated with a service. They see service facilities, equipment, employees, communication materials, other customers . . . all of these tangible are 'clues' about the invisible service . . . if unmanaged, the clues convey all the wrong messages about the service, seriously undermining the overall marketing strategy.

One of the tasks for design is to 'manage the tangible clues', which include the atmospherics of a restaurant's environment, leaflets, stationery, uniforms, and the overall corporate image and communications. Sisodia (1992) argues that 'a thoughtfully designed service can lead to great customer satisfaction. Good service design thus has a strong impact on perceived design quality.'

A new banking service such as a premium account has to be given an identity that reflects its status as an executive service, and this has to be reflected in the card itself and all of the literature associated with offering the service. In addition, the implementation of the account has to match its status and to ensure optimum customer satisfaction.

### Design and retail

In retail, design has to cater for a fast-moving market, in terms of the sales volumes and speed of stock turnover, so that McGoldrick (1990) argues that 'design has come to be recognised as a vital strategic function'. In the intensely competitive retail environment in the UK, design can help to differentiate products and to improve the retail environment. Food retailers like Sainsbury's lay their store out to maximize impulse purchase and to convey an impression of high quality and fresh produce. Green (1986) claims that 'the designer must create a store that encourages the shopper, once inside, to lower his/her psychological defences and become interested in the merchandise'. As well as displaying products to their advantage, design is used to communicate elements of a lifestyle for customers to aspire to. The fashion retailer Next presents images of lifestyles for people of different ages and pursuits, ranging from 'power dressing' for the professional woman of 20–40 to leisure wear for younger women. The product and the service mix of retailers are increasingly focused on 'homogeneous groupings' (McGoldrick 1990), so that food retailers, for example, may stock specialist food products that appeal to their more upmarket consumer.

## Design and innovation

> Good design can significantly add value to products, lead to growth in sales and enable both the exploitation of new markets and the consolidation of existing ones.
>
> (HMSO 1995: 143)

At the heart of technological innovation is design. Caldecote refers to design as 'the process of converting ideas into information from which a new product can be made' (Caldecote 1979). Product development is necessary to replace and update existing products, to diversify into new markets and to create new opportunities by innovation. Chapter 4 describes the process of product development and examines the role of industrial design and its links with R&D to produce a technologically innovative product in the construction tool market.

Figure 1.4 shows the design interfaces in the product development process.

It is well established that marketing has a critical role in the product development process, particularly during the early stages, which Cooper and Kleinschmidt (1986) refer to as the 'front-end' of product development. Marketing has a role in concept evaluation and the testing of detailed designs, and must also plan the market launch from the onset to ensure that the distribution channels are established and that the launch strategy has been considered (Biemans and Setz 1995). Design translates market requirements into concepts and develops these into the detailed design of products, it also provides the graphic design skills for print and promotional material to support the new product.

R&D is the domain of technologists, engineers and scientists who are concerned with developing new knowledge that can be incorporated into new products and processes. Designers, in this context, may use such knowledge in conjunction with existing design skills and expertise to generate new product concepts. In terms of innovation, then, design expertise often contributes to the delivery to the market of new technology in a form which can be used, for example the development of shape-memory alloy into bra underwires. Both R&D and marketing can drive innovation and product development (this will be discussed further in Chapter 3).

Firms vary enormously in the extent of time, effort and money they believe should be accorded to design and the extent to which design is carried out by professional design staff. Design-conscious firms employ professional design staff or retain design consultants, and take design seriously throughout the firm and allocate resources accordingly. Many firms, however, develop new products or modify existing ones without being fully aware of how the design process happens and where design is done by staff whose main job is something else and who do not accord it much time or effort. A recent survey (Walsh et al. 1992) of the organization of design in UK manufacturing companies showed that few companies have full-time design managers and designers. Most of design work and decisions about design were taken by managers who had full-time responsibility for another activity, such as R&D, marketing, production, etc. (Walsh et al. 1992). Walsh (1996) argues that design is not institutionalized in UK companies, as is the case for other functions, such as R&D and

*Figure 1.4* The process of technological or industrial innovation, showing the place of the design and development activity

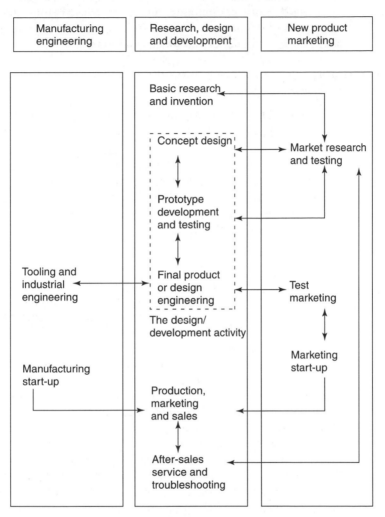

*Source*: Roy and Bruce (1984)

marketing. Hence the responsibility for creating design briefs, sourcing designers and managing the project is rather ad hoc and not formalized in UK companies. Perhaps this is one factor contributing to the high rates of project failure, estimated at 46 per cent by *International Business Week* (Power 1993).

It has been widely recognized that the interface between R&D and marketing is critical for effective product design (Gupta and

Wileman 1988); the same goes for that between design and marketing (Cooper and Jones 1995) (this will be discussed further in
Chapter 2). Poor communication between marketing and design
may result in unfocused design and failure to exploit design's
potential for product development and launch.

## Design and corporate communications
### Corporate identity

> It is virtually impossible to detect quality differences between
> the products of major financial service companies, or petrol
> retailers or the various chemical companies, for instance. This
> means that companies and their brands have increasingly to
> compete with each other on emotional rather than rational
> grounds. The company with the strongest, most consistent,
> most attractive, best implemented and manifested identity will
> emerge on top in this race.
>
> (Olins 1990: 70)

With the growth of mergers and acquisitions, the launch of new
companies and privatization of public organizations, corporate
identity and corporate communications have experienced an
upsurge of interest. In the UK, corporate identity is a major
component of professional design services. The merger of building
societies, the launch of trust hospitals and the creation of new
universities have provided investment in corporate identity design.
When two companies merge and create a new organization, decisions have to be made as to whether to subsume the identity of one
of the organizations into that of the other or to create a completely
new identity. The acquisition of Philips by Whirlpool is an interesting case. In Europe Whirlpool was not a known brand yet
Philips was regarded as a having a high reputation, and the con-
verse was true in the USA. Managers of Whirlpool decided to run
the two names in tandem in Europe, building the Whirlpool brand
image through promotion and graphic design, until customers had
begun to recognize Whirlpool and to associate this name with the
good reputation that Philips had always enjoyed. Eventually, the
name Philips was withdrawn in Europe and Whirlpool became an
acknowledged brand.

Corporate identity is the sum of the ways in which an organization presents itself to its various publics (see Figure 1.5) and
includes transport, publicity, advertising, environment, architecture and products. Corporate identity is concerned with the entire
communications plan and is integrated into the organization's

*Figure 1.5* The nine publics of a company image

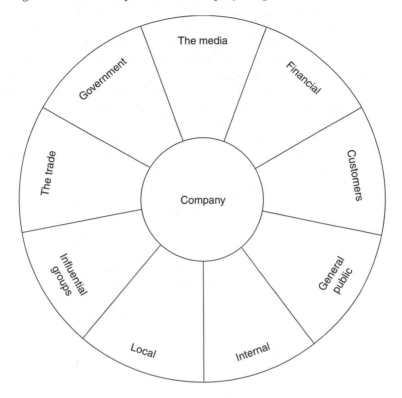

*Source*: Bernstein (1984)

philosophies, policies and activities. Michael Beirut, one of the Partners of the UK Office of Pentagram, a UK design group, refers to corporate identity in this way:

> in its fullest sense, corporate identity is the character of an institution or corporation as projected in its communications, its products and services, its property and facilities and in the attitudes and behaviour of its personnel. It is the sum of the ways in which the institution represents itself formally, as well as symbolically.
>
> (Michael Beirut; cited in Bruce 1994: 11)

Olins (1990) points out that the visual projection of a corporate culture not only helps internal cohesion but also plays a large part in showing the world what the company is like and how it can be expected to behave. Newall and Sorrell illustrate the use of corporate image as a cultural tool:

> The publisher Routledge was created by the merger of four publishing houses owned by International Thompson. The new company was slow to establish a profile in the market, A new corporate identity was commissioned to give the company a renewed sense of unity and purpose internally, and to enable it to compete more effectively outside. The design consultancy also advised on improving the publishers' own design and marketing processes. . . . According to Routledge's design manager the new identity 'was important in bringing everyone together, making everyone feel a part of the same company'.
>
> (*Independent on Sunday*, 21 May 1995)

A major problem with a new corporate identity is that companies often do not implement this correctly, so that the products of different divisions do not share a visual identity. This can lead to customer confusion and may serve to tarnish the image of the company over time. This issue of 'policing' the corporate identity to ensure that it is implemented consistently across numerous product ranges and services is of major concern and is discussed by the Head of Corporate Identity of the British Post Office in Chapter 5. Organizations produce corporate manuals which express the intention and objectives behind the corporate identity and give guides as to how to implement it consistently across the organization, so that the values of the organization are expressed visually in brochures, transport, letterheads, uniforms, products and environments. An example of a corporate manual is that of Caterpillar's *Communicating Caterpillar: One Voice* (1993). Figure 1.6 shows how the visual elements of the company reflect the espoused values of Caterpillar. The choice of typeface, illustrations and overall message and presentation are consciously made to demonstrate the quality of the company's products and service, and the high level of staff morale and pride in the company.

## Branding

The segmentation of the market and the positioning of a product to suit that segment is a core marketing activity. Branding is a means of delivering product values to a segmented market. For example, The Burton group in the 1980s used much the same device for Top Shop, Dorothy Perkins and Principles (see Figure 1.7).

Aaker (1991) defines a brand as 'a distinguishing name/and or

*Figure 1.6* Elements of corporate voice

*Source:* © Caterpillar (1994). Reproduced with permission of Caterpillar Inc.

*Figure 1.7* Burton Group branding and segmentation

| | | | |
|---|---|---|---|
| The young market: Dorothy Perkins | The style market: Principles | The teenage market: Top Shop / Top Man | The larger market: Evans |

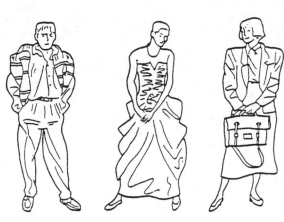

| | | |
|---|---|---|
| The men's market: Burton | The Knightsbridge market: Harvey Nichols | The family market: Debenhams |

*Source*: Walters and Knee (1989)

symbol (such as a logo, trademark, or pack) intended to identify the goods or services of either one seller or a group of sellers, and to differentiate those goods from those of its competitors'.

Brand names, symbols and slogans are important elements of the brand and to communicate branding the use of design is essential. Branding is often translated most effectively through the product attributes (for example, heritage and innovation and 'on the edge' are key values of Levi jeans) and their interpretation in the product design, product graphics, pack design and promotional design. One approach is to devise an integrated design, whereby the product, pack, promotional material and advertising reinforce the values of the brand. Terry's Chocolate Orange is a classic example. Here the orange taste of the chocolate, the shape of the chocolate product as an orange, with each piece shaped like an orange segment, and the pack design and point-of-sales literature all serve to reinforce the 'orangeyness' and 'uniqueness' of this product. Where the brand has been extended to bars of Terry's Chocolate Orange, the pack is similar to the boxed chocolate orange and each piece of chocolate is shaped as an orange segment.

For pack design, Southgate (1994) suggests there are two forms of brand values, those that are passive and active. Passive values are contained in brands, which over the years have acquired or evolved certain meanings – such as the association of Heinz baked beans with values like warmth, nutrition, motherhood and nurturing – from childhood experience and from advertising without them actually being suggested in the design of the package. Active values are communicated as specific values, rather than waiting for the values to become absorbed over time; for instance, the packaging of Baileys Irish Cream evokes feelings of warmth, tradition and Irishness.

In the corporate redesign of Fox's Biscuits, including the packs for their biscuit products (see Figure 1.8), the marketing manager used the new corporate identity to endorse the quality of the products, given that Fox's Biscuits were acknowledged in the market research as being perceived by consumers as a high-quality biscuit. The products are targeted towards different markets, for example 'Party Rings' and 'Rocky' are directed at children and Ginger Creams at adults, so these products have been given distinctive identities. The use of quality material and strong colours for the packs gives the products impact when they are displayed on the supermarket shelves. The repositioning of Fox's products has provided a consistent visual identity to their product range.

It is therefore essential that, as part of the marketing strategy, the aims and objectives of the branding are clear and the attributes of the brand are determined in conjunction with the market profile. These must be communicated accurately during the briefing to enable the designers to establish a common understanding and to design to it. Southgate recommends that the marketing team must communicate the brand's proposition and the personality to be reflected. 'Beyond these two key objectives, you might want to

*Figure 1.8* Fox's Biscuits before and after redesign
(a) Before: lack of coherent range identity

*Source*: Fox's Biscuits, Batley, Yorkshire (corporate document)

(b) After: coherent branding

*Source*: Fox's Biscuits, Batley, Yorkshire (corporate document)

define others in terms of perceived value (e.g. "make it look like it costs 50p more") or usage suitability ("reflect the brands strategic shift from breakfast to evening consumption" or target market ("broaden its appeal from teenagers to young adults").'

Design tools (shape colour, texture, typography, imagery) play a complex part in communicating branding and it is therefore essential that the designers and marketing personnel have a common understanding of the brand values they wish to communicate. They must also be able to assess how the tools used effectively communicate the brand values. Therefore a clear description of the brand values and strategy must be developed before design work begins. A few years ago, the 'brand promise' of Linda McCartney's vegetarian foods was 'to genuinely differentiate the brand from other convenience foods by providing a range of products according to the same principles and standard of Linda McCartney's own home cooking'.

A contemporary issue in the UK is that of 'copycat' branding. The main offender was Sainsbury's Cola, which used the same 'red' as that of Coca-Cola. Major UK retailers have used design to copy manufacturer's brands as closely as possible and then undercut these in terms of price. Brands that have an 'integrated design', like Jaffa Cakes and Terry's Chocolate Orange, may be more difficult to copy directly without retaliation by the manufacturer and this approach has been suggested as a way of countering the threat of 'copycat' branding (Curtis 1996). Curtis suggests that 'building on the emotional qualities of the brand and consistently reflecting them in all forms of marketing communication, including the packaging, is a powerful form of protection'. The visual element of the design can lead to technical barriers that may inhibit copying, for example the egg box-style packaging of the small Jaffa biscuits would require competitors to invest in new production techniques.

## DESIGN MANAGEMENT MODEL

Design management for a marketing professional is concerned with utilizing design expertise so as to achieve marketing's goals effectively. One definition of design management is that 'it is about managing those corporate expressive activities that generate products, services and corporate communications which aim to optimise customer satisfaction and business success'. Cooper and Press suggest that 'the management of design includes planning, organisation, implementation, monitoring and evaluation' (Cooper and Press 1994). In terms of using design effectively, marketing

*Figure 1.9* Four stages in the design process

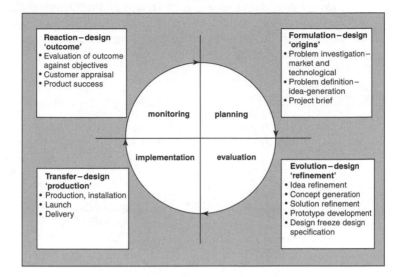

*Source*: adapted from Bennet et al. (1988)

professionals need to consider how design fits into their business, which design specialisms to use, the contribution design can make to their business, as well as developing skills in sourcing, briefing, liaising and evaluating design. The detail of managing design will of course vary from design discipline to design discipline and is also dependent upon whether design is insourced or outsourced. Figure 1.9 illustrates the design process and the issues which need to be managed by marketing professionals when working with designers. Essentially the design process can be broken down into four broad categories; Formulation, Evolution, Transfer and Reaction (Bennett et al. 1988). *Formulation* is concerned with identifying the design need and planning the problem definition. *Evolution* deals with the idea, concept and detailed design generation, *Transfer* covers implementation of the design and *Reaction* addresses the outcome of the design, for example customer acceptance. This model will be discussed in greater detail in Chapter 3.

## SUMMARY

Design's relevance to business and interplay with marketing has been the main theme of this chapter. The main intention has been to encourage marketing professionals to:

- understand the value of design to marketing and business;
- provide marketing information in a way that supports design and facilitates communication between marketing and design;
- be empathic to design and so encourage an effective relationship between marketing and design.

## ACKNOWLEDGEMENTS

Figure 1.2 is reproduced with permission from *Support for Design: Final Evaluation Report*, R. Shirley and D. Henn, published by the Department of Trade and Industry, 1988. Crown copyright is reproduced with the permission of the Controller of Her Majesty's Stationery Office.

Figure 1.3 is reproduced with permission from *The Design Agenda*, R. Cooper and M. Press, published by John Wiley & Sons, 1995. Copyright John Wiley & Sons.

Figure 1.4 is reproduced from *Product Design, Innovation and Competition in British Manufacturing*, R. Roy and M. Bruce, published by Design Innovation Group, Open University 1984.

Figure 1.5 is reproduced from *Corporate Image and Reality*, D. Bernstein, published by Holt, Rinehart & Winston, 1984.

Figure 1.7 is reprinted from *Long Range Planning*, 22(6), D. Walters and D. Knee, Competititve strategies in retailing, copyright 1989, with kind permission from Elsevier Science Ltd, The Boulevard, Langford Lane, Kidlington, OX5 1GB, UK.

## REFERENCES

Aacker, D. A. (1991) *Managing Brand Equity – Capitalising on the Value of a Brand Name*, The Free Press.

Bernstein, D. (1984) *Corporate Image and Reality*, Eastbourne: Holt, Rinehart & Winston (Cassell).

Berry L. L. and Seiders, K. (1992) 'Managing the evidence in service businesses', *Design Management Journal, Design in Service Industries, Managing the Evidence of Intangible Products* (1) (Winter): 97–102.

Biemans, W. and Setz, H. J. (1995) 'Managing new product annoucements in the Dutch telecommunications industry', in M. Bruce and W. Biemans (eds) *Product Development: Managing the Challenge of the Design–Marketing Interface*, Chichester: John Wiley & Sons.

Bruce, M. (1994) *Changing Corporate Identity: The Case of a Regional Hospital*, Cambridge, Mass.: Harvard Business Press.

Bruce, M. and Docherty, C. (1993) 'It's all in the relationship', *Design Studies* 14(4) (October): 402–22.

*Business Week* (1990) Design, the new buzzword of the corporate world in the nineties, Innovation Issue (15 June): 171.

Caldecote V. (1979) 'Investment in new product development', *Journal of the Royal Society of Arts* (October): 684–95.

Caterpillar (1993) *Communicating Caterpillar: One Voice*, Peoria, Ill.: Caterpillar Inc.

Cooper, R. and Jones, T. (1995) 'The interfaces between design and other key functions in product development', in M. Bruce and W. Biemans (eds) *Product Development: Meeting the Challenge of the Design–Marketing Interface*, Chichester: John Wiley & Sons.

Cooper, R. G. and Kleinschmidt E. J. (1986) 'An investigation into the new product process: steps, deficiencies and impact', *Journal of Product Innovation Management* 3(1): 71–85.

Cooper, R. and Press, M. (1995) *The Design Agenda*, Chichester: John Wiley & Sons.

Cross, N., Naughton, J. and Walker, D. (1991) Design Method and Scientific Method, *Design Studies*, October.

Curtis, J. (1996) 'Catch me if you can', *Marketing* (7 March): 28–31.

*Design* (1995 winter): 38–9

Dyson (no date) *The Story of the Dyson Dual Cyclone*, – Dyson Appliances Limited.

Farr, M. (1955) *Design in British Industry, a Mid-century Survey*, Cambridge: Cambridge University Press.

Glegg, G. L. (1995) 'The Design of Design Cambridge, Cambridge University Press', in R. Roy and D. Wield (eds) *Product Design and Technological Innovation*, Milton Keynes: Open University Press.

Gorb, P. and Dumas, A. (1987) 'Silent design', *Design Studies* 8(3): 150–6.

Green, W. R. (1986) *The Retail Store: Design & Construction*, New York: Van Nosbrand Reinhold.

Gupta, A. K. and Wileman, D. (1988) 'The R&D–marketing interface in hi-tech firms', *Journal of Product Innovation Management* 5: 20–31.

Gupta, A. K., Raj S. P. and Wileman, D. (1985) R & D and marketing dialogue in high-tech firm', *Industrial Marketing Management* 14: 289.

Heskett, J. (1980) *Industrial Design*, London: Thames and Hudson.

HMSO (1995) *Forging Ahead: White Paper on Competitiveness*, London: HMSO.

Kotler P. and Rath G. A. (1984) 'Design: a powerful but neglected strategic tool', *Journal of Business Strategy* 5(2): 16–21.

McCarthy, F. (1994) *William Morris: A Life for Our Time*, London: Faber & Faber.

McGoldrick, P. (1990) *Retail Marketing*, Berkshire: McGraw Hill.

March, A. (1994) *Design to Value at BNR/Northern Telecom: The Vista Modular Phone*, Boston, MA.: Design Management Institute

Mercer, D. (1992) *Marketing*, Oxford: Blackwell.

OECD (1987) *Science and Technology Indicators*, Paris: Organisation for Economic Cooperation and Development.

Olins, W. (1990) *Corporate Identity*, London: Thames & Hudson.

—— (1991) 'Corporate identity and the behavioural dimension', *Design Management Journal* (Winter): 42–5.

Pilditch, J. (1987) *Winning Ways*, London: Harper & Row.

Potter, N. (1980) *What is a Designer?*, Reading: Hyphen Press.

Potter, S., Roy, R., Capon, C., Bruce M., Walsh, V. and Lewis, J. (1991) *The Benefits and Costs of Investment in Design: Using Professional Design Expertise in Product, Engineering and Graphics Projects*, Design Innovation Group Report 03, Milton Keynes: Open University.

Power, C. (1993) 'Flops', *International Business Week* (13 August).

Roy, R. and Bruce, M. (1984) *Product Design, Innovation and Competition in British Manufacturing*, Working Paper WP-02, Milton Keynes: Design Innovation Group, Open University

Roy, R. and Potter, S. (1993) 'The commercial impacts of investment in design', *Design Studies* 14(2) (April): 171–95.

Service, L., Hart, S. and Baker, M. (1989) *Profit by Design*, London: Design Council.

Shirley, R. and Henn, D. (1988) *Support for Design: Final Evaluation Report*, London: Research and Technology Policy Division Assessment Unit, Department of Trade and Industry.

Sisodia, R. S. (1992) 'Designing quality into services', *Design Management Journal, Design in Service Industries, Managing the Evidence of Intangible Products*, 3(1) (winter): 33–9.

Southgate, P. (1994) *Total Branding by Design*, London: Kogan Page.

Sparke, P. (ed.) (1986) *Did Britain Make it? British Design in Context 1946 to 1986*, London: Design Council.

Walsh, V., Roy, R., Bruce, M. and Potter, S. (1992) *Winning by Design: Technology, Product Design and International Competitiveness*, Oxford: Blackwell.

# 2 Marketing and design: a working relationship

*Margaret Bruce and Rachel Cooper*

> In a world where many new products are similar in function and
> even performance, a product's design – its shape, its look and
> above all its image – can make all the difference.
>
> (*Business Week* 1994)

## INTRODUCTION

Since the mid-1970s, manufacturing industry, in particular, has
identified that the two central factors determining the competitiveness of firms have been internal efficiency and the management of
external relationships with their suppliers (Lamming 1993). Companies have turned to partnering, using preferred suppliers and
building up long-term relationships.

For a number of years, design expertise has typically been
outsourced and partnered. Indeed, in the service sector, design
skills usually have been supplied by external design firms. None
the less, there are three different approaches to integrating design
expertise: in-house capability, outsourcing and a blend of these
two. In some cases, a 'temporary' team may be created by using a
number of different external suppliers for a given product development (Bryne et al. 1993). Whatever the source of design expertise, whether in-house or external, it has to be integrated with other
areas of the organization to form the new product or service
offering. Different management skills will be needed for different
situations; for example, sourcing and commissioning skills are
required by marketing professionals for design outsourcing. The
interface between marketing and design, and how this is managed,
is the theme of this chapter.

## SOURCING DESIGN

A trend to outsourcing of design is discernible in Britain, and accompanying this trend is the growth of the design consultancy profession (McAlhone 1987). A number of factors have contributed to the trend to design outsourcing. First, the increasing complexity of products and their shorter life-cycles demand expertise from a range of different sources, so that companies collaborate for various reasons, including developing new technology, spreading the costs and risks of new product development, and entering new markets (Dodgson 1993). Second, the use of technology in the design process has facilitated a change in practice, as Francis and Winstanley note:

> Firms are facing a high degree of competition and as the nature of the design process is changing (with the greater use of computers and technical expertise) then the opportunities for changing organisational forms are increasing and the pressures for switching to forms perceived as more effective are intensifying.
>
> (Francis and Winstanley 1987)

Third, design expertise is being used by service organizations, which have traditionally had few or no in-house design skills and so have consistently outsourced design expertise. To manage this effectively, service organizations like British Telecom and Royal Mail (see Chapter 5) have dedicated design managers to source, brief and liaise with external design firms. These design managers manage the relationships with the external design suppliers and so contribute to the success or otherwise of the design project.

### Approaches to design management

Three types of approaches to design management exist, namely: in-house design function; solely external expertise; a mixture of in-house and external design expertise (*see Part II* ). Each of these has benefits and costs.

### *In-house design sources*

Design skills lie within the firm and can be located in a design department, or be dispersed through R&D, production or marketing. As well as full-time design staff, other personnel such as the

Technical Director may be counted as additional design resources. In-house designers may be expected to generate income by serving as consultants to other companies.

### External design sources

Design competence lies outside the firm and design professionals are selected and commissioned to carry out the design activities required by the firm. Design managers – or those with the responsibility for design – source, commission, liaise with and evaluate the design skills. A 'temporary team' is an extreme example of an external approach. Indeed, Bryne et al. refer to this thus:

> a temporary network of independent companies – suppliers, customers, even erstwhile rivals . . . to share skills, costs and access to one another's markets . . . this new evolving, corporate model will be fluid and flexible – a group of collaborators that quickly unite to exploit a specific opportunity. Once the opportunity is met, the venture will, more often than not, disband.
>
> (Bryne et al. 1993)

### Combination of design sources

Design capability comprises a mix of in-house and external design skills. The external design professional is brought in to inject additional resources to ensure that the project is completed on time, or to put in fresh ideas, or to provide a specific expertise.

## Benefits and costs

The strength of an in-house approach to design management is that the designers are 'intimately aware of company practices . . . and are always on hand to give advice or deal with problems that may arise through the stages of product development . . . also they are more closely integrated into the overall design team' (British Productivity Council 1975). However, the danger is that they may either lack integration or become complacent and fail to provide innovative ideas. By contrast, external design professionals may make fresh inputs and may not be hampered by the politics and culture of the firm. Yet, they may make mistakes in moving from the concept to development stages because of their insufficient knowledge of the firm's practices (Potter et al. 1991). Fear of leakage of proprietary knowledge is another potential problem (Leverick and Littler 1993): how trusting can one be and how much information should the external designer have?

A blend of in-house and external design expertise appears to overcome the problems and build on the positive aspects of each situation. However, the integration of the in-house and external professionals has to be managed carefully to ensure that they are truly working together. The tension between fear of giving away commercially sensitive information and the need to build up an open and trusting relationship is particularly acute. Whatever the approach adopted, the interface between the design resource and

*Table 2.1* Comparison of approaches to the location of design

|  | *In-house* | *Outsource* | *Mixture* |
|---|---|---|---|
| *Purposes* | Accessible | Solve short-term problems | Flexible |
|  | Integrated within company practices and product development team | Relieve workloads |  |
|  |  | Access new ideas |  |
|  |  | Access specialist expertise |  |
|  | Cost-efficient | Easier to abort unsuccessful projects |  |
|  |  | Cost-efficient |  |
| *Management characteristics* | Encourage creativity | Evaluation of work more intense during the design process | Creation of design team is complex |
|  | Less anxiety over control factors |  |  |
|  |  | Level of contact higher in the initial relationship stage |  |
|  |  | Choosing the designer is critical |  |
|  |  | Communication factors uppermost |  |
|  |  | Fear of leakage of proprietary information |  |

*Source*: Bruce and Morris (1995)

other functions has to be managed and the nature of this interface considered, planned and integrated within the firm. Different approaches to the location of the design expertise are shown in Table 2.1.

## Company summaries

Three brief summaries of approaches to using design are presented below. Company A represents the 'in-house' approach, Company B is indicative of the 'outsourced' approach, Company C illustrates the 'temporary team' approach and Company D uses a blend of in-house and external design skills.

---

### COMPANY A: IN-HOUSE DESIGN EXAMPLE

Company A designs and manufactures mostly 'white goods' for the consumer market. An in-house design department is used whose role is perceived as mainly 'appearance' designing by the Design Manager, since the 'nuts and bolts' of the product basically remain the same from project to project.

Different appearances are evaluated in a presentation to marketing where the design proposals are compared in terms of the 'bottom-line cost versus appearance' compromise. Good rapport with marketing is critical as this leads to generation of appropriate solutions by design first time round.

The Design Manager argues that in-house designers have a level of familiarity with the company that puts any external designer at a disadvantage. When external design consultants have been used, they have slowed the design process, and for these reasons the use of external designers is not considered a 'serious option' for the foreseeable future. The Design Manager admitted that in-house design departments can become 'stagnant' leading to lower work rates and less creativity when compared with outhouse designers, but he saw the advantages as:

- cost (because they are a fixed overhead);
- familiarity with the firm's production, marketing and corporate culture;
- stability;
- appropriateness of design expertise;
- control of the resource (to produce appropriate and creative work);
- proprietary nature of the work is guaranteed.

The relationship with external consultants has in the past been on an arm's-length basis, where the contact between the consultant and other personnel at Company A was tightly controlled. Controlling the work of consultants was considered to be the major headache because the fact that they were external made it difficult for a client to monitor their work. Thus the key to design management for Company A is to allow the designers to be creative, but at the same time to make sure their work is appropriate.

## COMPANY B: EXTERNAL DESIGN CONSULTANCY EXAMPLE

Company B is a subsidiary of large electrical company. In 1980 Company B diversified from a spring production business (mainly for seatbelts in the automotive industry) into the design and manufacture of a pedestrian barrier system that made use of innovatory tensioned cloth webbing to guide pedestrians (usually to control customer queueing in banks and post offices, etc.).

Since the diversification, external design expertise has been utilized. The Marketing Director has a strong relationship with one particular consultant and associations with several smaller ones. Designers form part of an integral development team which consists of sales, marketing, production, engineering, and quality personnel. Suppliers are considered to be 'development partners'.

The team decided on a three- to five-year development strategy from which short-term tactical product development plans were created, which were then explained to the design consultant. The external designer was bought in to be briefed informally and to take part in 'brainstorming' exercises with the development team. This activity resulted in a product specification which was mutually agreed upon within the team. Whilst generating concepts was seen as the consultant's responsibility, evaluation of the consultant's work was undertaken by the whole team. Throughout the development process the product was constantly re-evaluated, to check its relevance to market requirements which might also be changing.

The Marketing Director believed that consultants should be viewed as extensions of in-house expertise: 'if you don't know anything about a subject and you hire an outside consultant, it may not help you because you don't know what you're talking about. You have to have a knowledge base to start with.' The trigger for using the design consultant was the company's lack of confidence about dealing with a particular task itself.

When buying design, the Marketing Director sees the personal characteristics of the consultant as the most important consideration, since other tangible aspects (reputation, quality of work) are to be expected as a minimum. He describes how he met the design consultant at a presentation, where 'I listened to what he had to say and I thought I could understand what this guy's talking about'; thus mutual language is seen as an important factor. Trust is another important ingredient of the partnership. Trust is about communication, for example talking about issues in the same way. The Marketing Director explains:

> if I can't trust him, I can't involve him, and if I can't involve him, I can't give him the information he needs to be effective. You'll get a much faster and better-quality result with the guy if you put everything on the table at the beginning.

The Marketing Director believes that mutual language and trust, enhanced by good communication, leads to better-quality solutions. Design management is therefore seen as managing the link between customer needs and the design input. Whilst controlling the resource is important, the Marketing Director also suggests that creativity requires freedom:

> I think you have to give them the freedom to let them do it. You have got to choose the right person otherwise you won't trust them to do some free thinking. Quality of input is down to the consultant used.

## COMPANY C: TEMPORARY TEAM

Within a service company new product development may entail the use of a number of independent suppliers and their integration with an internal team. For example, in the development of the Co-operative Bank's 24-Hour Banking network – which used advanced technology to provide videoconferencing facilities, cash and deposit machines in unmanned kiosks – an internal team with skills in marketing, technology, operations and distribution was set up. The Distribution Manager was in charge of the day-to-day running of the project, and he was supported by the CEO and other senior managers.

The external team was made up of different technology suppliers, the kiosk manufacturer, shopfitters and the corporate identity and graphic design company. Some of these companies had long-term relationships with the bank, others were new suppliers. Some of the suppliers knew each other from previous projects, others did not. The project manager was the prime source of contact within the bank for the suppliers. The external suppliers were not encouraged to work together as a team; the preferred approach was for the Project Manager to liaise with each supplier in turn, discuss progress with the internal team and then instruct the external suppliers to carry out further work. This approach to the project management of the 'temporary team' facilitated control and direct communication between the project manager and a given supplier.

## COMPANY D: COMBINATION OF IN-HOUSE AND OUTSOURCED DESIGN

Company D is a subsidiary of a large textile-producing plc which manufactured garden and car products for large car/DIY retailers. Internal R&D were supported by external product designers and their skills and expertise were integrated to produce new products. Product development was driven by the needs of the key accounts.

The company had built up a long-term relationship with a product design firm, which was regarded as beneficial because 'the designer knows our markets and our business and knows what we want. We consider them as an employee and we are working with them, rather than them working for us'. Initially the design firm was chosen on the basis of its reputation, but after a number of projects track record was the main grounds for continuing the relationship.

In terms of benefits, the company noted that using an external designer was cheaper than maintaining an in-house resource; the budget for a given project was discussed with the designer and the optimum design for the budget was produced. Despite the good working relationship certain difficulties were identified:

■ *accessibility*: problems might not be sorted out immediately, but depended on the design firm 'fitting these in' with other projects for their other clients;
■ *familiarity*: in-house staff were more involved with the project and had been involved with its modifications and upgrades;
■ *briefing*: consultants might not always appreciate the nuances of the project and so time and effort is taken to ensure that the external designer fully understood the nature of the project.

## Management implications

For all the companies, control and communication problems were of uppermost concern. These were dealt with in various ways:

■ time was taken in the selection of the designers – for external designers pitching was involved and also some design project work was undertaken to ensure that the level of design skills was satisfactory;
■ the brief was defined early and formed part of the contract, rather than evolving as the design work progressed;
■ intense level of contact in the initial stages of the design project was established via regular meetings – this also facilitated close monitoring of external designers' work;
■ familiarity with the design buyer's market needs and production processes were regarded as assets that in-house designers would have, compared with external designers – however, project managers were aware of this and therefore made specific efforts to overcome this problem, e.g. through intensive briefing and in-depth discussion;
■ long-term relationships were preferred because of their stability, loyalty and trust, which facilitated a creative and open atmosphere.

## MANAGEMENT AND INTEGRATION OF EXTERNAL DESIGN SKILLS

The decision to outsource design is driven mainly by cost and control factors. The design buyer's previous experience and personal preferences have a role to play, so a wide range of design management practices exists. Design management practices for outsourced design entail the procurement, commissioning and project management of the design resource, and issues of compatibility influence these practices. In addition, the design supplier has to decide whether to use a preferred supplier(s) and invest in building a longer-term relationship, or to switch suppliers, which could be costly in time and effort, or to use a rosta of preferred suppliers and chose from the rosta the most appropriate supplier for a given task. Again, a wide variety of practices exists. Public-sector organizations tend to switch suppliers and buy in design on price factors in the main. FMCG companies tend to have a roster of preferred suppliers, and other practices are evident elsewhere. In general, manufacturers tend to build up longer-term relationships with a preferred supplier.

Two dominant patterns of design relationships are evident in practice, namely long term and close, and short term and distant (see Figure 2.1). Long-term relationships may have perceived benefits in attaining security, trust and understanding (Bruce and Docherty 1993). A comparison of the relative merits of long- and short-term relationships is shown in Table 2.2.

Cultivating long-term relationships requires investment of personal time and effort, as well as the development of a modus operandi for design projects. The relationship between the design

*Figure 2.1* Matrix of design relationships

| | |
|---|---|
| Close/family-like Long-term | Arm's-length Long-term |
| Arm's-length Short-term | Close/family-like Short-term |

*Table 2.2* Relative merits of long- and short-term relationships

| Short-term advantages | Long-term advantages |
|---|---|
| **Comparison purposes**<br>Having a relationship with more than one consultant enabled the client to compare quality and efficiency factors between consultants.<br><br>**Cost**<br>Relationships were open to market forces.<br><br>**Access to different expertise**<br>This gave the client more choice in the type of expertise required.<br><br>**Time**<br>Consultants were used to relieve short-term in-house design workloads.<br><br>**Compatibility**<br>If a short-term relationship with a consultant is 'difficult' it gives the client the freedom to choose a more compatible designer partner | **Familiarity**<br>This improved the effectiveness of design input from project to project.<br><br>**Stability**<br>Once a project had been completed successfully with a consultant, management anxiety and uncertainty about the relationship and product development was in general reduced.<br><br>**Continuity**<br>Retaining the same consultant ensured that the brand proposition within and, if required, across product ranges remained the same. It also made the initial stages of each new project much easier because the 'process' of using the same consultant remained consistent. |

*Source*: Bruce and Morris (1995)

buyer and supplier has to be managed so that design is effectively integrated into the client organization. This involves two levels: at a project level, on a short-term basis; and at a relationship level, on a long-term basis. This integration is influenced by compatibility between the buyer and supplier, which has different elements: the characteristics of the individuals involved, the type of expertise required and the respective company cultures and modus operandi. Figure 2.2 depicts a model of the different phases involved in design relationships from initial contact to project completion. Contact in some form has to be maintained between projects to foster continuity, if a long-term relationship is to be established. Good design, a positive personal relationship and company compatibility have to dovetail for a long-term relationship to evolve. The model in Figure 2.2 sets out the types of decisions marketing professionals need to make at different phases of the design pro-

*Figure 2.2* Phases in design relationships

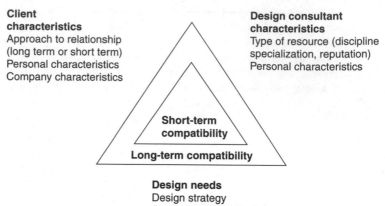

**Client
characteristics**
Approach to relationship
(long term or short term)
Personal characteristics
Company characteristics

**Design consultant
characteristics**
Type of resource (discipline
specialization, reputation)
Personal characteristics

**Short-term
compatibility**

**Long-term compatibility**

**Design needs**
Design strategy
Customer requirements
Product requirements

*Source*:  Bruce and Morris (1995)

cess. They need to ask which approach will give the most effective and quality of design for the same cost.

Once the design expertise has been sourced and the project is underway, the knowledge created has to be integrated into the business context. The ability of a firm to exploit external knowledge – that is, to recognize the value of new, external and meaningful information, assimilate it and apply it to commercial ends – has implications for its innovative ability, which Cohen and Levinthal (1990) refer to as a firm's 'absorptive capacity'. This entails the linking of 'internal' and 'external' networks (Biemans 1995), that is, the transfer of knowledge across and within different parts of the company.

One of the implications of the effectiveness of the interfaces inside an organization is their impact on the integration of external networks, and hence the ways in which external suppliers and their knowledge are used. 'Unless an organisation knows how to foster collaborative relationships internally, then it won't be good at making such relationships outside,' claims Don Ciampa CEO of Rath & Strong Consulting Firm (cited in Biemans 1995: 148). One example is that of market research (Brown and Ennew 1995) where external suppliers were commissioned to research the potential market opportunities for a new brand of chocolate. From their research, the agency recommended to its client that they should not invest in new product development. Part of the marketing group disregarded the research and went ahead anyway, and this only ended in commercial failure two years later. Internal politics were such that those who disagreed with the market research report had the power to override it.

Biemans (1995) cites different approaches to the creation of 'teamnets', that is, the combination of focused small groups of people within a network, or disparate groups of suppliers. Kodak, for example, has an Early Production Supplier Programme, which was created to involve suppliers closely in the design and manufacture of new products. Boeing involved customers, as members of their design/build teams, in the creation of the new 300-seat 777. Howard and Guile suggest that 'membership of (cross-functional) teams may be quite flexible and may even include suppliers, customers, consultants and members of technical advisory groups, as needed' (Howard and Guile; cited in Biemans 1995: 150).

Jevnaker (1995) describes a Norwegian furniture company which utilized a design consultant and where the collaboration led to innovative design (e.g. Balans chair) based on a new approach to seating. The first contact between the designer and CEO was on a casual basis, and the CEO took a risk to see if there was a market for such a radical design. The chair was exhibited at a major trade fair and considerable interest was shown in the product, which convinced the CEO to invest in manufacturing the chair. However, the product did not sell well, and so to stimulate sales the company adopted a strategy of educating its salesforce and those of its distributors in the ergonomic value of the chair, and emphasis on this benefit boosted sales. New product concepts were commissioned from the designer and the relationship between the company and designer became close, with the designer spending part of each week in the company. However, a change in the senior management of the firm affected the relationship and the designer had to exert time and effort in engaging the new managers with the design activity. This he did by demonstrating different concepts, getting the management team to try out different products and educating them in ergonomics, which influenced the form and function of his designs. In time, the new management team and the designer discovered effective ways to work together and gained a sense of mutual respect for each other's expertise. Jevnaker refers to this process as 'inauguration' and 'acknowledgement', that is, the education of non-designers into the 'way of seeing' of the designer, so that they share the same vision and have empathy for each other's roles and responsibilities. So, instead of the new management team dismissing the designer, they continued to employ him/her and to recognize that his/her specific skills meshed with those of the firm to produce distinctive products that were commercially viable. Over time, both companies 'learnt by doing' how to work together effectively to produce a stream of innovations.

Obviously managing and integrating external design skills requires an understanding of the role of design in the company's overall strategy to enable effective design sourcing, in conjunction with design management policies and good project planning. These will be discussed in Chapter 3.

## Marketing–design interfaces in new product design

I perfectly understand the importance of design. But that is not to say that my education, experience or natural instincts lead me with confidence to produce it myself, or back others to produce it on my behalf. I believe that a large number of managers have exactly the same problem.

(Sir Christopher Hogg, Chairman of Courtaulds, speaking at the SIAD Design Management Seminar 1985; cited in Walker 1990)

The integration of design expertise into particular projects and the ways of sustaining design knowledge are the focus here, in particular in the marketing–design interface. It is clear that, in terms of the new product development (NPD) process, unless the organizational climate is supportive and the key functions work together effectively success may not be achieved. Much management research has focused on the interface between marketing and manufacturing (Souder 1988; Cooper and Jones 1995); both industry and academia have placed the emphasis on building up awareness of the importance of being market-oriented, of understanding the customer, improving the use of technology and using tools and techniques for more effective manufacture. In the past few years quality has become an issue that has been used to focus all functions and to develop cross-functional relationships (Griffin 1992; Hauser and Clausing 1988).

A University of Strathclyde survey (Hart and Service 1988) that examined the relationship between product design strategy, design management and company performance in 369 British companies identified that the following characteristics were among those common to the top performing companies:

■ market-led orientation;
■ use of design as competitive tool;
■ multi-disciplinary approach to new product development;

- adaptability and willingness to change;
- good company image;
- continuous product improvement;
- representation of design at Board level;
- top management commitment to new product development;
- attention to technology and market trends.

The Strathclyde research suggests that the effective interface of design and marketing had a positive effect on business performance. Braun, the German consumer electronics company, that regards itself as the epitome of 'good design', provides an example. It is a 'design-oriented' firm and its strategic orientations reflect its design culture (Freeze 1990). Design is represented at the highest management level and the company's mission statement centres around ten design principles (see Table 2.3). Freeze points out that Braun has an uncompromising commitment towards the pursuit of excellence in performance-oriented design. Every product designed and manufactured by Braun must adhere to these principles of 'good design'. This focuses both marketing and design professionals on this topic.

Other research supports the findings of the Strathclyde study and also indicates that the success or failure of NPD can be influenced significantly by the interface between the marketing and design functions (Rosenthal 1990). In addition, it is also necessary to examine the dynamics of each of the interfaces, specifically those within the design function and those between design and all the other key function areas. Cooper and Jones

*Table 2.3* Braun's ten principles of good design

---

- Good design is innovative.
- Good design enhances the usefulness of a product.
- Good design is aesthetic.
- Good design displays the logical structure of a product; its form follows its function.
- Good design is unobtrusive.
- Good design is honest.
- Good design is enduring.
- Good design is consistent right down to its details.
- Good design is ecologically conscious.
- Good design is minimal design.

---

*Source*: Freeze (1990)

*Table 2.4* Common areas of weakness in new product design across six UK companies

| | |
|---|---|
| New product development | Unclear roles and responsibilities<br>Badly chosen projects with no clear project goals<br>Inadequate funding and resourcing of projects<br>Poor communications<br>Not using multidisciplinary teams<br>Little toleration of failure<br>Lack of encouragement of innovation |
| Design | Overburdened with routine work<br>Slow response to the needs of the market<br>Unable to do anything challenging<br>Resistant to change |
| Marketing and design | Marketing not understanding the design process<br>Lack of clear information supplied to design<br>Little mutual respect between functions<br>Lack of market research and no coordination with sales |
| Product briefs and specifications | Late arrival<br>Too brief, vague and ambiguous |
| R&D and design | Little contact between R&D and design<br>No awareness of current research being undertaken within the company<br>Little encouragement to use new technology, materials or processes<br>Lack of a good technical library |
| Manufacturing and design | Design not understanding production implications<br>Production constraining design<br>Production and manufacturing not being involved early enough in the project<br>Not using the same components for prototypes as are intended for production |

*Source*: Cooper and Jones (1995)

(1995) studied a number of UK companies to diagnose the weaknesses of design interfaces in NPD and found several indicators of NPD problems (see Table 2.4). From this study it was clear that in those situations where difficulties arose there was little understanding of others' roles and responsibilities, that marketing did not understand the design process and as a consequence design was overburdened with routine work.

Hopkins (1981) claims that there ought to be a continuous interaction between marketing and design throughout the product development programme. Not only do designers need to know about the product, the competition, the target market and the price, but, as well as having information on the characteristics of the consumer, they also need to be regularly updated on any changes in their requirements (Dace 1989). This range of information needs to be presented clearly and must, at all times, be appropriate to the needs of the designers (Slade 1989). In order to achieve this successfully, it is often recommended that marketing should fully understand the design process and that there should also be regular communication between marketing, production and manufacturing to ensure that all products are appropriate to the company's current or planned manufacturing capability (Rothwell and Whiston 1990).

As one of the primary means of communicating product information from marketing to the rest of the development team, the initial brief and the subsequent specification have been identified as critical documents. Usually written by marketing, the brief ought to be clear and concise, because a vague and ambiguous brief can be the source of major problems in the project (see Chapter 3). Furthermore, early discussion of the brief allows design to comment on it and feed back their understanding before acceptance (Rosenthal 1990). This ensures that all parties understand and agree with the briefing document and that design do not have to clarify omissions later on. Although involvement of all of the NPD functions means that the specification may take longer to prepare, it is also important that this document should be communicated clearly before any detailed design work is undertaken.

## Company summaries

Two cases from the study by Cooper and Jones (1995) are presented here; these identify some of the main problems of the marketing design interface.

---

### COMPANY A: A LARGE INTERNATIONAL MANUFACTURER OF DOMESTIC APPLIANCES

The analysis for Company A identified a number of important areas.

Individual roles and responsibilities were not made clear to all, and projects were felt to be neither well chosen nor well funded. Projects were not considered to be well managed;

there were no clear project goals, nor was there good communication between personnel. Furthermore, NPD was not felt to occur in a creative environment; nor were personnel well motivated. Multidisciplinary teams were not used, and key functions identified more with their separate departments than with the team as a whole.

The contribution of design was not recognized, and design felt burdened with routine work.

Marketing did not understand the design process and was therefore unable to provide design with the necessary information at the appropriate times. There was no clear idea of how market research was undertaken and coordinated with other marketing areas.

Design was not aware of what R&D was undertaken by the company, the use of new technologies was not encouraged and it was felt that a good technical library was not available.

Neither production nor manufacturing was considered to be involved early enough, while design felt constrained by production and were not made to understand the implications of their design decisions.

## COMPANY B: A LARGE MANUFACTURER OF CONSUMER PRODUCTS

For Company B the conclusions were more specific to the functions and their interfaces.

Design staff in particular were not happy with their role and position within the company. They did not feel that their responsibilities were clear and were scared of making mistakes. They thought that resources were wasted and that the reasons for terminating projects were not communicated to them. They tended to identify more with their department than with the team, and considered that their contribution was not recognized. In addition, other functions felt that design did not respond quickly to the needs of the market and had an insufficient input into NPD.

Although it was felt that design undertook its role within the company effectively, marketing neither respected design, nor were in turn respected by design, and were not felt to understand either the design process or the needs of design. Designers did not feel that enough market research was undertaken and considered that it typically addressed only the present and not future demands. In addition, managers felt that marketing was not innovative.

Although R&D was well integrated with design, it was considered that a good technical library was not present within the company, nor was information on new materials and processes made available to design. Moreover, the use of such new technologies was not encouraged.

The relationship between design and production was generally effective. However, design felt that production constrained design and a close interaction between the functions in the early stages of projects was considered to be lacking.

## Marketing and design styles

Walker (1990) argues that these problems are deep-rooted and lie in the different 'psyche' of marketing and design disciplines (see Table 2.5). Marketing are trained to be adept with words and numbers and to develop their analytical powers; whereas designers are trained to be visual, emotive and analytical. They are located in two separate worlds that have different professional styles.

Conflicts between design and management can and do arise. Part of the designer's culture is based on individuality and originality and a desire to be creative. Designers work intuitively as well as imposing a rational and analytical structure on their work. Designers are comfortable with uncertainty and coming up with solutions to problems. Their research for inputs into the creative process entails 'wandering around' to collect visual material, photographs, competitors' products, to watch people's reactions to existing articles, to observe the body language and expressions of those providing them with the design brief and to have some feeling for what the organization is about and its goals. They may ask 'awkward' questions whilst searching for this kind of input into the design process. They may look different and talk differently from other managers – wearing bold colours, distinctive shapes and textured fabrics, as well as using a distinctive language, for example referring to the 'sculpture' of the pack of a TV set, or the 'softness of the corner' of a desk, etc.

By contrast, marketing as presented in most textbooks (for example Kotler 1994; Dibb et al. 1994), is based on rationality, measurement and certainty, and on teamwork and decision-making. Visualization as a form of communication is not common; numeracy and literacy are more highly prized. Conformism is more likely to yield promotion and job security than individuality. So, a potential culture clash between design and management is

*Table 2.5* Marketing and design polarities

| Characteristics | Managers | Designers |
|---|---|---|
| Aims | Long term<br>Profits/returns<br>Survival<br>Growth<br>Organizational<br>durability | Short term<br>Product/service quality<br>Reform<br>Prestige<br>Career building |
| Focus | People<br>Systems | Things<br>Environments |
| Education | Accountancy<br>Engineering<br>Verbal<br>Numerical | Crafts<br>Art<br>Visual<br>Geometric |
| Thinking styles | Serialist<br>Linear<br>Analysis<br>Problem-oriented | Holistic<br>Lateral<br>Synthesis<br>Solution-led |
| Behaviour | Pessimistic<br>Adaptive | Optimistic<br>Innovative |
| Culture | Conformity<br>Cautious | Diversity<br>Experimental |

*Source*: adapted from Walker (1990)

present. This may be effective in 'sparking off' new ideas, but it can mean a rejection of more radical design solutions and result in 'me-too' design. Designers are increasingly aware of this 'culture clash', and UK designers, in particular, are aware that their design work has to be commercially viable and that they have to use a language that builds bridges with managers if their design ideas are to be accepted. Often designers and production engineers use a very different language to describe the project; for example, in one company visited recently by the authors, the production manager wanted to specify the design time for given a project tightly and to allow for no possibility for change once designs were being agreed, and he joked about the designers' use of words like 'soft', 'curvy', etc. He wanted a shade, tone and hue of a colour, for instance, to be given to the designers, that is, to build in more constraints into the design process. From the designers' viewpoints these constraints may be so constricting that the designers would feel inhibited in their creativity.

None the less, the two 'worlds' are finding ways to bridge the communication gap: designers are learning to operate in a commercial world and to direct their creativity to serve the goals of their client's organizations, rather than producing designs that they themselves like regardless of the client's needs; and marketing professionals are recognizing the commercial benefits of using professional designers and are developing design management skills. Walker (1990) points out that it is unlikely that one person can have all of the characteristics of a designer and marketing professional and so a 'working partnership' is required that builds on the relative strengths of each area. It is the differences in perception, attitudes, processes and skills that make designers and marketing professionals important to each other. As Walker (1990) simply puts it: 'they need each other.'

Cooper and Jones suggest that the marketing and design interface could be enhanced by:

1   *Understanding*: this means each function understanding not only its own role and responsibility but also those of others in the team.
2   *Awareness*: each function and team member must be aware of, and respond to, the needs of the others during the process.
3   *Communication*: good communication in terms of frequency and content must occur between functions, both at the beginning of a product development programme, in order to develop an accurate product concept description or design brief, and throughout the process in terms of the findings of market testing and product testing through to launch.
4   *Commitment*: a culture of commitment to the project must be evident from the outset. That commitment must be based on respect and understanding of the value of all functions contributing to the design and development process
                              (Cooper and Jones 1995: 95).

These aspects are present in situations where an effective marketing–design interface is in place. The following examples illustrate this.

One company that has recently developed a new product family of industrial products is Ingersoll Rand (see Chapter 4). In the market for construction tools, major innovations have been rare since the mid-1950s, although incremental improvements to products is commonplace. Within a year of launch Irgo-Pic was the market leader and was a highly successful product. The head of the product development team considered two main factors to have led to its success: first, the small, close-knit, interdisciplinary product development team; and, second, the continuous involvement of the user in the product development process. The product development team comprised marketing, design and engineering managers, all of whom were equally responsible for the decisions made throughout the product development process. This ensured that tasks were carried out in parallel, and that a blend of marketing and technical managers visited key customers together to ascertain their attitudes to and views of the company's products and those of their competitors.

In BNR/Northern Telecom a multidisciplinary team was made responsible for product design (March 1994). This team comprised engineers, product designers, graphic designers, psychologists and marketing specialists. User requirements were continually monitored with the aim of identifying those product attributes that converged with customer values and market trends, and this information was fed into the early phases of product definition and established target requirements for the design group. For this company, user needs were paramount in terms of product differentiation and in establishing a proprietary basis for competition. All those involved in product development had to be accountable for user needs; for example, the industrial designers adhered to three guiding principles: easy to recognize, easy to choose and simple to use.

The user-orientated approach to market research was emphasized at the idea and concept-definition stages of product development, but so as to maintain user/customer focus such research was necessary throughout the process, with collaborative inputs from market research, design and the technologists.

## CONCLUSIONS

The dimensions of the marketing and design interface have been the overriding theme of this chapter. It is clear that there are different modes of working and thinking that prohibit a full integration of the two, but an empathy for each other's capabilities and expertise would encourage synergy. Marketing and design do need each other and the Chapter 3 provides some insights into how to foster an effective relationship.

## ACKNOWLEDGEMENTS

Figure 2.2 and Tables 2.1 and 2.2 are reproduced with permission from 'Approaches to design management in the product development process', M. Bruce and B. Morris, in *Product Development: Meeting the Challenge of the Design – Marketing Interface*, M. Bruce and W. Biemans (eds), published by John Wiley & Sons, 1995. Copyright John Wiley & Sons.

Table 2.3 is reproduced from *Braun AG: The KF40 Coffee Machine*, K. Freeze, published by the Design Management Institute.

Table 2.4 is reproduced with permission from 'The interfaces between design and other key functions in product development,' R. Cooper and T. Jones, in *Product Development: Meeting the Challenge of the Design – Marketing Interface*, M. Bruce and W. Biemans (eds), published by John Wiley & Sons, 1995. Copyright John Wiley & Sons.

Table 2.5 is reproduced from 'Managers and designers: two tribes at war?', D. Walker, in *Design Management: A Handbook of Issues and Methods*, M. Oakley (ed.), published by Blackwell, 1990.

## REFERENCES

Biemans, W. (1995) 'Internal and external networks in product development: a case for integration', in M. Bruce and W. Biemans (eds) *Product Development: Meeting the Challenge of the Design–Marketing Interface*. Chichester: John Wiley.

Brown, A. D. and Ennew, C. T. (1995) 'Market research and the politics of new product development', *Journal of Marketing Management* 11: 339–53.

Bruce, M. and Biemans, W. (eds) (1995) *Product Development: Meeting the Challenge of the Design–Marketing Interface*, Chichester: John Wiley.

Bruce, M. and Docherty, C. (1993) 'It's all in a relationship: a comparative study of client–design consultants', *Design Studies* 14(4): 402–22.

Bruce, M. and Morris, B. (1995) 'Approaches to design management in the product development process', in M. Bruce and W. Biemans (eds) *Product Development: Meeting the Challenge of the Design–Marketing Interface*, John Wiley: Chichester.

Bryne, J. A., Brandt, R. D. and Part, O. (1993) 'The virtual corporation', *Business Week International*, (8 February): 36–40.

Business Week (1994) 'Why Italian design is sweeping the world', *Business Week* (3 September).

Cohen, W. M. and Levinthal, D. A. (1990) 'Absorptive capacity: a new perspective on learning and innovation', *Administrative Science Quarterly* 35: 128–52.

Cooper, R. G. (1993) *Winning at New Products: Accelerating the Process from Idea to Launch*, 2nd edn, Reading, Mass.: Addison-Wesley.

Cooper, R. and Jones, T. (1995) 'The interfaces between design and other key functions in product development', in M. Bruce and W. Biemans (eds) *Product Development: Meeting the Challenge of the Design–Marketing Interface*, Chichester: John Wiley.

Craig, A. and Hart, S. (1992) 'Where to now in new product development research?', *European Journal of Marketing* 26(11): 2–49.

Dace (1989) 'Japanese new product development', *Quarterly Review of Marketing* 14(2): 4–13.

Dibb, S., Simkin, L., Pride, W., and Ferrell, O. C. (1994) *Marketing: Concepts and Strategies*, 2nd European edn, London: Houghton Mifflin.

Dodgson, M. (1993) *Technological Collaboration in Industry*, London: Routledge.

Francis, A. and Winstanley, D. (1988) 'Managing new product development: some alternative ways to organise the work of technical specialists', *Journal of Marketing Management* 4(2) (Winter): 249–60.

Freeze, K. (1990) *Braun AG: The KF40 Coffee Machine*, Boston, Mass.: Design Management Institute.

Griffin, A. (1992) 'Evaluating QFD's use in US firms as a process for developing products', *Journal of Product Innovation Management*, 9: 171–87.

Gorb, P. and Dumas, A. (1987) 'Silent design', *Design Studies* 8(3): 150–6.

Hart, S. J. and Service, L. M. (1988) 'The effects of managerial attitudes to design on company performance', *Journal of Marketing Management*, 4(2): 217–29.

Hauser, J. R. and Clausing, D. (1988) 'The house of quality', *Harvard Business Review* (May–June): 63–73.

Hopkins, D. S. (1981) 'New product winners and losers', *Research Management*, 24(3): 12–17.

Howard, W. G. Jr and Guile, B. R. (eds) (1992) *Profiting from Innovation*, New York: Free Press.

Jevnaker, B. (1995) 'Developing capabilities for innovative product designs: a case study of the Scandinavian furniture industry', in M. Bruce and W. Biemans (eds) *Product Development: Meeting the Challenge of the Design–Marketing Interface*, Chichester: John Wiley.

Johne, A. and Snelson, P. (1988) 'Success factors in product innovation: a selective review of the literature', *Journal of Product Innovation Management* 5(20): 114–28.

Lamming, R. (1993) *Beyond Partnership: Strategies for Innovation and Lean Supply*, Hemel Hempstead: Prentice-Hall.

Leverick, F. and Littler, D. A. (1993) *The Risks and Rewards of Collaboration: A Survey of Collaborative Product Development in UK Companies*, Manchester: Manchester School of Management, UMIST.

McAlhone, B. (1987) *British Design Consultancy*, London: Design Council.

March, A. (1994) *Design Value at BNR/Northern Telecom: The Vista Modular Phone, Case Study*, Boston, Mass.: Design Management Institute.

Potter, S., Roy, R., Capon, C., Walsh, V. and Bruce, M. (1991) *The Benefits and Costs of Investment in Design*, Milton Keynes: Design Innovation Group, Open University.

Rosenthal, S. (1990) *Building a Workplace Culture to Support New Product Innovation*, Boston Mass.: Boston University Manufacturing Round Table.

Rothwell, R. and Whiston, T. G. (1990) 'Design, innovation and corporate integration', *R&D Management* 20(3): 193–201.

Souder, W. E. (1988) 'Managing relations between R&D and marketing in new product development projects', *Journal of Product Innovation Management*, 5(1): 6–19.

Topalian, A. (1989) 'Organisational features that nurture design success in business enterprises', *Proceedings of the Conference on International Engineering Management*, Toronto.

Walker, D. (1990) 'Managers and designers: two tribes at war?', in M. Oakley (ed.) *Design Management: A Handbook of Issues and Methods*, Oxford: Blackwell.

# 3 *Using design effectively*

*Margaret Bruce and Rachel Cooper*

Design is everything to the success of our products. We demand
great creative vision that works in the real world and design that
encourages intuitive interaction with our products. We only
work with people we can trust to challenge us, to run with a
leading edge idea and be dedicated to our success.
(Brian Hinman, President and CEO, Polycom Inc;
cited in ID March April 1996)

## INTRODUCTION

It is clear that the effective use of design is a crucial contributor
to the effectiveness of business activities and to overall
corporate success. This chapter discusses the most important
aspects of managing design and provides tools and guidelines
for doing so.

First, it is important to understand the role design plays in a
business or organization. An effective tool for doing this is often
described as a design audit. This needs to be followed by the
development of a policy for the management and use of design
by the organization, and then good design management practice.
This chapter will therefore discuss the process of auditing design
and developing a policy for design and the practice of managing
the design process.

## MANAGING DESIGN STRATEGICALLY

Managing design 1: when undertaking a design audit, decide:

1   What aspects of design in the organization are going to be
audited.
2   How: by external auditors or internal auditors?
3   Which method: benchmarking, best practice, focus groups?

4   What timescale?
5   What should result: reporting and action?

## Auditing design

In undertaking a design audit organizations are attempting to define the role of design in their business. There have been numerous approaches to design audits, from the short analysis of design sensitivity given to us by Kotler and Rath (1990) and the checklists presented by Topalian (1983), to the detailed audit programmes developed by Morton for the Design Council (Cooper and Press 1995). The aspects of an organization's business to which they have been applied is also random. These aspects are related to the reasons which drive the audit process; for instance, the business may be trying to reposition itself in the marketplace or to develop a cohesive approach to product design and development. Cooper and Press (1995) provide us with an overview of the issues which should be addressed by design audits (see Figure 3.1). These are as follows:

1   The environmental issues which impact corporate strategy and design strategy, such as legislation, market trends, competitor trends. For instance, there are international telecommunications standards for signalling, and therefore a UK telecommunications company developing networks must not only comply with national standards such as BT's, but also with the international standard D7S, otherwise they may be excluded from world markets.
2   The corporate culture, the levels of design awareness, including values and vision, the design strategy (implicit or otherwise) and the silent design decision-making. Frequently organizations have no understanding of how design impacts their business or indeed what design means to them. This must be understood and the values articulated and communicated through design, otherwise the customer will always receive confused messages. For instance, a rail company communicates its values through the quality of its service; this is reflected in the carriage's interior design, the quality and presentation of the food, the uniforms and the travel documents. If these are poor, no matter how efficient the journey, underlying negative perceptions may result from the traveller's experience.
3   The 'management' of the design and design projects, and the design processes and design skills available. Too often design is commissioned and managed in a random manner by various individuals in organizations. This is often evidenced by a

*Figure 3.1* The complexity and the levels an organizational design audit might address

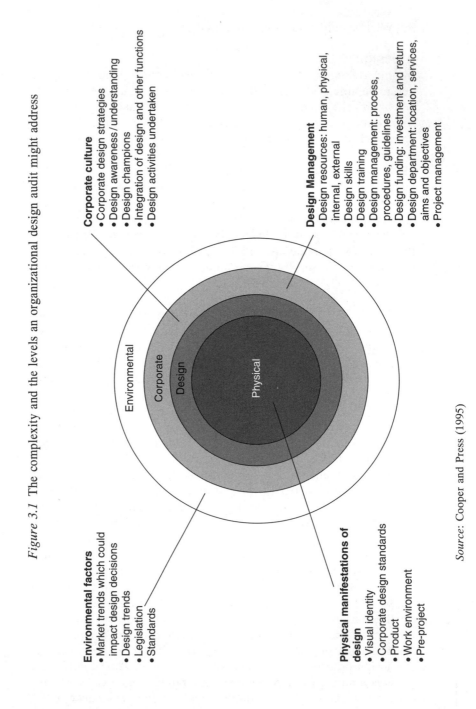

**Environmental factors**
- Market trends which could impact design decisions
- Design trends
- Legislation
- Standards

**Physical manifestations of design**
- Visual identity
- Corporate design standards
- Product
- Work environment
- Pre-project

**Corporate culture**
- Corporate design strategies
- Design awareness/understanding
- Design champions
- Integration of design and other functions
- Design activities undertaken

**Design Management**
- Design resources: human, physical, internal, external
- Design skills
- Design training
- Design management: process, procedures, guidelines
- Design funding: investment and return
- Design department: location, services, aims and objectives
- Project management

Environmental

Corporate

Design

Physical

*Source:* Cooper and Press (1995)

plethora of dissimilar interpretations of the corporate logo or typeface on literature. It also results in overrun budgets and time.

4   The physical manifestations of design; the product/service, place and communication in all the organization's activities. Analysing the design of all manifestations of design can not only marshal an appreciation of the aesthetic and functional aspects of the company's use of design, but also lead to competitive benchmarking and recommendations for improvements.

Clearly what one audits is dependent on what is important to the business, and also on the resources available to support an audit programme. In the first instance the business requirements of an audit need to be considered by defining the audit's overall aims and objectives.

The aims and objectives of design audits will vary between organizations. However, the potential aims of a design audit might be:

■ to advise and direct strategic change (e.g. noting competitor activity and market forces might suggest the need to reposition the whole company through a corporate identity change);
■ to improve the overall standard of product design as compared to competitors (the design audit, having assessed the products and benchmarked against competitors, can inform an improvement process or product semantic);
■ to develop a design policy manual;
■ to monitor policy implementation;
■ to improve design standards (e.g. having set targets for design standards or policy, the audit monitors current position in order to inform and advise on methods for improvement).

In terms of undertaking a design audit there are no existing tools. Cooper and Press make recommendations, suggesting that:

if one is concerned with product design management, one might choose the Design Council approach using the BS7000 standard against which to benchmark the activity. If one was concerned with a product, one might use the relevant tools such as Design for Manufacture, or Value Analysis. However, if these are considered too prescriptive for the subject, then a methodology must be used that is appropriate. Methods include developing a checklist of issues or questions to ask, questionnaires and interviews both structured and unstructured. There are also observational techniques, as in the 'Journey' method, recording all relevant design activity and measuring it using a pre-defined criteria, for instance, of what is acceptable, good or poor.

(Cooper and Press 1995: 215)

There are, in fact, a number of issues to consider and plan when developing a design audit, as Cooper and Press (1995) suggested:

- What will be the subject of the audit?
- What are the aims and objectives ?
- Who is responsible for commissioning the audit?
- Who will undertake the audit – external, internal or a combination of personnel?
- What questions will be addressed?
- How will the data be collected – interviews, questionnaire, checklists, focus groups, user testing?
- What criteria will be used?
- When will the audit be undertaken?
- What outcome is expected from the process?
- How are the findings to be used or implemented?
- Who is responsible for acting on the recommendations?
- How much will the audit cost?
- How will the audit be evaluated?

Design audits provide valuable information from which a policy for design and design management can be constructed. It is therefore worth investing in a rigorous audit.

## Developing a policy for design

Managing design 2: when developing a design policy:

1  Identify management responsibility for design.
2  Determine design values.
3  Determine design skill and competency requirements.
4  Determine design procurement process – pitching policy.
5  Develop a process for managing design.
6  Develop design policy awareness training.

Frequently organizations fail to consider their policy for design, not only in terms of how design is managed but also its contribution to the business. Every manifestation of the company's products and communication will say something to its customers and stakeholders about how the company sees its business and its customers, how much it is concerned about its employees and also the environment. Take, for instance, an airport. Not only must the interior design service reflect the needs of the customers, it must also operate effectively for its employees. In addition, whatever publicity it uses must show concern for the environment, on which it is undoubtedly having an impact.

The outcome of a design audit is usually a report, which forms the basis of a design policy, and such a policy would ideally cover some or all of the following:

■ Who manages design?
■ What do they manage?
■ What skills are required?
■ What should be in the design brief?
■ What type of system of management and monitoring will be used?
■ What training and awareness programmes are to be developed?
■ What design skill and competencies are required?
■ What type of design orientation and style is required?
■ Are designs are to be outsourced or in-house?
■ How are designers to be recruited?
■ How is the design pitching process to be organized?
■ What are the core values to be reflected in the corporate identity, products and services?
■ How will the business ethics and environmental policies be reflected through design?

A good design management policy will set out guidelines for the management of design, for example in terms of skills and competencies, procedures and evaluation criteria.

## MANAGING THE DESIGN PROCESS

Managing design 3: when planning for a project:

1   Determine the objectives of the project.
2   Define project plan and determine key milestones.
3   Appoint project leader or manager.

In order to manage any process one must understand what it is. There are many models of the design process, frequently developed by specialists in one discipline or another, predominantly engineering design (Pugh 1991) or architectural design (Lawson 1990). Four basic stages of the design process can be identified, as described by Bennet et al. (1988) and as shown in Chapter 1 (see p. 31). These are *formulation, evolution, transfer* and *reaction* (see Figure 3.2). These four stages are very generic and are therefore appropriate because they can be attributed to the design process involved in most design disciplines and elaborated upon for specific applications.

The design process is not necessarily sequential. Research (Cooper 1995) indicates that success in a project, particularly in new product development, occurs when activities run to some extent simultaneously or concurrently – for example market testing and design during prototype development. Many companies use phase reviews or stage gates to monitor the process and formally approve work, in order to move to the next phase. A lack of a clear design management process or project plan often leads to poor team commitment and little project ownership.

Obviously, such design management process programmes can be generic or specific. It is generally recommended that a generic process is developed, to be adapted later for specific projects. Hozelock (the UK garden equipment manufacturer), for instance, use a simple template, modifying it according to project needs. In order to manage and monitor design projects effectively against the programmes, a project leader or manager needs to be given responsibility. Research indicates that a product/project champion

*Figure 3.2* Four stages in the design process

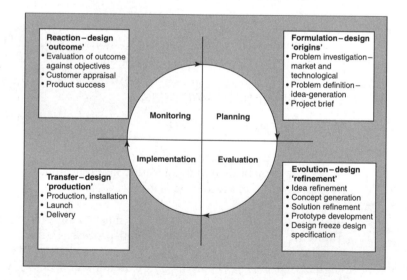

*Source*: adapted from Bennet et al. (1988)

(Roberts and Fusfield 1991) can create a culture and climate which leads a project to a successful conclusion. Project leaders frequently remain the only consistent aspect of the project teams as outsourcing, and even the use of internal resources, is a matter of bringing together competencies as and when the project requires it (see company case below).

## PRODUCT DEVELOPMENT PROCESS

In 1991 a major UK FMCG manufacturing company reviewed recent launches of a number of their products and identified a number of problem areas as follows:

- the planning process in neither case recognized the complexity of the projects; timings were optimistic with little/no allowance for the implications of the potential need to revise components in the light of initial production experiences;
- the objectives/goals of each project were changed during the course of the developments without sufficient regard to the implications of the change in terms of previously set deadlines;
- there was clear evidence that there was a lack of real commitment by team members to achieve the project goals, i.e. there was no ownership by the team of the project objectives;
- communications both within the team and across functions were poor;
- there was an absence of go/no-go milestones in both projects. (Such milestones are project stages at which the work is reviewed and decisions made as to whether to continue.)

Success factors were identified as:

- market and consumer research gained early;
- concept defined and worked to;
- focus;
- drive;
- ownership and product champion;
- teamwork;
- supplier involvement;
- product and packaging testing;
- marketing support planned and delivered.

As part of an action to address these issues the company developed a new product development process which began at 'idea' stage and had clear milestones. This was endorsed by senior management. Parallel working and teamwork were seen as an essential part of this process. A training programme for all functions and levels was used as a means of introducing the process and developing the culture to support it.

## The design process

### *Formulation – design 'origins'*

Managing design 4: when selecting the team:

1   Determine the skill requirements of the team, including all interdisciplinary contributions.
2   Appoint the project team.
3   Source designers.
4   Determine roles and responsibility, in particular those of the designers.

Formulation refers to early planning and need recognition. This may be prompted by a number of factors, for instance a perceived gap in the market, a new material, or software. Indeed, a combination of a number of factors such as marketing opportunity and technological development or a customer request may stimulate the need for design activity. This early idea capture, need recognition and project assessment is rather a 'chicken and egg' situation as far as managing design is concerned (see Figure 3.3). In some companies and situations (Figure 3.3-A), a need will be recognized, for example in corporate publicity, to develop a brochure or sales material. It would then follow that a manager (usually marketing) is given responsibility for determining how to source and manage the design and development. In other cases (Figure 3.3-B) such as product design, a company may have permanent functions whose responsibility is to generate new ideas and develop the concepts. ICL, for instance, uses a Technology Division whose responsibility it is to search for market and technological new product or service concepts. At this stage, ideas are fairly loose, general and 'fuzzy'. None the less, whichever approach is adopted, a business decision must be made to explore the opportunity or react to a situation and to make further progress. This should be

*Figure 3.3* Two models of where design starts in the design process

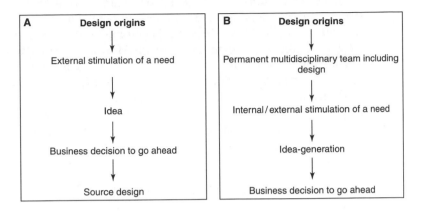

done by assessing the idea against predetermined criteria such as the business strategy.

At this stage, then, a project development team may take the initiative to develop the idea further, or a brand/product manager may have the remit to commission design. In this case decisions must be made on the type of contribution required from the designer. For instance, the development of the design brief may require input from the designer and the appointment of designers must therefore occur before the problem definition. It is crucial, therefore, that the project leader/manager determines how design is to be used during the project.

Designers frequently believe that their role must be set in a wider context. For example, in the development of a corporate identity for London Transport the client (London Transport) may have thought the objective was to create graphic unity for the organization. However, as Jeremy Rewse Davies (designer), commented:

> my task as I saw it was to try to unify the disparate parts of the organisation with design without attempting to change or fight against the political and management agenda. The central plank of the task was to install into the various companies a culture based on design excellence with the familiar corporate symbol and typeface as a starting point.
>
> (Rewse Davies 1995: 27)

Designers' roles in organizations tend to develop as their skills are better understood and when they are taking a more strategic role in product development. They are becoming 'product innovation suppliers'. *Business Week* (1995) quoted Gianfranco Zaccai, President of Boston-based Design Continuum: 'We are now doing their research, applying their core technologies and conceptualising future product lines. Design is becoming much more strategic, a lot more like Management Consultant McKinsey.' It is therefore crucial for the company to define its own need in terms of the contribution of the designer. This relates further to decisions on whether to outsource design skills or to develop an in-house competency, or indeed a combination of the two. (This was discussed in Chapter 2 and is illustrated in the Bankpoint and Texas Instruments cases below).

---

## OUTSOURCING DESIGNERS: BANKPOINT

The Co-operative Bank wanted to introduce a fully automated banking service delivered by state of the art technology that provides 24-hour banking. Bankpoint encompasses individual automated telling machines, as well as stand-alone unmanned Kiosks and full-service Bankpoint branches. The timescale was very short for such an innovative project.

### Choice of design agency

The key criteria were reputation and past experience. Hans Billman, Network Manager of the Co-operative Bank, expressed the reasons for their choice in the following way: 'we knew the designers, we trusted their capabilities and knew that they would know straight away what sort of design the bank was looking for.'

At the first meeting with the design agency, Tin Drum Associates, it was clear that the bank team did not have a precise idea about Bankpoint's identity or its branding. The relationship facilitated a trusting environment which enabled the frank discussion and exchange of sensitive and strategic information about the bank's future distribution strategy. This enabled the designers to express appropriately the underlying needs of the bank through design. Steve Glennon, Managing Director of Tin Drum Associates, recommended that the bank should exploit this new opportunity very carefully, which meant paying attention to the Kiosk's image and defining Bankpoint's identity. The designer's first task was to produce a three-dimensional model of the Kiosk, and this helped the client realize its potential.

The designer's familiarity with the client had made it

easier to reassess the original brief, to identify the problems and share the problem-identification stage of the project.

## USING IN-HOUSE DESIGNERS: TEXAS INSTRUMENTS

In the case of Texas Instruments (TI), Tracy Rice, Group Product Marketing Manager in TI's educational products group, describes how Texas Instruments was at the crossroads. In the face of competition from traditional toy companies, Texas Instruments could abandon the electronic educational toy market it had created or it could fight back with innovative new products. It chose the latter option and used a marketing-driven design team. The educational products business manager hand-picked and hired a staff of aggressive marketers. Other groups, such as industrial design, engineering and European marketing, contributed as needed and leadership shifted from one group to another as various expertise came to the fore in the programme. Representatives from TI's Industrial Design, Graphic/Package Design, Human Factors, Engineering Marketing and Market Research groups all participated, but extra support was needed in industrial, graphic and human factors design.

Source: Rice (1991).

### *Selecting design consultants*

Managing design 5: when selecting designers:

1  Determine criteria for selecting designers
2  Determine skill requirements
3  In-house sourcing:
   ■ assess their weakness and strengths;
   ■ determine the need for additional design advice.
4  Outsourcing:
   ■ shortlist designers;
   ■ implement pitching policy;
   ■ draw up criteria for selection;
   ■ interview designers;
   ■ draw up contract/design brief;
   ■ determine roles and responsibilities.

If a decision has been made to use outsourced designers, the question often arises of who to use and where to find them. Frequently the easy route is to ask a colleague and just contact the first name which arises. However, this can lead to problems – for example, the designer may not have the appropriate skills. In the first instance one must decide what type of design professional is needed: graphic designer, interior design or interdisciplinary. It is often appropriate to draw up a list of requirements as follows:

■ What experience must the designer have?
■ What type of previous experience would be ideal?
■ What type of visual and style statements are required?
■ What would be the definition of the designer's role?
■ What type of relationship is expected?

Shortlisting and interviewing design consultancies using requirements criteria as a basis for evaluating them is an effective method of sourcing design.

In order to present themselves to a client, designers are often asked to 'pitch'. Pitching (see 'What the Clients Say' case) often requires that the design consultancy develop their ideas on a project and present them to the client in competition with other design consultancies, as a way of helping the client choose the design consultancy they want to work with. This may indeed be an appropriate manner in which to make comparisons between design groups. However, frequently the work is expected to be done without any payment, which encourages unfair competition between those who can afford to devote time and expenditure to a free pitch and those who cannot.

---

## WHAT THE CLIENTS SAY

The Jenkins Group research into annual report design buyers found that free pitching was on the increase in the annual reports sector. The following comments provide a client's-eye view of the issue.

### The free pitch
■ 'We could make a comparison of their ideas and costs – we gave them a guideline brief in terms of the themes we wanted to express and the audience for the report.'
■ 'We were testing the chemistry. We wanted to see if the

ideas were sensible and focused and it was useful to get the best of the ideas presented.'
- 'It meant we could get ideas and costs from three independent sources.'
- 'We didn't expect any creative work for free. One design company did present free creative work, but it didn't make any difference to our decision and we did not appoint them.'

### The credentials pitch
- 'The credentials presentations gave us a quick look at what was available and was the most effective method of selection.'

### The paid creative pitch
- '[The paid creative pitch] gives you a demonstration of good ideas for the report from a range of agencies. It also keeps the incumbent on their toes to have to re-pitch – they continually have to give good service and ideas.' (This company paid from £500–£1,000 to companies it did not appoint.)
- 'We wanted to establish the design route early on through the creative pitch, with the initial shortlist of four having been drawn up from their previous work. I feel very strongly that creative work from any agency should be paid for' (Malcolm Scott, Scottish Power, which pays £1,000 per pitch).

Source: Gilchrist and Mistry (1995).

### Design, client, team relationships

Developing a relationship between the client company and the design team is vital to the success of any project. Some companies have a roster of preferred design suppliers, whilst others will select them according to a specific need. Lou Lenzi, General Manager of Design, Thomson Consumer Electronics' Americas Design operation, believes that 'there's a delicate balance involved in keeping a handful of design agencies you can turn to and speak to in shorthand. But by the same token, you don't want to nurture a stale list' (Pearlman 1995: 70).

Another issue is that of building up an effective rapport between the client and design supplier. Oakley (1992) emphasizes the importance of the chemistry between personalities (the factors affecting client–design relationships were discussed in Chapter 2). Oakley is particularly concerned that frequently a design group will query a design brief, often one that is too prescriptive. They need to understand the corporate culture and company activities to develop appropriate interpretations. As John Sorrell, Director of Newall and Sorrel Design Consultants, indicates:

> When I go into the company and discover they are poisoning the people with appalling food, or they are not welcoming people properly, or their factories are dinosaurial in their design, then it is part of my job to tell the client that this will not serve them well.
>
> (cited in Oakley 1992)

The issues of understanding what a designer can do, bringing them into the team and managing them are critical to the successful use of design. Indeed, Sir Tim Bell, adviser on communication strategy to Margaret Thatcher and Lord Hanson, believes a company should see an all-round communications strategist (like himself) before going near a designer: 'People actually create identities that have no purpose to them whatsoever: they're just arty or a nice colour' (Oakley 1992). This suggests that in order to achieve the best results a company should ensure that it understands exactly how it will use designers and what skills it requires. It must have expert advice on sourcing and briefing designers and this may mean it is more cost-effective to use a design management or communications strategist, either in-house or outsourced, to undertake this activity.

Once a team has been chosen it is important to draw up a contract with the design consultancy indicating how you expect them to work, the project plan, the milestones and the billing stages. This contract may or may not include the design brief, depending on the stage at which the design group is brought into a project.

---

## TEAMS AT THOMSON: THOMSON CONSUMER ELECTRONICS PROSCAN

Thomson Consumer Electronics Inc. has become a familiar name among the winners of the Industrial Design Excellence Awards competition.

Nothing illustrates Thomson's commitment to good design better than its Proscan big – TV line. This year, Lenzi's (general manager of design for Thomson) team focused on making these increasingly sophisticated television sets easy to use. They began by improving the item consumers pick up first after they uncrate their TV – the manual, normally written in either Japanese English or techno-English. Thomson assembled a team of cognitive psychologists, creative writers and engineers to write a new guidebook, one that would encourage users to doodle around with Proscan's Features.

The centerpiece of Thomson's customer-friendly effort is a graphical user interface with icons similar to those normally found on a PC. Selecting the graphic guides with the remote control, viewers can perform dozens of tasks. They can change picture quality, program personal viewing menus and get answers to vexing questions. Lenzi and his team also outlawed complicated remote controls. Proscan's remote has only eight buttons, compared to the 40-plus found on the average remote. It controls power, channel changing and volume, plus the on-screen graphic menu.

The in-house design team, recognized for their well orchestrated efforts included: Sheila Augaitis, user interface designer; Steve Schultz, manager, video and accessory products; Rich Scheer, student designer; Richard Bourgerie, principal industrial designer; Gretchen Barnes industrial designer; Doug Goodner, programme manager; video and accessory products; Doug Satzer, senior industrial designer; Rob Hube, account manager, colour television products.

The International Design Excellence Awards jury was most impressed by the team's efforts to consider the human factor. 'They worked really hard at making it easy for the customer to use,' says Elizabeth Powell, a vice-president of design for Sony Signatures, the licensing arm of Sony Corp.

Other comments on the design from the jurors: 'The designers obviously have plenty of free rein. . . . You can see the process of experimentation with the conceptual models, which allows the team to develop feedback and

> enthusiasm that is not always easy to achieve in a large corporation.'
>
> Source: Kelly (1995: 48 and 70) and Pearlman (1995).

## Design brief

Managing design 6: when managing the generation of a design brief with the team:

1  Incorporate a requirements capture process.
2  Translate market research and stakeholder requirements for design interpretation.
3  Ensure a common understanding of the brief.

A design brief is a statement of the general objectives and requirements of the envisaged project and is a crystallization of the views of those commissioning the design. A poorly considered and ill-constructed design brief can result in mistakes that can be costly and time-consuming to rectify subsequently (Walsh et al. 1992). The British Standard on Product Design Management, issued as BS7000, notes that:

> The importance of the design brief cannot be over-emphasised. An inadequate design brief is a dangerous document: it may mean that management does not know what it wants, but it certainly means that the designer is misinformed about what is required. . . . It is regrettable that many designers are obliged to work to briefs that are inadequate − or even non-existent.

A fairly typical and good brief would contain certain key elements. These are:

- background to the company;
- corporate strategy and its relationship to the brief;
- the design problem − attribute definition;
- consumer and market information.

The brief does not have to be a long document, but the preparation of the brief needs to be considered carefully and information from a number of sources has to be collected. Background information provides a rationale for the project and helps to ensure that the design project corresponds to the corporate values and reflects the organization's overall strategy. The design problem is stated, perhaps as a general issue, or with a great deal of detail about the product attributes, the materials to be used and the desired functionality. Consumer and market information is valuable as it focuses on the type of customer, the type of market that the company is aiming at and the price parameters for the project. The market information is often neglected, even though this provides valuable information about the target market, competitive products, price and distribution. Designers need such information in order to develop their understanding and synergy with the user, which will then enable them to use the most relevant 'design tools' to create a targeted product. Such design tools include choices of materials, colours, shapes, surfaces and functions.

One example of a comprehensive brief is that for a well-known chocolate bar and its packaging. This set out the financial objective in terms of profit, market share and return on investment. If the product did not break even in two years, then a decision would be made to gradually withdraw it from the market. In this case, the product or brand manager acted as the coordinator of the project, acquiring input from each part of the organization to put into the brief. For example, production had to consider the feasibility of making the proposed product and the costs of doing so; R&D had to consider the texture, taste and possible changes to taste over the product's shelf life, and so on. The final documentation was substantial and had to be thoroughly checked before it was 'signed off' and the resources secured to invest in the design and development of a new chocolate bar.

Briefing for a service organization often takes a similar route. The rationale and need for change, the design problem and the market information have to be put into the brief. Manchester City Council's brief for the corporate identity for the 1994 Commonwealth Games bid (i.e. logo, graphics and merchandise) is an example of the form such a brief can take (see box below). The rationale and background of the brief referred to Manchester as a 'vibrant and ambitious city that is multi-cultural, has a heart and soul and is a welcoming city, friendly to visitors from all over the world' and as leading Britain towards the new Millennium'. The corporate identity had to capture and convey to people throughout the world the essence of the city. In addition, certain functional specifications were laid out for the logo and supporting material.

# MANCHESTER COMMONWEALTH BID BRIEF AND LOGO

1 Following the announcement on 2nd February that Manchester had been nominated to be England's Bid City to host the Commonwealth Games in 2002, the Bid Committee, in association with the Commonwealth Games Council for England (CGCE), are now looking for a corporate identity which will represent Manchester locally, nationally and internationally until the decision in Bermuda in November 1995, and possibly through to the Games themselves in 2002.

2 The Commonwealth

The Commonwealth family is made up of 66 nations each of whom have one vote on the Commonwealth Games Federation, the body which will decide the host city for the Commonwealth Games. The nations vary tremendously in size, from continents such as Australia to tiny Pacific islands: however, in this instance each has the same say.

There are strong governmental links within the Commonwealth family, all are inextricably linked by the sharing of a head of state and by language. However, we should be careful not to overstress these links as many Commonwealth countries have spent a number of years asserting, and are proud of their independence.

3 Manchester 2002

The following aspects of Manchester and Manchester's bid should be taken into consideration:

- Manchester is an ambitious City which has a vibrancy lacking in many other English cities. As well as talking about regeneration and changing the City for the better, there are visual physical improvements taking place. For example: the Velodrome, Victoria Arena, Concert Hall.
- Manchester is a truly multi-cultural City which lives in harmony. Many of the Commonwealth countries have representation within the population of Manchester. This gives the City a cosmopolitan air of which we should be proud.
- Manchester is leading Britain towards the new Millennium. We have become an emerging force over the past 3 years – demonstrated by having been awarded City Pride

status by the Government in November 1993 – and now we intend to make our mark as a truly world class city, as a city in which to work, live, visit and invest. Manchester's strengths are numerous, amongst them are the excellent integrated transport infrastructure. Europe's largest education campus, a major media and financial centre, and a centre for the arts, culture and music. The list is endless.

■ Manchester is a dynamic city, we achieve and we deliver. This can be attributed to the unanimity of purpose amongst all sections of the community. Manchester has realised that the only way to move forwards is to do so in partnership with other agencies within the City. The result is that from schoolchildren and members of local communities to Chief Executive and Chairman of multinational companies, all are involved in the City and all are supportive of its ambitions.

■ Manchester has a heart and soul and is a welcoming city, friendly to visitors from all over the world. It does not have a single icon which is instantly recognisable such as Sydney's Opera House and Paris's Eiffel Tower, but it has something far more intangible which ensures it remains at the forefront of youth culture, of music, and which ensures that many students choose to study in Manchester, and stay afterwards.

■ England has never held the Commonwealth Games and in 2002, which is the year of the Queen's Golden Jubilee, it is felt that the chances of Manchester securing the nomination are very high. It is an opportunity for the Commonwealth to show its bonding and unity. England will be inviting all other members of the Commonwealth family to share in the greatest celebrations ever held, the Games of the new Millennium, to share in the celebrations for the Queen's Golden Jubilee.

■ Manchester is the front runner in the race to host the Commonwealth Games in 2002. We are the only City thus far to put our names in the ring as contenders. However, the closing date for other contenders in the race is not until May 1995 so there is no place for complacency. To counteract any late bids from within the Commonwealth, Manchester wishes to portray itself as supremely confident, the City which all others have to catch.

## 4 The Logo

As was demonstrated with the 2000 Olympic Bid, a logo of this nature will have numerous uses and target audiences. However the following aspects should be taken into consideration during initial design work:

4.1 The identity must be both distinctive and forward looking and work in the following arenas:

a) Locally: The identity must be something with which the local community and businesses can identify. It must generate a sense of civic pride.
b) Nationally: This is the English Bid. We would hope that we will secure the backing of the national Government as well as national companies and the media.
c) Internationally: Both within the Commonwealth and throughout the rest of the world, the identity must be distinctive and confident. It must identify itself with Manchester, a City which is going places and which will deliver.

4.2 The identity must transcend age, race, sex and situation. It must be all things to all people, whilst recognising that the final decision will be made by the 66 members of the Commonwealth Games Federation.

4.3 As a corporate identity for such a major international event, the logo must be able to be brought to life graphically. It needs to suggest energy and movement.

4.4 The uses of the logo are numerous, for example:

Literature; Advertisements; Posters and Banners; Merchandise; Signage, Street Dressing; TV; Vehicles; Buildings.

The logo must therefore work equally well in colour, black and white, at all sizes, and in the moving image, television in particular.

4.5 The Manchester 2000 Olympic Bid logo served us well, it helped to establish Manchester as the British Bid graphically, and it created a clear and instantly recognisable identity.

We are open to discussion and proposals as to whether the Commonwealth Games logo should retain links with the past and with a traditional approach. However there is the belief that we should now create a new and totally different identity for 2002, devoid of any specific 'British' images or links with the Olympic Bid (the flames and bowl are not a part of the Commonwealth opening and closing ceremonies).

Now is the time to create a unique logo for Manchester in its own right, which will have a distinctive identity and personality. Two such examples were Barcelona's 1992 Olympic Games logo linked to the mascot Cobi, and Sydney's 2000 Olympic Bid design which included the 'Share the Spirit' theme.

## 5 Further Considerations

The wording which will accompany the logo should include 'Manchester' and '2002'. However the Committee has made no formal decision on whether the words 'Commonwealth Games' or 'England' or the word 'Bid' should also be included. This aspect is an area in which design groups can put forward their own opinion.

## 6 Timescales

We are looking for an initial response from design groups by Monday 11th April. This will include sketches of initial ideas and the thought process behind the design.

From these submissions a short list of 4 design groups will be selected and final submissions will be made by 29th April. We aim to have a finalised corporate identity in place by end May.

## 7 Costings

The competition for the corporate identity which will take Manchester 2002 forwards will take the form of a free competitive pitch with no rejection fees being made available.

However, a sum of . . . will be paid to the Designers of the winning design in return for total rights to that identity. This will mean that any aspect of the corporate identity for Manchester's bid for the 2002 Commonwealth Games will be, without exception, the property of the Manchester 2002 bid committee.

## 8 Conclusions

The design for the Manchester bid for the Commonwealth Games 2002 is one which we hope will have a long life span. This brief offers designers the chance to become involved in a process which we hope will be ultimately successful.

Source: Manchester City Council, reproduced with permission.

There are very different practices in design briefing: a design team may be informed that 'two new cookers are needed', with no other information forthcoming; and, at the other extreme, extensive documentation of the brief, covering quality, cost, production, servicing, relationship with current products and planned future products, may be developed. In practice, good results can come from the two extremes of briefing. When designing Junior Pro Children's Golf Clubs for Dynamic Precision Casting (Taiwan), designer Raymond Smith remarked that 'the design brief called for clubs that would serve three different age groups – 6 to 8 years, 9 to 11 years and 12 to 14 years – other than that we were given a free hand, (Pearlman 1995: 72). Such informal methods of briefing can work if the project concerns minor modifications, or if the individuals involved know each other well. But in the majority of cases, this approach is likely to be inadequate. Research has shown that the factor that most significantly distinguished commercially successful firms from others was the care they took in drawing up a comprehensive marketing and technical specification at the start of the project (Walsh et al. 1992).

It can be argued that a vague brief encourages creativity by giving freedom to the designers. On the other hand, this approach can waste time, as design effort has to be spent on defining the problem and unsuitable designs may be devised which require ongoing modification. It may be the case that the designers ignore the brief if they regard it as inhibiting their creativity or goes against their professional judgement. This points to the need for a collaborative team approach where designers are involved with others in devising the brief. It also suggests that policy must be made on the way in which briefs are generated and issued to designers.

## Requirements capture

Managing design 7: when doing requirements capture/market research:

1  Identify key stakeholders in the idea/concept.
2  Choose techniques for accessing information on their requirements, visions and future needs.
3  Translate market research and stakeholder requirements for design interpretation.
4  Plan research for concept/prototype testing.

As part of the development of a design brief and the design concept it is important to establish the key attributes which are to be incorporated into the design. Often this is referred to as defining the customer needs or the end-user requirements. However, there many more stakeholders in the development of a 'product' (product, place or communication). Each stakeholder will have needs, both current and future, which need to be accessed understood and incorporated (if approved) into the design.

There are potentially two issues in requirements capture. First, the marketing and design team must identify the design stakeholders and develop methods for eliciting the information from

*Figure 3.4* Stakeholders in design

| **A mobile phone** | **A retail outlet** | **A company letterhead** |
|---|---|---|
| Manufacturer | Franchisee | Author Secretary |
| Production R&D Marketing | Installation and maintenance | Printer |
| Distributor Sales Installation and maintenance | | Customer Supplier |
| End-user | Customer | Recipient of letter |

them. Second, they must also undertake traditional market research to access market intelligence. To identify stakeholders in the design requires that as many of the design team as possible use network analysis to plot the stakeholders and their potential needs. Figure 3.4 illustrates potential stakeholders in three specific design areas. The Rockwater case (below) illustrates the need to understand all the key stakeholders, not just to develop a detailed concept brief but to uncover potential problems with the concept and the underlying the brief.

## THE ROCKWATER STORY – PART ONE

### A new corporate identity for Rockwater

Lloyd Northover were asked to design a corporate identity for a company. This was based on a potential merger of two diving companies, 2WT and Merex. The brief for creating it centred on trying to catalyse cultural cohesion between two companies that had previously been the keenest of competitors. Responding to this difficult situation, the process included comprehensive research on the industry and interviews with a substantial cross-section of employees, clients and outside experts in this business. This research revealed very different company culture, and a degree of antagonism, so much so that the merger was called off.

However, a year later when 2WT merged with Socon, Lloyd Northover received the brief to create a corporate identity for the new company. It was fortunate that the previous year's exercise had provided a solid grounding in the industry. They still needed, however, to define a brief, catch up on trends in the business, get to the root strengths of the constituent parts and clarify the future aspirations of the chief executive and his new team.

First we wanted to see how the industry scene had changed in a year. In the fast-moving, volatile world of offshore oil and gas, a lot can happen in that time. We noted changes and tracked how competitors were faring in the market. And with this information we were able to articulate the kinds of challenges the new company would be facing. We also conducted a visual audit of communication materials, environments and equipment and interviewed a cross section of employees and a sampling of clients.

(Lee 1991: 23)

The goals here, were twofold:

1    To uncover practical issues – to know how the business would be structured and run, and to understand on what and where the visual identity would have to be implemented, documenting the physical dimensions of the design problem.
2    To unearth the core values of the companies – determining strengths on which to build and weaknesses to be overcome and gaining insights regarding the kind of organization managers and employees felt the new firm could and should be.

### The brief

The key points with respect to the factual components of the project were that the name and the visual identity of the new company must:

■ position the company as capable of substantial engineering/project commissions rather than simply as diving contractors;
■ express the integrated capability of the new company to offer expertise above and below the water line;
■ position the company as one integrated firm and not a joint venture;
■ be suitable for an industry leader;
■ reflect and amplify service and quality messages;
■ underline safety as being of paramount importance;
■ work internationally in the offshore market in applications from lapel buttons to vessels and underwater equipment;
■ be easy and economical to reproduce in all regions.

As to the perceptual dimensions of the work, it was felt that the new company must embody the following qualities and characteristics:

■ more brain, less brawn;
■ professionalism;
■ integrity, honesty, straightforwardness;
■ stable and substantive, mature, authoritative, responsible;

■ human, approachable;
■ closer to client;
■ here for the long term.

The project resulted in a successful corporate identity as discussed later in this chapter.

Source: Lee (1991).

## Market research

Market research is obviously an important element in the require-ments capture process. Market information is, however, required throughout the design process (whether it is design for corporate communications or new product development), from the justifica-tion for allocating design resources, through assessing and choos-ing design concepts, to consumer testing and post-launch evaluation. This has been recognized by numerous studies (Walsh et al. 1992; Potter et al. 1991; Cooper and Kleinschmidt 1988; Leonard-Barton 1991). It is therefore worthwhile considering mar-ket research's role at this early stage and throughout the design process. It should certainly be planned into the process from the outset. What is required is an approach to market research that asks what will help to elicit the kind of information that is helpful to the design function. Designers need qualitative information about atti-tudes to a given 'product' or idea, the environments in which the product is to be used, as well as fairly precise information about the proposed target markets.

Take an example of a kettle and consider the end-user needs, especially where the kettle is to be used and for what purposes. The kettle may be on a kitchen top and used to boil water to make tea or for cooking purposes, and it may be typically used by someone who has a good grip of the handle of the kettle. The kettle may be used on the floor in someone's office. It may be used to carry hot water to fill a hotwater bottle and used by an elderly person who is arthritic and so has a poor grip. A metal texture for a kettle on the hob may denote it is cold to a child and so she or he may be tempted to touch the surface. Functionality in terms of perfor-mance – i.e. that it boils water quickly, that it is easy to hold and pour – may be important. Aesthetics too may be important – for example, the Italian company Alessi has been highly successful in producing 'designer-label' kettles that push aesthetic considera-tions to the forefront. So customer needs have to be examined in detail – where will the design be used, by whom, for what purpose and at what price?

Market testing of prototypes, either graphic or product, is desirable for customer acceptance and user feedback before manufacture, implementation and launch. Kotler and Rath suggest that 'designs need not be market-sourced but at least they should be market tested. Consumers should be asked to react to any proposed design because often consumers have ways of seeing that are not apparent to designers and marketers'. (Kotler and Rath 1984:19). Obtaining customer reactions to prototypes and mock-ups can help to avert expensive errors and potential failures by identifying design changes wanted by users before the product is in production.

Many methods of market testing prototype designs, mood boards or graphic mock-ups exist, from gathering informal comments from employees or at trade shows, to product clinics (Holt 1987). Walsh et al. (1992) found that a fairly common method of evaluating acceptance before market launch was to get comments on prototypes from customers, which were often distributors and specifiers rather than end-users. More formal methods were costly and time-consuming, especially for smaller companies. Successful companies may do much more: Lego tends to subject all of its prototypes to extensive user trials by schoolchildren. Many observers relate the need to focus on the customer and product testing as applying only to product design. However, this is not necessarily the case; indeed technological advances offer the opportunity and the need to test all types of 'product', from packaging through to interior design.

Differences have been found to exist between successful and less successful companies (retail, service and manufacturing) in their approaches to market research (Walsh et al. 1992). Overall, more successful firms tend to gather market intelligence from a wide variety of sources and feed this information into the planning and design process. They use feedback from sales staff and customers, carry out market surveys and monitor competitors' products, as well as setting up user panels. Less successful firms tend to rely on sales staff feedback and collect information from customers in an informal and ad-hoc way (see Table 3.1).

Market research techniques can be applied to suit different purposes depending on the aims for which they are required, for example focus groups to explore new concepts, scenario building to visualize future product directions. Leonard-Barton (1991) has developed a typology of different techniques to see to what extent

*Table 3.1* Market sources of information for design

| I | II |
|---|---|
| Senior management 'feel for the market' | Customer feedback/ inquiries/complaints Service reports/warranty claims Trade shows/exhibitions Technical/trade literature Market surveys |
| Sales/market statistics | Developments in related industries Competitors' products User groups/customer panels |
| Sales-force | Workshops involving engineers, marketers, customers and users, etc. |

*Source*: Walsh et al. (1992)
*Note*: Commercially successful firms in study B employed sources listed under both I and II. Less successful firms tended to use only I.

market research techniques are used for different design purposes (see Figure 3.5).

## Translating market research

Criticisms have been made of traditional, quantitative approaches to market research on the basis of their descriptive and historical nature (Alexander 1985). They tend to produce quantitative data about the design outcome after market launch, such as potential market share, which may be too general and imprecise to help in design. Qualitative information, such as how the intended design is to be used, by whom and for what purpose, and problems users have with current products all constitute more appropriate information at the outline design concept stage.

The designer's role is pivotal in translating market information into concepts which the users can relate to and comment on. In many companies, particularly those which have traditionally been technology-led, market research information tends to be presented to R&D, design and engineering in quantitative form. Although this may well be interpreted into graphical representations or descriptions of product-use scenarios, many designers, especially those who work in more customer-oriented environments, prefer to

*Figure 3.5* Market information employed in design

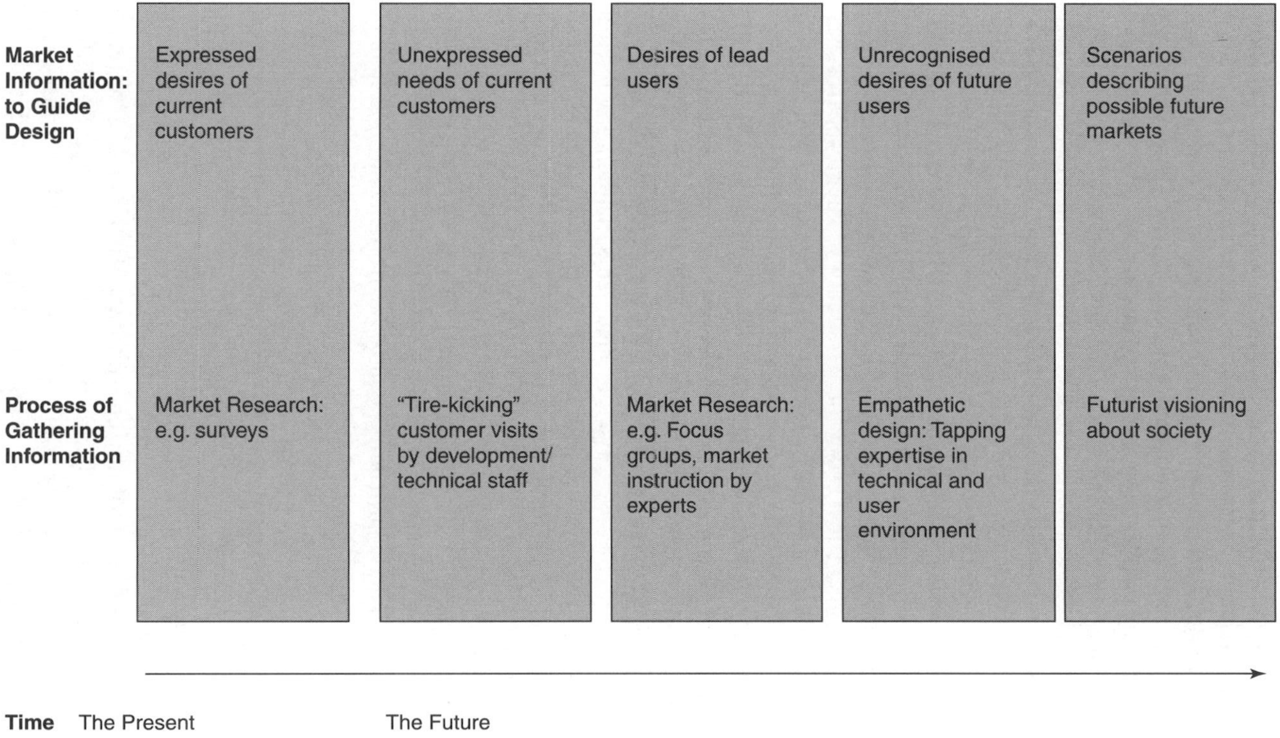

| Market Information: to Guide Design | Expressed desires of current customers | Unexpressed needs of current customers | Desires of lead users | Unrecognised desires of future users | Scenarios describing possible future markets |
|---|---|---|---|---|---|
| **Process of Gathering Information** | Market Research: e.g. surveys | "Tire-kicking" customer visits by development/ technical staff | Market Research: e.g. Focus groups, market instruction by experts | Empathetic design: Tapping expertise in technical and user environment | Futurist visioning about society |

**Time**   The Present                    The Future

*Source:* Leonard-Barton (1991)

have more qualitative information about the end-user and the type of attributes the product may require (Alexander 1985).

One common technique used to communicate this information effectively is theme boards. Transmitting market intelligence through a theme board is a means of achieving an understanding between design and marketing, and is useful to clarify aesthetic and functional attributes. By putting together relatively simple visual montages, it is possible accurately to describe the type of person for whom the product is to be designed. Images of the type of car they may drive, the clothes they may wear or the restaurants they may eat in give a very simple but reliable impression of the target user. Likewise, boards composed of images of other products which have similar characteristics, colours or planned working environments can also provide a highly efficient means of indicating what sort of product is required, not in technical detail but more in feel, style or personality. Theme boards have been used frequently where 'design' is a central feature of the product, for instance with fashion, textiles and small domestic appliances. The IT technology available to create and relay both still images and live action is an obvious medium for interpreting and visualizing market research.

Alternatively, some companies develop scenarios and set the scene for the use of a product. This method involves actually telling a story about people and the products, for instance describing fictitious couples or individuals, their daily lives, perhaps even their use of a product or behaviour in a situation (e.g. how they shop for groceries, the process they go through and what guides their decisions). This type of information helps the designer to focus on the sensory and functional problems. Understanding consumer behaviour is important to the designer, who in many cases is carrying out her or his own 'market research'. It is the cognitive and emotional issues and their evolution which are of interest to the designer and aid them in the creation of product ideas for the consumers' future needs, rather than just their present wants (Woodhusyen 1990). This methods also guards against the designers drawing too much from their own personal experiences.

Another common way to convey market intelligence is to use analogies. Describing one product as being like a Land Rover Discovery and another as being like a Lotus clearly differentiates the two, and defines the first as tough, reliable, easy to maintain but secure and the second as sleek, fast, sophisticated and expensive. Although cars are usually the best analogy because they are the products which people most easily recognize and they have distinct target markets, others – such as colours, landscapes or even personalities – are equally effective.

Yet another effective means of determining the product concept and conveying market intelligence is to use metaphor as a definition. Clark (1991) gives the example used by Honda to describe the characteristics of its 1990 Accord: 'A rugby player in an evening suit.' This metaphor captured the 'personality' of the project and was translated into key attributes such as 'rugged but fair', 'socially recognizable', 'polite', 'sportsmanlike', 'strong and secure', 'orderly', 'likeable, 'bright and elegant'. These attributes were in turn translated into features: for example, 'friendly' became a soft touch interior; tough, a larger engine and improved reliability in extreme conditions. Metaphor can therefore be used to capture the feeling of the product throughout the development process and to develop product specifications which everyone in the product team can relate to.

More successful firms, such as Ingersoll-Rand (see Chapter 4) have developed an approach to marketing which helps them achieve good design. At Ingersoll-Rand this is wide-ranging and probes for motivational information in order to understand what users want by involving them in the product development process and eliciting ideas they may have for product improvements and developments. Another example is Philips, the Dutch electronics giant, which also engages in creative marketing exercises; for example, in the 1980s it introduced a Youth Task Force to identify product opportunities for the teenage market. A series of workshops with in-house designers, marketing staff and potential users created the concepts that led to the highly successful, innovatively styled 'roller radio' range and subsequently to a whole series of audio products, 'Moving Sound', for the youth market (Blaich 1990).

Translating market requirements and other stakeholder requirements effectively is crucial to the success of the next stage of the design process: concept development. This is where the designer interprets such information into the development of a design. The formulation stage therefore constitutes the 'origins' of the design activity; it involves planning the team, selecting the designers, developing the design brief and the stakeholder requirements. Without this sound foundation the next stages in the design process are often confusing and unsatisfactory.

## Evaluation–design 'refinement'

### Concept development, the idea, brief, concept cycle

Managing design 8: during concept design:

1   Support creative design idea-generation.
2   Provide information and contacts to aid the designers in their idea and concept search.
3   Test design concepts.
4   Revise design concepts.

The process of idea generation, brief development and concept development is often iterative. An idea arises, market research is undertaken, the idea is modified, a brief is generated, followed by design concept development and testing, which frequently leads to further refinement of the idea, the brief and the concept (see Figure 3.6). Many companies desire to rush through this process, in an attempt to reduce 'time to market'. This, in most cases, is false economy: too many projects fail because the early concept planning and testing has been overlooked, which results in the need for costly changes later in the production process or failure in the market. It is much more time- and cost-effective to make changes and test concepts at the earlier stages than later on in production.

Frequently the development of the concept, in design terms, demands input from a wide variety of sources (see Rockwater

*Figure 3.6* Design origins cycle

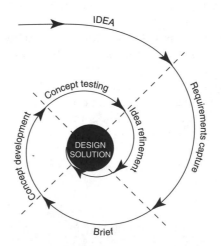

case). These ideas do not arise 'out of the blue' but are almost always stimulated by something in the experience of the designer, or an image that may give the designer the starting-point for the problem. For example, when describing the two Kata eyewear series, Blake Kuwahara (Pearlman 1995: 66), principal designer at eyeOTA Kata, said collection one, Gaia, paid 'homage to the earth with a series of nature inspired creations . . . taking inspiration from the shapes and forms in nature, hints of leaves, twigs and stone motifs found in the side of the frames are meant to be reminders of the wonderfully simple forms from nature that we often encounter and frequently ignore', and collection two, Ethos, 'was inspired by the purity and fluidity of human motion' (Pearlman 1995). Holt (1987) argued that creative design ideas arise from a 'fusion' between the designer's perception of a problem and possible means of solving it. Designers themselves suggest that they need to visit exhibitions, go to trade shows, look at an extensive range of reference material, etc., as sources of creative stimuli (Howie 1989). Often, however, the designer is expected to remain in the confines of the office developing ideas on limited sensory experiences. Design managers have to ensure designers are exposed to appropriate sensory stimulation.

## THE ROCKWATER STORY – PART TWO

### Developing the name

*In developing a name for a new company, arising out of a merger, Newall and Sorrell had to consider how to generate ideas.*

Since the name would, in a first impression, have to carry the full weight of the brief, it was decided that the best method to develop it was to put together a team made up of lateral thinkers from 2WT, Smit and the design consultancy. This group would conduct brainstorming sessions and having the clients involved would improve the chances of getting to an appropriate result quickly.

Broad categories were identified as a focus for these meetings, but it was made clear that at this stage anything goes. While the selection of a short list of names is largely an intellectual process – a rational evaluation against a predetermined set of criteria – the generation of options from which to choose was a freewheeling, intuitive process. There were at least three gatherings with representatives from 2WT

and Smit and, in between, the design consultancy team continued to generate additional names. Other suggestions also
came from employees of the two companies.

The value of including such diverse views was immense.
Not only was it possible to firm up a common vision, but
having been part of the process, the client participants were
readily able to get their respective internal approval systems
to support the final short list.

Source: Lee (1991).

Walsh et al. (1992) mention several sources that can provide
designers with ideas and solution concepts, including:

- competitors' products;
- experience of new and related technologies, materials and
components;
- current ideas from the design community, from magazines, exhibitions, etc.;
- creative thinking and problem-solving by individuals or groups,
using informal meetings, discussions and the use of techniques like
brainstorming;
- searches of patents and technical literature;
- suggestions and ideas from customers, users, dealers, suppliers,
etc.;
- experimentation and testing.

Obviously much of this idea sourcing is frequently done independently by designers (especially outsourced designers), to enable
them to invigorate their creative and visualization abilities. However, the process cannot be separated from the activity of requirements capture. The process of requirements capture stimulates idea
generation and, similarly, the process of environment scanning to
generate ideas reveals and tests the requirements. This iterative
process is again frequently rushed. However, it is an extremely
valuable stage in the design process. It tends to throw up potential
problems, focus the team, the company and the designer's mind on
requirements and, as a result, strategy. For instance, as a designer
uses colour and type in concepts for a pack design, his or her
choice will lead the client/company to consider how accurately the
colour or the typeface represents the aspirations of the company
and/or targets the appropriate customers. The example of Texas
Instruments (below) shows hows design concepts and strategy
were clarified.

## TEXAS INSTRUMENTS (TI): IDEA-GENERATION/ REQUIREMENTS CAPTURE AT THE CONCEPT STAGE

*In the development of a new range of products the design team had to establish the broad platform of products and their design.*

The scope of the work became integrating the market research into conceptual maps that would guide the creation of a strategy and road map, for presentation at the Toy Fair 1988. Here, the biggest challenge was to seamlessly bring technology, the physiological characteristics of children and the educational goals into a reality that would simultaneously fulfil the needs of parent and child alike.

To help achieve this, a design and communications room was set up. This was the place where technical and design members of the task force could visually and logically map specific product characteristics. For instance, information about what a child could do at the age of four was plotted against desired learning and comprehension principles and the ability of that age group to accept and perform various tasks. This facilitated decision-making and clarified the optimum balance among design and engineering criteria.

On the broadest front, the goal of this creative effort was to generate a complete picture of TI's entire electronic educational toys programme, materials that would ultimately be presented to retailers at the Toy Fair. This included a positioning theme and statement, facts about how this related to product design, packaging and future products and samples of communication elements such as manuals, data sheets and literature.

Source: Rice (1991).

Ideas and concepts do not relate entirely to the customer or end-user or the designer's own intuition; another factor comes into the equation very early: that is, the technology to be used, for example the materials, functions and methods. Designers frequently search for innovation in the materials they use and the technology available for production. They use that knowledge in conjunction with all the other information to take creative leaps and make connections in order to devise a new concept and an appropriate solution. For example, in designing the Berkley SP 2000 Integrated Spin

Reel Fishing rod, the designers (IDEO) used a fibreglass pole which had a different molecular structure from the rod handle, which meant that 'users are able to feel the vibration that travels down the pole as the fish takes bait. In the past you had to keep one finger on the line to feel that vibration' (Pearlman 1995: 78). Much of the credit for the design was given to the IDEO's in-house fisherman for suggesting various features and testing the final product. However, the creative links were made between the user, the designer and the technology and materials available.

Another example where information was combined to make creative leaps was the development of Fed Ex's corporate identity. In devising the new aircraft livery, the designer eliminated much of the purple paint used in the fleet's previous garb. This reduced the surface temperatures of the plane by 40 per cent, amounting to considerable energy and cost saving.

This design iteration and problem-solving process occurs in both concept and detailed design stages and is frequently overlooked by the client/company. Yet unless the design process and the requirements capture process are managed in a transparent and conversational environment the interaction never occurs and the potential creative leaps are lost.

## Concept selection

Managing design 9: when selecting the design concept:

1   Develop the criteria for evaluating design concepts.
2   Determine methods of evaluating design concepts.
3   Organize the team to assess concepts.

After this initial period of idea generation and concept development, the designer(s) will provide alternative solutions for evaluation and selection. Selection is a critical point. Frequently in smaller companies two or three senior managers have been known to sit around a table and make decisions based on their own experience and preferences or, in some cases, to refer aesthetic or 'ephemeral' decisions to their friends, wives or secretaries. This is less common today. However, the selection procedure still involves a level of 'adhocracy' due to poor planning.

The selection of the design solution should always refer to the original design brief; the selection panel should include all company stakeholders, i.e. those who will be involved in the production or use of the design. If design solution involves the development of a product, the user/stakeholders should, where

*Figure 3.7* Semantic differential for concept evaluation

Corporate colour: emerald green

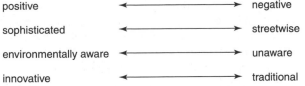

| positive | | negative |
| sophisticated | | streetwise |
| environmentally aware | | unaware |
| innovative | | traditional |

feasible, be included, through focus groups, interviews and panel testing both inside and outside the company.

In some instances the designers may present concepts which have moved away from the original brief. This may have occurred through continuous interaction with the stakeholders and the company. It is worth recording and monitoring those changes to ensure the decisions are not random but are consistent with the company's strategy, market and technology plans.

Semantic differentials can be used as a tool to assess the degree to which the solution answers the original design brief. The simple example in Figure 3.7 illustrates the assessment of whether a particular colour accurately represents the values. Changes do occur during the design development and these should of course be noted and measured.

## Design development and prototype testing

Managing design 10: when developing the detailed design:

1   Test alternative prototypes and detailed design.
2   Determine how the test will take place.
3   Consider the use of key stakeholders in tests.
4   Provide access to the stakeholder to enable the designers to get original feedback.

At the end of concept stage the design is translated into detailed layouts drawings, or prototypes, or mock-ups for testing and further evaluation. In graphic design fairly firm decisions can be made, such that the detailed design stage probably involves some production activity such as photographic work, page layout or typesetting. A full-scale mock-up of the design may be produced. For the Co-operative Bank's Bankpoint, the kiosk was developed and located in a garage beneath the bank's headquarters in

Manchester for consumer testing before the national rollout of the service took place.

In product design, concept approval leads on to further detailed design and development of numerous aspects of the product. In the development of the Apple Power Book, detailed development involved alternative devices to control the cursor, followed by alternative approaches to the integration of the trackball in parallel with detailed design comparisons of internal and external floppies (March 1994a). In such a detailed development selection will be ongoing and require several user tests and trials to revise and refine the design. In Apple's case Irene Wong of the user test lab ran most of the test research. She encouraged the designers and other team members to sit behind one-way mirrors to watch videotapes of the tests and to attend user feedback sessions. Tests were conducted with Apple employees, whose hand size and height covered the full spectrum from very small to very large. There were several rounds of testing undertaken by Wong.

Rigorous testing and refinement leads to a focused and clear understanding of the product attributes and resultant design specification.

## Specification

Finally, in whatever design context one is operating there is a need to freeze the design, to determine the design parameters and develop a specification.

The original brief has now to be transformed into detailed instructions to make the product, or the new interiors, or the printed literature. This product specification details the parameters that define the product, for example the accuracy to which a measuring instrument operates. The marketing specification is a detailed version of the brief that describes the target market, price and requirements of the product ideally required by management and the customer. The technical specification translates the marketing and business requirements into more precise technical parameters.

## Transfer–design 'production'

Managing design 11: when producing the design:

1   Determine and agree the specification.
2   Ensure the specification is detailed enough for production and commonly understood.

3    Manage the transfer into production.
4    Continue to develop launch plans.

Once the decision has been made to go ahead with the given design – that is, all the relevant tests have been conducted, design changes made, and the specifications amended – the design is put into production and implemented. This process will vary according to the complexity, innovation and type of design. Obviously a complex computer product requires a different production and manufacturing process from that of an annual report. Plans must be put in place for the implementation of the design – this includes production or build and launch. The generation of such plans involves, yet again, a combined team of people skilled in the design, production/construction and launch of the designed 'product'.

In retail/interior design, for example, the effort taken to transform all the retail outlets for a major retailer is enormous, and so the implementation of the change will not occur overnight but be planned over a particular timescale. The rollout programme for a new corporate identity for a hospital is shown in Figure 3.8. Informing the various publics – medical staff, patients, etc. – of the change to the corporate identity involved different events that were planned to take place over a few months.

The relationship between the design and its launch can so frequently be overlooked, yet it can be an essential element in the success or otherwise of the whole design and development programme as illustrated by the OK Soda Identity Programme, where Coca-Cola saw the launch design as an integral part of the design programme. ID's Design Annual Review describes the launch of OK Soda:

> In contrast to Coca-Cola's mainstream advertising campaigns, the sales pitch for OK Soda was delivered deadpan, with flat graphics and borrowed vernacular. . . . Though design is not meant to appear important to this 'anti-design' brand soft drink for teenagers, the diffident selling tactic, drab-grey and communist-red colourways, clumsy hand rendered type and cheap spy novel illustrations effectively translated across all media. Created entirely by Wieden & Kennedy, the identity was launched with a chain letter, followed by print advertisements and TV and radio spots promoting a toll-free number (1–800–I–FEEL–OK) with implicit references to answering machine vernacular, party lines and instructional tapes.
>
> (Pearlman 1995: 126)

*Figure 3.8* Columbus Hospital rollout programme

1992 Name Change Communication Timeline for Target Audiences

| | Jan | Feb | Mar | Apr | May | Jun | Jul | Aug | Sep | Oct | Nov | Dec |
|---|---|---|---|---|---|---|---|---|---|---|---|---|

**1 Employees/Auxilians/Retirees**
Present name change rationale, naming system, new logo and opening weekend plans
  • to Directors at Management Council
  • to Managers at Interdepartmental
Condense presentation for employee update

People re. view info re. upcoming name change/employee event/public events
Communications re. ID badge conversion
Employee event and contest
Provide information re. policy on use of old materials after 25/9
End of year audit of materials in use
Instructions re. answering telephone

**2 Physicians**
Presentation of name change rationale
Announcements in doctors' rounds
Office staff luncheon topic
Physician/spouse event
Convert brochure racks
New Rolodex
Notification to out-of-county referral MDs
Special Christmas gift to reinforce the change
Mailing of commemorative brochure

**3 VIPS**
Quarterly VIP letter topic
Health Issues topic
Brunch
Mailing of commemorative brochure
Personal individual meetings, also Rotary and other groups
Focus 2000 tour

**4 Media**
Press release on name change rationale
Media luncheon
Press kit distribution; explanation of name and logo, inclusion of stat and colour
Use of new name

**5 Public**
Early announcement of name change
Newspaper ads re. Grand Opening
Newspaper campaign re: new services
Billboard campaign
Radio announcements
Direct mail postcard
Newspaper insert on Grand Opening weekend
Public Open House Event
Convert all public communications to new name by 25/9
  • stationery
  • bills
  • patient items
  • brochures etc.
  • develop 1993 communication plan

**6 Legal/Regulatory/Other Assoc. Groups**
Trademark name
Notify all agencies, vendors, banks, etc. of new name and conversion date
Change all internal forms according to rollout plans

*Source*: Design Management Institute case study

Ideally, planning for this stage of 'implementation' should begin in parallel with the early work at formation and evaluation to form a (holistic) plan of the 'product', its development and its introduction to use.

## Reaction–design 'outcome'

Managing design 12: post launch:

1  Develop a method for collecting reactions to the launch design.
2  Maintain a library of information on market/stakeholder reactions.
3  Institute a continuous improvement process or make case for next design and development.
4  Review the design management process for the project and inform future projects.

Once the design is in use or in the marketplace, it is important to gauge reaction to the design and to pick up any problems and potential problems as early as possible. Problems do occur. For instance, one chocolate bar, launched as a major new brand, sold extremely well for about six months and then sales fell dramatically. Consumer tests showed that the core values of the brand – the shape, concept and mint taste – were well accepted, but the mint filling was of a very runny consistency and the outer chocolate layer was too thin, so that it was a messy product to handle. These problems were rectified by a new recipe and the new product was relaunched at a lower price point initially to build up sales.

Customer confusion can be the result of a new corporate identity which has not been implemented properly across all the divisions of the company, so that the products of one division may not share the same visual cues as those of another division (Clipson 1984).

Technology also tends to create user problems where functions are not effectively communicated or easy to use; for example, video-banking machines that act as remote sales machines of financial services as well as other products, such as holidays etc., have been found to be underutilized. In this case the customers often do not know that the machine offers services other than the delivery of cash and may also be unsure of to how to use it.

These kinds of problems should perhaps have been predicted during the design brief stage. However, problems arise with usage and therefore post-launch evaluation is important, as well as a mechanism to feed back these issues to the design team for product improvement and modification (see Encarta case).

## ENCARTA 95: A REDESIGN

The way William Flora saw it, Microsoft Corp's Encarta was a software programme that looked too much like a software programme. So Flora took on the challenge of redesigning the interface on Microsoft's multimedia CD-ROM encyclopaedia. The original version of Encarta had too much clutter on the screen. It looked more like a serious spreadsheet than a 'warm and fuzzy consumer title'. The programme contained dozens of buttons, distracting users from its main focus to help them uncover the nuggets of content they needed to tackle school papers or other research chores.

The newly designed interface on Encarta 95 was meant to amplify and not overwhelm the content, a great deal of which was fresh information. Flora's team cut the number of buttons in half. The Designers also switched to an understated, less-vibrant palette that is easier on the eyes. And users can change the size of article text or choose a flexible screen layout that lets them display – or hide – article outlines.

Source: Baig (1995: 53).

The most common form of post-launch evaluation is in terms of sales and payback. If the design fulfils the commercial and financial targets and expectations it is regarded as a success. Little effort is expended on assessing whether the design could have met the targets even better, or really to find out what went wrong. And yet it would be valuable for companies to collect this information to help them to learn for future projects.

The objectives set out in the brief in terms of functionality, brand values and so on can be used as assessment criteria to discover how well the design is meeting its expectations. One study that was conducted of a convenience food product found that even though the sales targets were more or less achieved in the short term, the product was not attracting consumers from the intended target market. Indeed, consumers from this target market were quite sceptical about the product and the pack design, especially when compared with competitive products (Burrill 1994). And yet the company itself had not carried out such post-launch evaluation, even though this information is helpful for the long-term development of the product.

Reaction also involves assessing the bottom line. John Simmons, Director of Newell and Sorrell Design Consultancy, explains that when the publisher Routledge was created by the merger of four publishing houses owned by International Thomson 'the new company was slow to establish a profile in the market, due to a credibility gap internally and externally . . . A new corporate identity was commissioned and after three years Newall and Sorrell conducted a design audit which showed sales had increased by a third and Routledge had moved from No 3 to No 1 in its market, with barely any advertising. The Routledge design manager saw the identity as important in bringing everyone together, making every one feel part of the same company' (Carter 1995).

### Incremental design

Updating and improving a design after its market introduction can affect competitive success (Georghiou et al. 1986). Companies like British Aerospace and Lego continuously extend their product range to exploit the design and technology they have developed. Improvements based on customer and user feedback can lead to new developments, like the example of a hi-fi supplier who changed the colour of one of its amplifiers and improved the sound in accordance with customer and dealer feedback, and showed that sales of the new version were nearly double of those of the original design. Designers should always be aware of the need to reassess a design; for instance, in response to the question 'what features would you like to include if another Ti series camera is produced', Tsukaha and Suyama, the designers of the Nikon 28Ti Quartz Camera, said: 'Before we begin a new camera we will conduct extensive market research to determine the needs of photographers. Their experience in using the 28Ti, combined with our research will guide us toward future designs' (Pearlman 1995: 68). Tsukaha and Suyama sum up the design cycle and how important it is to manage it effectively. It is up to the design manager to harness the skills of the team, but particularly the design skills, which for so many companies have been lost as a core competence.

## CONCLUSIONS

This chapter has illustrated that design must be managed at two levels. First, it must be managed strategically through the use of design audits and the development of policies and strategies for design to be effectively integrated into the marketing process. Second, it must be managed at a tactical level throughout the design cycle, that is, from design origins through design refinement and design production, to design outcome, as shown in Figure 3.2. These levels together outline the roles and responsibilities of design managers within a marketing context.

## ACKNOWLEDGEMENTS

Figure 3.1 is reproduced with permission from *The Design Agenda*, R. Cooper and M. Press, published by John Wiley & Sons, 1995. Copyright John Wiley & Sons.

Figures 3.5 and 3.8 are reproduced with permission from 'Market information employed in design, Leonard Barton inanimate integrators: a block of wood speaks,' *Design Management Journal* vol. 2, no 3, published by the Design Management Institute, 1991.

Table 3.1 is reproduced from *Winning by Design*, V. Walsh, R. Roy, M. Bruce and S. Potter, published by Blackwell Business, 1992.

## REFERENCES

Alexander, M. (1985) 'Creative marketing and innovative consumer product', *Design* (1): 41–50.

Baig, E. (1995) 'A dandy encyberpedia: Microsoft Encarta', *Business Week* (5 June): 53.

Bennett, D., Lewis, C. and Oakley, M. (1988) The Design of Products and Services pp 46–69.

Blaich, R. (1990) 'The global, regional and national product dilemma', paper presented at the Financial Times Conference Product Strategies for the Nineties, London, 15–16 October.

Burrill (1994) Evaluation of package design: a focus on supplier/ Customer Perceptions', MSc dissertation, UMIST.

*Business Week* (1995) Annual design awards, winners – the best product designs of the year', (5 June): 44–54

Carter, M. (1995) 'How to look like a Winner', *Independent on Sunday* (21 May).

Clark, K. (1991) Product Concept Development in the Automotive Industry, Design Management, Research and Education Proceedings, May.

Clipson, C. (1984) *'The Competitive Edge: The Role of Design in American Corporations' Business/Design Cases*, Ann Arbor, MI: Architecture and Urban Planning Research Laboratory, University of Michigan, Ann Arbor.

Cooper, R. G., (1995) 'The fourth generation process', *Journal of Product Innovation Management*.

Cooper, R. G. and Kleinschmidt E. J. (1988) 'Pre-development activities determine new product success', *Industrial Marketing Management* 17: 237–47.

Cooper, R. and Press, M. (1995) *The Design Agenda*, Chichester: John Wiley & Sons.

Georghiou, L., Metcalfe, J. S., Gibbons, M., Roy, T. and Evans, J. (1986) *Post Innovation Performance: Technical Development and Competition*, London: Macmillan.

Gilchrist, A. and Mistry, B. (1995) 'Out on the pitch, what is free?', *Design Week* (25 August): 8.

Holt, K. (1987) *Innovation: A challenge to the Engineer*, London: Elsevier.

Howie, A. (1989) 'The role and management of design issues in the NPD process – a study of confectionary', MSc dissertation, UMIST.

ID (1996) Bleck Design Group advertisement, March/April: 14.

Johne, A. and Snelson, P. (1990) *Successful Product Development*, Oxford: Blackwell.

Kelly, K. (1995) 'Annual design awards: sofa spuds never had it so good', *Business Week* (5 June): 48–70.

Kotler and Rath (1984) 'Design – a powerful but neglected strategic tool, *Journal of Business Strategy* 5(2): 16–21.

Kotler, P. and Rath, G. A. (1990) 'Design: a powerful but neglected strategic tool', *Journal of Business Strategy* 5(2):

Lawson, B. (1990) *How Designers Think: The Design Process Demystified*. 2nd edn, Architectural Press. London:

Lee, S. (1991) 'The Rockwater story', *Design Management Journal* (winter): 22–8.

Leonard-Barton, D. (1991) 'Inanimate integrators: a block of wood speaks', *Design Management Journal* (summer): 61–7.

March, A. (1994a) 'Apple Power Book: design quality and time to market', *Design Management Institute Case Study* (March): 3–21

March, A. (1994b) 'Paradoxical leadership: a journey with John Tyson', *Design Management Journal* 5(4) (fall).

Oakley, A. (1992) 'The identity problem', *Management Today* (August): 54–9.

Pearlman, C. (ed.) (1995) 'Consumer products, 41st annual design review', *International Design Magazine* (July–August): 64–85.

Potter, S., Roy, R., Capon, C., Bruce, M., Walsh, V. and Lewis, J. (1991) *The Benefits and Costs of Investment in Design*, Milton Keynes: Design Innovation Group Report.

Pugh, S. (1991) *Total Design, Integrated Methods for Successful Product Engineering*, Wokingham: Addison-Wesley.

Rewse Davies, J. (1995) 'The Roundel and the corporate image of London Transport', *Design Management Journal* (winter): 22–8.

Rice, T. (1991) 'Teaming strategic marketing with design', *Design Management Journal* 2 (2) (spring): 59–63.

Roberts, E. B. and Fusfield, A. R. (1991) 'Staffing the innovative technology-based organisation', *Sloan Management Review* 22 (spring): 19–34.

Topalian, A. (1983) *Summary Notes on Corporate Design Audits*, London: Alto Design Management.

Walsh, V., Roy, R., Bruce, M. and Potter, S. (1992) *Winning by Design*, Oxford: Blackwell Business.

Woodhusyen, J. (1990) 'The relevance of design futures', in M. Oakley (ed.) *Design Management*, Oxford: Blackwell.

# PART II
*Cases*

# 4 *Design partnerships practice: Irgo-Pic*

*Margaret Bruce and Barny Morris*

## INTRODUCTION

This is a design management case study of Irgo-Pic, a hand-held construction power tool, designed and manufactured by Ingersoll-Rand and Buxton Wall McPeake Design Consultancy.

## INNOVATION IN PRODUCT AND PROCESS DESIGN: INGERSOLL-RAND'S IRGO-PIC

Ingersoll-Rand's design process for a new construction tool, Irgo-Pic, is the focus of this case. The initiative for the product design was changing health and safety requirements for the European market, particularly in Germany, which led to new market opportunities. The company's success in substantially reducing time to market and quickly gaining market acceptance for the product is attributed to the multidisciplinary team approach used, the effective integration of the design consultant into the team and customer inputs at critical points in the product development process. This case describes the design process from setting up the in-house team, sourcing the design consultant, briefing the designer to rapid prototyping and production. Customer visits and the inputs of a user group were effective in getting customer feedback into the design process.

## PRODUCT DESCRIPTION

The new Irgo-Pic demolition tool was designed to bring together power and comfort. Traditionally, powerful construction tools were heavy and uncomfortable to hold for any length of time and considerable hand and arm vibration was experienced by the user, which were health and safety risks. Irgo-Pic was 10 kg but delivered the performance of 13 kg competitive tools. This was achieved by an innovative design that combined advanced materials (polymers and plastics), engineering developments (Vibra-Smooth isolator) and ergonomic design (grip areas and handle to spread force, reduce stress and give protection to the operator's hands). The product with a T- and D-shaped handle is illustrated in Figure 4.1.

## COMPANY BACKGROUND

Ingersoll-Rand is a multinational company with a turnover exceeding $4 billion and it is one of the top Fortune 500 companies. The company has manufacturing operations in seventeen countries and a worldwide sales and distribution network. Ingersoll-Rand manufactures a range of industrial products, including process plants, mining equipment, automated assembly systems and construction tools.

## POWER TOOLS GROUP, UK

The UK division is part of the International Power Tools Group, alongside sister plants in the US. The UK manufactures, sells and markets hand-held air-powered tools, such as scalers, chippers, drills, impact tools and sand-rammers for use in all industries where air power is used. Traditionally, the design and development of all products has been the responsibility of the US plant in Pennsylvania.

## EUROPEAN DESIGN CENTRE

Ingersoll-Rand's strategy has been to broaden its customer base and to manufacture more of its products abroad. Europe was envisaged as a major emerging market and the company planned to set up a European Design Centre responsible for new products for Europe. The intention was to develop and market products with European equity, rather than American. The philosophy of the centre would replicate that of other parts of the company, namely use product design teams, concurrent engineering, user groups and rapid prototyping. A starting-point for this was needed and the Irgo-Pic construction tool was the first project designed, developed and marketed by a European team.

The aim was to set up, as a long-term commitment, a European Design Centre for Ingersoll Rand that was responsible for new products for Europe. Part of the initiative involved employing Graham Dewhirst as a Design Engineer. However, John Schofield,

*Figure 4.1* The Ingersoll-Rand Irgo-Pic

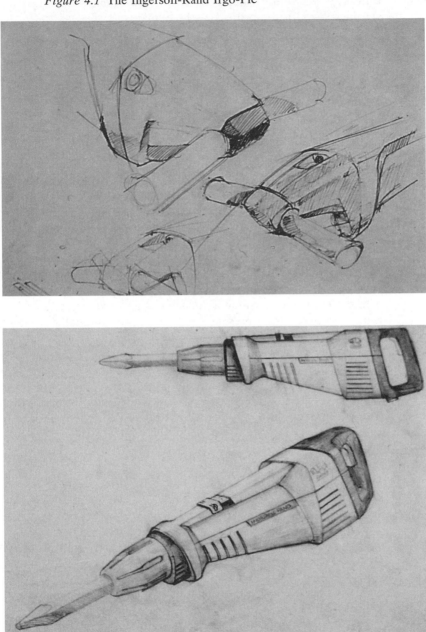

*Source*: Ingersoll-Rand, UK

European Marketing Manager and Product Champion, needed a starting-point for the project, as he explains:

> We had nothing. We had no in-house experience of developing products from scratch. We had no supplier base. This has positive and negative benefits. Starting from fresh meant that we could do what we wanted; however, the rest of management saw it as 'opening a can of worms' as they weren't sure how it was going to work.'

John Schofield was highly motivated to become involved with setting up the design centre because he saw very clearly the potential of changing market conditions and market opportunities, and wanted to sell a product that had European equity, rather than American. It was decided to base the organization of the project along similar lines to Project Lightning (an air-powered grinder) which ran in the US, where product design teams, concurrent engineering, user groups and rapid prototyping were used to develop products quickly and effectively. As John Schofield comments: 'It was not so much a decision as an acceptance that if we were to collapse the timeframe with a market-orientated product, there was no other way to be organized.'

## THE DESIGN TEAM

The aim was to bring to market within twelve months and within budget a product in the 10 kg weight range that would be best in class for:

- Power;
- Vibration;
- Ergonomics.

The product also had to break even within three years.

John Schofield had the responsibility for setting up a design team. He decided that the team approach would be best used as a way of cutting down the development time from four years, as was typically the case for new product development in Ingersoll Rand, to one year.

However, a number of questions were raised by top management. Could the company organize an efficient and effective design team? Who would be the members of the team? Would this team be able to manage the process having little experience of new product development? Would they be able to source external design expertise successfully? Would the project be to schedule, meet all customer requirements and still be within budget?

After much discussion, John Schofield managed to gain support for his idea and a small full-time team was put together, consisting of representatives from Marketing, Design Engineering, Manufacturing from within the company (i.e. John Schofield, Graham Dewhirst, Dave Hill), and Product Design was sourced externally. Dave Hall had been with Ingersoll-Rand on the 'shop floor' for almost thirty years, and so knew the capability of the UK manufacturing plant and what it could or could not make.

This core team was given sole responsibility for all the decisions made concerning the project, and reported to a steering committee made up of directors of different functions. John Schofield persuaded his peers that this was the only way to get real commitment:

> Unless you give the team the authority to do the job, they won't take any of the responsibility for it. It helps get the motivation. By getting everyone in the room together it meant that everyone knew what was going on. We all believe that everyone can contribute to the design of the product, not just the engineers, and not just the core team members either.

Each team member contributed on an equal footing. This meant that they bounced ideas between each other, giving different views on subjects that were not ordinarily within their traditional area of expertise. Normal traditional hierarchical forms of authority were also forgotten. Instead, project leader's duties were rotated amongst the group so that different people took command at different times.

Control was exercised through goal-orientation, so that the team collectively focused on achieving tasks and the satisfaction accruing from solving problems together, rather than individual conformity to meeting a series of established milestones, or from subservience to an authority figure. The members of the team viewed their relationships with each other as being akin to a marriage; whilst there was bound to be conflict (since the free flow of opinions and ideas was encouraged) the members always made up afterwards! Dave's personality, particularly his sense of humour, 'kept the banter going' whenever there were heated discussions in the team.

## THE STEERING COMMITTEE

The steering committee oversaw the team but, in fact, took no part in the team's decision-making process. The committee could advise and guide the team, but not make any of the final decisions. Its responsibilities were:

1   To set and concur with the team vision for the project.
2   To review change in the scope of the project.
3   To review changes in time, budgets and key product features.
4   To project status and milestones.
5   To remove strategic barriers.

The committee consisted of top management from Finance, Quality, Purchasing, Manufacturing and the General Manager. The committee knew at any given point in time what the team had done, where the team were, and the team's direction for the next few weeks. This could only be achieved by the core team and steering committee interacting closely together throughout the project. Occasionally conflict arose when the traditional bosses of the members of the core team found it difficult to accept that Project Gemini took priority over other projects.

## MARKET ANALYSIS

Market research and analysis were carried out throughout the project's duration. The type of information, and the means of generating and collecting market information were carefully planned, in order that an appropriate marketing strategy could be put together.

The main areas that the team had to consider were:

■ market research that would generate product specifications, e.g. user needs/customer needs, industry regulation and legislation, product positioning;
■ sales: past, present and predicted (and estimations of market size and value);
■ competitor information.

## MARKET RESEARCH

Remaining close to the customer was an overriding concern of the product development team. Accordingly, the team worked closely with a core user group, which consisted of the following:

- Ingersoll-Rand distributors;
- competitor's distributors;
- salespeople (Ingersoll-Rand staff);
- end-users.

The user group members (UGM) were compiled mainly from Europe, although regular input was also solicited from America, Canada, South America, Asia and the Pacific Rim. The fifty to sixty members of the group were used to evaluate concepts and to verify that the product was 'on the right track' in terms of the product specification's ability to satisfy market requirements. Most of the user information and specifications were compiled via close interaction with the UGM. Three approaches were used to talk to the UGM:

1  The UGM were asked for product feature preferences.
2  The UGM were then asked for direct requirements in order to create a 'wish list' of product features.
3  Finally the UGM were asked what product features they disliked.

The Team had difficulty in getting customers to articulate exact and precise needs in the abstract, so throughout the product development process the UGM were shown a number of competitor tools (and in the final stages of the process, prototype tools) to elicit a better response. The team found that having tools in front of them to criticize tended to focus the UGM's attention on key issues.

John Schofield already knew that health and safety features of power tools were becoming important as purchase criteria for Ingersoll-Rand's customers. This demand was driven primarily by health and safety regulations that were laid down to protect the end-user. Whilst at the time there was no regulation in force that limited the use of tools with a high level of vibration, the pace of regulation in the industry, particularly in Europe, suggested that this would soon become an issue. John Schofield identified that the European market was ahead of the American market in terms of concern for health and safety legislation at work, and a concern for the ergonomics of the product. John Schofield explained that:

We have legislation two or three years in advance of the US market. We have an opportunity for designing products specifically for the European market, which will not only benefit us in Europe, but give us a product advantage in the US market.

## PRODUCT POSITIONING

The intention was for the product to be the best on the market. There was no premium sector of the market, and John Schofield wanted to break away and create a new market with a radically designed product. This was reflected in his approach to his pricing strategy, where his starting-point was to see how 'high' he could go rather than, as is more usual, how 'low' he could go.

## VALUE ANALYSIS

Ingersoll-Rand and Atlas Copco (including Chicago Pneumatic or Consolidated Pneumatic in Europe) were the only two worldwide suppliers in the construction tool market. However, each major geographical market had its own indigenous manufacturer, who challenged strongly in that area. Using competitive benchmarking (see Table 4.1), John Schofield categorized the following competitor products into a particular power/weight/vibration/cost ratio – low weight (in the 10 kg range), low vibration and low cost coupled with high power being the optimum for hand-held tools.

## MANAGING THE DESIGN CONSULTANT

The in-house team needed additional expertise to design and develop a new product that entailed a vibration-reducing device, known as 'Vibra-Smooth Isolator', which would give a competitive edge over other available products and would meet customer requirements for a tool with less vibration. Whilst this concept was proven in theory, it was unclear whether the device could work in practice or even be engineered into the product, along with a new body shell, within the allotted time. A chronology of events for the whole project is presented in Table 4.3.

To examine the feasibility of exploring the technology in the new product design, a product design specialist, Buxton Wall McPeake (BWMc), was employed. As time to market was a critical factor, the design consultancy was asked to report back quickly. A major factor in the choice of this consultancy was its willingness to come up with designs to meet the client's schedule. John Schofield also sought a design supplier that would become part of the team; as he commented:

> the designer had to take on some of the responsibility and put his own stake in as well . . . we didn't want someone to come and listen to our problems, go away and solve them and come

*Table 4.1* Value analysis

|  | Product Weight (kg) | Blow energy (Nm) | Power (p.h.) | Vibration (ms-2) |
|---|---|---|---|---|
| Irgo-pic (I-R) | 11.20 | 29.00 | 1.37 | 6.70 |
| Atlas Copco Tex11 | 12.40 | 12.00 | 0.59 | 11.10 |
| C.P. FL22 | 10.40 | 12.00 | 0.57 | 7.90 |
| Maco P43 | 13.00 | 29.00 | 1.32 | 17.30 |
| Maco P105 | 8.40 | 18.00 |  | 17.60 |
| Compair U9 | 11.75 | 14.00 | 0.59 | 18.80 |
| Bohler A140 | 11.50 | 11.50 | 0.64 | 20.50 |
| Thor 16D | 8.20 | 8.00 | 0.49 | 16.20 |

back with a solution . . . we wanted someone who was part of the team.

An empathy for this approach was reflected by Bob Buxton, one of the partners of the design company. He stated that 'You have to tell the client everything, otherwise at the end of the product, the product is not acceptable. This takes a lot of time, and typically we have put in more time than we wanted to'.

It is worth noting that other specialist companies were sub-contracted to implement the design tasks, notably for injection moulding and tool-making.

## DESIGN AND DEVELOPMENT PROCESS

The project was divided into four design and development stages:

1  Briefing.
2  Feasibility study and detail design.
3  CAD development.
4  Rapid prototyping and tooling up.

### Briefing

The design company and the in-house team met in early January to discuss the details of the project. John Schofield was cautious because he wanted to make sure that the working relationship and the envisaged design quality were right. The briefing at this stage was very informal, as John Schofield explains:

What I'm looking for, is a new image for the product. I don't just want the product to be a market beater functionally, I want our customers to be able to look at a product, and know it instinctively to be made by Ingersoll-Rand.

The team was still undecided as to whether to incorporate the Vibra-Smooth isolator. Whilst some members of the core team wanted to do some minor modification to the existing prototype, others wanted to make use of the Vibra-Smooth device. Time was running out and the possibility of starting a new design was not viewed with particular relish given the pressure they were all under. Before making a final decision, they decided to welcome some fresh input from BWMc. Whilst the Team described their requirements, Bob Buxton made small 'thumb-nail' sketches. Graham, the Design Engineer, commented later to the rest of the team that he was particularly impressed with the way the consultant 'put pencil to paper' and started sketching in this initial discussion. This briefing was critical for a number of reasons as the consultancy needed to know:

1   How the product was to be made.
2   The effect the additional Vibra-Smooth device would have on the internal geometry.
3   The type of material and process to be used for the moulding, and how it was to fit to the inner mechanisms.
4   What other existing Ingersoll-Rand products there were, and how this new product was to fit into, or be a departure from, the existing range.
5   The critical elements in the design as perceived by the end-user and customer.
6   How project management was organized.
7   The number of units (as batches) to be produced in the first and second years.
8   The handle configurations.

As Bob Buxton walked around the Ingersoll-Rand factory and was shown the existing product range by Graham Dewhirst and John Schofield, he soon realized that the product was going to be used in a fairly tough environment. Bob Buxton thought back to his student days. He had worked on a building site and on motorways during summer vacations and remembered the way the workmen had treated the tools, for example leaving the tools exposed to all weather conditions, never cleaned and treated roughly. Bob Buxton believed that as a designer, these briefing situations were invaluable in absorbing 'the approach' or 'the culture' of the company.

## Design considerations

During the briefing process, Bob Buxton realized that the Vibra-Smooth device would give the product immense added value. If the Vibro-Smooth device was to be included in the product, it meant a new product image and a change in dimensions, so that from an industrial design standpoint they would have to start again. Bob Buxton's view was that the Vibra-Smooth device should be included and he saw this as an opportunity to do something very different. Eventually they managed to persuade John Schofield that a radical redesign had greater benefits than the modified product.

With the team united, the steering committee were convinced that this was the way forward since their worry was that a 'me-too' product would be developed. It was decided that an initial feasibility study conducted by the design consultancy would allow other possibilities to be explored. John Schofield appreciated the idea of an initial trial period as this allowed him to evaluate the work of BWMc and the potential of the working relationship that was to ensue. Bob Buxton was enthusiastic not only at the prospect of redesigning the product from scratch, but also because he was entrusted with some freedom in this process by Ingersoll- Rand. Aware that time was short, John Schofield gave BWMc less than two weeks to come up with a conceptual design for the product. Lack of time also meant that Ingersoll-Rand were unable to give BWMc any payment for services rendered up front; thus BWMc had to take John Schofield on trust at this initial trial stage.

## Feasibility

BWMc was given two weeks to produce concept designs with the Vibra-Smooth isolator integrated into the product and designs without this feature. A critical design consideration was that of the handle. The tool was to be used in a variety of situations and so interchangeable 'D'- and 'T'-shaped handles had to be available. The barrel of the tool, which tapered towards the pneumatic chisel, was the common component for each of the handles and so the best solution was to arrange a universal fixing system between the different types of handle and the main barrel, which was durable enough to withstand the environment in which the product was to be used. However, this meant that the fixings used to attach the handle to the barrel had to be hidden by styling of the product to disguise these fixings.

## The presentation

Following a two-week period, BWMc returned to Ingersoll-Rand with some conceptual sketches (see Tables 4.2 and 4.3 and Figure 4.2). Bob Buxton had been told of the project time constraints, and whilst normally in a Stage One project situation he would show a range of proposals to his client, he homed in on only one proposal to save time. To illustrate his proposal, full-size two-dimensional representations were produced, along with a cardboard cutout of the product for the core team to evaluate. Back-up sketches were also brought.

When the colour illustrations were unveiled, the reaction to the concept from the core team was very positive. Bob Buxton's instincts were right about the proposal, and the concept was considered for further development. What surprised the consultants

*Table 4.2* Project history in brief

| | |
|---|---|
| December 1991 | Initial meeting with Ingersoll-Rand (IR). Briefing to design a new power tool. |
| January 1992 | Initial concept work carried out for a nominal fee. Accepted well by IR staff. Buxton Wall McPeake (BWMc) asked to set out a design programme. |
| January 1992 | Initial development work: liaison with IR team and Thomas Wright Ltd, tool-maker, and CTR Plastics, moulder, both of Liverpool; prepare layout drawings, make full-size foam model. |
| February 1992 | Design T-handle; liaison with Joe Langford, Human Factors Services, for advice and evaluation of handle sizes and ergonomics in general.<br>    Advice on materials and design details. Visit Formation with drawings; Formation produce three-dimensional CAD model, then SLA model. |
| April 1992 | CAD model to tool-maker. SLA model used as pattern for polyurethane castings for prototypes. Design work continues on nose ring, exhaust insert, etc. IR tests prototypes. |
| May 1992 | Detail engineering drawing of T-handle. Liaison with tool-maker and moulder. |
| June 1992 | Prepare definitive visual for final version of product with T-handle. |
| October 1992 | Finish T-handle foam model for photography. |
| November 1992 | Product launch for D-handle version. |
| May 1993 | Product launch for T-handle version. |

*Table 4.3* Chronology of events in detail

| | |
|---|---|
| mid-December 1991 | Initial Discussion between Ingersoll-Rand and Buxton Wall McPeake (BWMc). |
| 6 January 1992 | BWMc Project Briefing at Ingersoll-Rand, and initial feasibility study by BWMc signifying the start of Stage One. |
| 12 January 1992 | Presentation to Ingersoll-Rand team. End of Stage One. |
| 13 January 1992 | Debrief at BWMc. |
| 4 February 1992 | Fax sent of breakdown of consultancy costs and of the product costings (not including the design of the T-handle). Ingersoll-Rand were very focused on completing the job rather than on the cost of the job. |
| 12 February 1992 | Bob Buxton visits Ingersoll-Rand to discuss engineering details with Graham Dewhirst. |
| 13 February 1992 | Creation of a sculpted model from foam by BWMc. Bob Buxton gains John Schofield's approval to enlist the help of an ergonomics consultant. Ergonomist is sent the original model made by the first design consultancy. |
| 19 February 1992 | Received relevant ergonomic data on the product. |
| 17 March 1992 | Visit to Gloucester to see Formation Engineering, and to explain detailed general arrangement drawings. |
| 27 March 1992 | BWMc receive fax from Formation that the CAD model has been completed. |
| 30 March 1992 | BWMc change the outside of the foam model to incorporate the fixing bolts for the handles and the ergonomic specifications. |
| 16 April 1992 | Ingersoll-Rand invoiced by BWMc for work completed in Stage Two.<br>    Stage Two involved BWMc working very closely with Ingersoll-Rand, such that over 35 hours were spent in meetings between the two companies between early February and late March. |
| 13 April 1992 | Meeting with Formation Engineering to approve pattern for tooling up. |

*Table 4.3* Continued

| | |
|---|---|
| 15 April 1992 | Meeting with tool-maker to progress the casting of the injection moulding tool. |
| 28 April 1992 | Preparation of final detailed GA. Remodelling of certain details required by the tool-maker.<br>    After mid-April much of the liaison with the tool-makers and moulders was carried out by Graham Dewhirst, the Design Engineer, as Ingersoll-Rand had financial constraints concerning the commissioning of BWMc to do this. |
| 19 May 1992 | BWMc still working on the T-handle. |
| 30 May 1992 | Preparation of component drawings. Sorting out the nose ring detail, exhaust baffle and moulding the D-handle. SLA. Project was a 'mad scramble' towards the end. |
| 3 June 1992 | Logo label added to the moulding/casting. |
| 6 June 1992 | IR polyeurethane castings. |
| 21 July 1992 | Ridge for nose ring completed. Tool-maker makes wooden pattern for carbon electrode to spark erode. Also polypropylene exhaust baffle snap fit finished. |
| 3 November 1992 | Product launch for D-handle expected. |

was the reaction to the cardboard cutout model. Graham Dewhirst remarked on how this gave a very clear indication of scale and of the ergonomic problems involved.

The two companies discussed how to progress from concept stage to product development. Bob Buxton was asked to cost the components that made up the barrel housing and handles, and was given the name of the moulder and tool-maker, which had been previously sourced by Ingersoll-Rand.

John Schofield again reiterated the time pressure on the project. He felt that this could not be stressed too much. They had already spent over nine months of their allotted time, and had another nine months to go. This meant that the exterior of the product had to be designed, developed and manufactured well within that timescale. Bob Buxton voiced his worry about proceeding from development to manufacture without a prototyping stage.

How are we going to have time to produce an appearance model? It's important to realize that once we reach the tooling-up stage, it's very difficult to change the design at that point

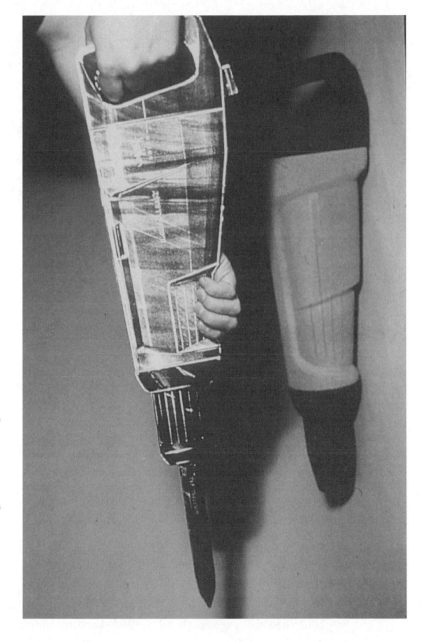

*Figure 4.2* Two-dimensional representations of product

and so it's far better to model the product now whilst the design is still on paper. Are you confident that the design will be exactly what you want?

Bob Buxton had known other clients miss out this important stage in the development process and then regret it later on. However, John Schofield had already paid for a prototype from the previous consultancy, and felt that with time running out, it was best to proceed to full manufacture as quickly as possible. He also knew that the earlier the product was produced, the more advantage it had over its competitors, and the higher price premium the market would be prepared to pay for it. He believed that Bob Buxton was able to visualize the product well enough without the need for an appearance model, and so took the risk that Bob's expertise would avoid the need for another prototype.

## Feasibility study and detail design

Whilst BWMc started work on the external casing of the product, Graham Dewhirst was still, at this stage, completing details for the Vibra-Smooth device and testing the product, right up until the end of March of year one. Bob Buxton needed to stay in constant contact with Graham, in case any significant developments should occur. He noted that:

> We received sketch drawings with general sizes of components, and where they fitted internally. Elements were still changing such as the diameter of the isolator and the barrel, because these were still being developed, and this affected the appearance obviously. That's the frustrating stage where things keep changing. Everything's fluid, but again, you have to expect that. It's a normal part of development.

Bob Buxton now knew enough about the moulding to produce some preliminary detailed development drawings that would enable the tool-maker and moulder to put some more exact costs together. These drawings were done manually, but more detailed views had to be worked out using BWMc's CAD software.

By the beginning of April, the team knew that all of the components would fit together without any problems occurring. They knew how they were going to mount the internal components and the exhaust baffle had also been finalized. As Bob Buxton comments:

> We spent quite a lot of time detailing the bosses [where the bolts attaching the handle to the casing were located], and the rib

sections that connected the bosses to the case, so a lot of the later development was to do with those sorts of details. There was more work inside this moulding than there was outside.

## CAD development

One of the reasons BWMc were chosen by Ingersoll-Rand was for their expertise with CADCAM (computer-aided design/computer aided manufacture), and particularly rapid prototyping using a process known as stereo-lithography.

The process of using such technology was divided into stages:

1   The design was developed to a detailed design stage, similar to the traditional design process.
2   The detailed development work was translated from a two-dimensional to a three-dimensional solid model using sophisticated CAD software. (NB This development stage could have been reduced, or missed out entirely, if the product had been detail-designed with CAD to begin with.)
3   The CAD model was then loaded into a stereo-lithographic machine, which, through a chemical process, can actually reproduce physically the shape designed on computer.
4   The resultant shape was finished off quickly by traditional model-makers and used by the tool-maker as a pattern. Using a spark erosion process, this pattern was used to form the metal injection moulding tool.
5   The moulder then used the tool to make the plastic moulds traditionally.

Whilst BWMc produced all the information necessary for Stage One of the process, other companies were subcontracted to produce the three-dimensional model on computer, to produce the tools and to make the plastic moulds.

## Rapid prototyping and tooling up

Rapid prototyping was an expensive but quick and effective method of moving from drawings on paper to prototypes that could be used for the core mouldings for manufacture. The client had not used this approach before because its cost had been prohibitive (conventional methods were slower but less than half the cost), but the urgency to move the product into the market rapidly justified the high cost. Indeed, one of the reasons for the client's choice of BWMc was its ability to work with sophisticated technology in both the design and manufacturing process.

Before the product design could be finalized and put on to CAD, the design team, tool-makers and moulders had to reach agreement about the production method. A major consideration was to produce either a one-piece moulding or a clam-shell arrangement (i.e. a mould that was in two halves). The former approach meant that the exterior of the product would be seamless, but the production cost would be higher because of the complexities involved. John Schofield was adamant that the customers would prefer a flawless finish; any seams would appear as a product weakness. And so the one-piece moulding was the route taken.

Bob Buxton was anxious to make sure that the translation of the drawings into a three-dimensional shape were executed well, and this involved continual liaison with the tool-makers. He noted that:

> The product may look a fairly simple thing, but it's actually tricky to model on computer because of some subtle blends and changes. Nonetheless, you rely on someone else's interpretation, unless you are there the whole time. The point is that you can change a model on CAD quickly and easily because it's a virtual model.

The major part of BWMc consultancy work finished once their drawings had been translated into the three-dimensional CAD model. BWMc's input from this point was to finish off some small details (such as the exhaust baffle plate) and generally to be accessible for advice to the Ingersoll-Rand core team should the need arise.

## FROM DESIGN TO MANUFACTURE

It was not until July 1993 that most of the details of the product were completed. With Graham Dewhirst now overseeing the process from three-dimensional CAD model to manufacture, Bob Buxton did not see the 'real' design until the moulders were starting trial production runs.

It was at this point that Bob Buxton noticed a small, almost unnoticeable flaw in the exterior of the product: where the barrel body met with the end nozzle section a slight ridge was apparent. This had been caused purely by the CAD solid modelling process. When the company had translated Bob Buxton's drawings, the model had been divided into two separate sections and then 'joined' on screen. Because of the limitations of computer screen definition technology, the join looked perfect. However, once it was transformed into a 'real' solid model, the ridge became evident.

Bob Buxton was tempted to change the model to rectify the flaw; however, as he explains:

At the end of the day there was so much time pressure the ridge remained although it was feasible to it take out. When I went down to the tool-maker and saw the carbon electrode used to spark erode the tool, I really should have got some Wet and Dry (sandpaper), there and then, and removed the detail. I think I would have been thrown out of the workshop if I had done that, because it was a fairly traditional workplace! I think this is a good illustration of the process and it's pitfalls. Its essential to have the designer right the way through the process.

## EPILOGUE

The product was launched on time and was successful. The new Irgo-Pic demolition tool was designed to bring together power and comfort. Despite the worst worldwide recession in recent years, the Irgo-Pic has proved to be a success. In terms of the power to vibration ratio (e.g. the more power the more vibration), Irgo-Pic is a leader and is way ahead of the competition, such that in 1993 Ingersoll-Rand sold twice as many units of Irgo-Pic in Europe as of the previous model in the previous year. Lack of vibration was immediately recognized as the main selling point, but with the coming of the final stages of the EU Machinery Directive, and the increasing awareness of the damages caused by exposure to hand and arm vibration, the ergonomics of the tool have become an important feature too. John Schofield commented:

There are many things learnt during the project and which besides being brought into the next project, will also be applied to Irgo-Pic – continuous improvement is the name of the game! The Irgo-Pic is the start of the 'right' product image for Ingersoll-Rand. The image of the future will be one of modern styling and super efficiency which are instantly recognizable as Ingersoll Rand's.

## ACKNOWLEDGEMENTS

The authors wish to acknowledge the support and interest of John Schofield, Marketing Manager, Ingersoll-Rand, and of Bob Buxton, Partner, Buxton Wall McPeake; and also thank the ESRC for supporting the research.

# 5 A dedicated approach to design management: Royal Mail

*Margaret Bruce*

## INTRODUCTION

The process of design management is the focus of this case. The Identity Team of Royal Mail manages the organization's corporate identity and also provides a project and design management service to other parts of the organization. The Identity Team acts as an internal design management consultancy and is self-financing. The activities of, for example, sourcing external design and print suppliers, briefing and liaising with suppliers are all undertaken by the design managers of this unit.

## ROYAL MAIL'S IDENTITY TEAM

The Identity Team is part of RM Consulting, an internal consultancy business within Royal Mail, which was created from a restructuring of Royal Mail. RM Consulting employs 1,000 people and has a turnover in excess of £50 million per annum. The Identity team consists of between fifteen and twenty people from diverse backgrounds, which range from graphic design, to marketing, to consultancy.

The primary contract of the Identity Team lies with Royal Mail's headquarters to manage its corporate identity. David Griffiths, Royal Mail's Identity Manager, regards this task of the team thus:

> We're guardians of the identity and committed to using the management of design as a business resource. We're about identity, brand and resource management and are expert resource managers, putting people and resources together from within the Royal Mail and outside to achieve objectives.

The mandate to manage the company's visual identity entails interfacing with those parts of the organization that are dealing with communications: marketing, public relations, community action and internal communications. This is a company with 165,000 employees spread across seventeen major business units. The Identity Team runs seminars, publishes guidelines and has published a CD-ROM-based corporate identity manual, and interfaces with a wide range of external suppliers, including designers, printers and clothing manufacturers. The team has an educational role to inform internal staff and outside suppliers about the corporate values that are expected to be conveyed, as well as taking a firefighting role if things begin to go wrong.

## CORPORATE IDENTITY: 'MASTERBRAND'

Central to the corporate identity are the values of being purposeful, inspiring, innovative, successful, international, expert, natural/human, reliable and genuinely caring. These types of values are expected to be captured throughout the organization's corporate identity and are summed up in the phrase: 'building and fulfilling relationships'. Royal Mail is renowned for providing good design, even though it does not have a formal design policy.

Recent changes centre around the shift from a public-service orientation to one that is customer-friendly and customer-focused. One facet of this is the design and implementation of a new range of postboxes.

## RENEW THE POSTBOX

The last significant wave of postbox design and installation was over 100 years ago. In the 1990s new sites were needed. The old postboxes located at street corners all over Britian serve a function and service it well; people still post letters in them. Furthermore, as historical artefacts they are watched over by English Heritage and local preservation societies. For these reasons the old boxes could not be uprooted, even if Royal Mail wanted to do so. 'The indoor postbox, designed for use in retail and other indoor environments, came about through a desire to improve opportunities for our customers to post their mail', says Keith Fender, Delivery and Access Marketing Manager.

It's Royal Mail putting postboxes where our customers want them, as opposed to where they have always been. The way things are at the moment, we have 1890s technology in 1950s locations and we are almost in the twenty-first century. People drive past the old corner postboxes to get to the supermarket, and when they get there, there's nowhere to post a letter. The new indoor box means that situation is set to change.

As well as offering greater access to the postal service, the new postboxes in supermarkets and shopping malls are supposed to support the sale of greetings cards, stamps and other postal peripheries and increase the presence of Royal Mail as a brand in new locations. Supermarket chains are keen to attract the new breed of one-stop, out-of-town shopper in any way they can, and the increasingly customer-focused Royal Mail is keen to collaborate, using design as part of the marketing mix.

Royal Mail has been working with the international design consultancy IDEO on a range of new postboxes. Nick Dormon, designer and project manager at IDEO, has been involved in the project from the beginning and he regards the need to change as being market-driven. As Dormon explains:

When the business managers realized there were new things happening out there, they decided they needed to do something. That was the push, really. Of the new postboxes, the Indoor Box is probably the most significant because it came from a marketing opportunity.

From IDEO's point of view, the design of a potentially ubiquitous object like a new postbox presented a range of challenges new to the consultancy. At every point in the process, issues of heritage were combined with functional issues to keep the integrity of the Royal Mail identity intact.

## CORPORATE IDENTITY ISSUES: KEEP THE CAP

Pillar-box red with a black pedestal and cylindrical in shape, the new glass-reinforced plastic (GRP) boxes conform to what Royal Mail calls its 'three-dimensional design [3D design] form standards'. One of the most important elements of the new design is the cap, originally designed to throw off rainwater. Although indoors the need for it is questionable, customers like it and equate it with the most traditional and reliable elements of Royal Mail's high-street presence. Now, minus the beading and casting details on its century-old counterparts, the cap has become an iconic feature of the newly responsive and strategic Royal Mail 3D identity.

The materials for the new box had to be changed for strictly functional (or perhaps foundational) reasons. Cast iron, from which postboxes are traditionally made, though 'perfect' for the outdoor box, is unsuitable for indoors, simply because street boxes sit in two-foot deep concrete foundations and have to be lowered into position by crane. The Indoor Box is made of GRP and can be easily carried in and bolted into place.

There are currently seven new designs for street furniture, including metered mailboxes and a new town postbox. All are either under development or about to be rolled out. Among them is a rural postbox designed to replace the old tiny-mouthed version which prevents the posting of anything bigger than the slimmest of letters. Standing on a black stainless steel post, the new cast-iron box includes the features – cylinder, black pedestal, cap – which are now the immovable constants in Royal Mail's street identity.

## TWO-DIMENSIONAL MATTERS

If Royal Mail is pleased with its new design work, it is in part because it is being made to work hard at pushing and carrying the company's visual identity. Like the 3D project, work on the corporate identity has been going on for a long time. Consultants Sampson Tyrell began to redefine and renovate the identity as long ago as 1988, and since 1993 Landor Associates have been advising on just how the graphic identity should be applied to the three-dimensional designs.

David Griffiths is clear about the role of the Identity Team in Royal Mail's ongoing transformation from plodding public servants to competitive company. Says Griffiths of the Identity Team:

> Our job, given that we have a decentralized structure, is not to manage everything. We are there as facilitators and enablers regarding the integrity of the identity. The new postboxes have been commissioned by a number of different management teams within the business. The common linkage is a commitment by the business to getting the identity right on them, and the role of the Identity Team is a facilitator in that process.

The company is currently teaching itself to think strategically in a fast-changing market, to prevent the brand suffering in the future. Its Masterbrand programme is designed to permeate every working process and facet of the organization, from advertising through to the street furniture and the new postman's uniform being developed.

## PROJECT AND DESIGN MANAGEMENT

David Griffiths perceives the role of members of the Identity Team thus: 'fundamentally we're politicians and diplomats who are constantly on the offensive and so we have good intelligence networks throughout the organization to pick up issues and problems to do with the identity'. His intention is to 'make people self-managing and self-policing, to help them to be equipped to succeed'. The guidelines and corporate manuals produced by the Identity Team provide a framework to help others reinforce and maintain the corporate identity. Essentially, the Identity Team provides design leadership and strategic guidance to the departments it works with and it helps with tactical implementation, for example preparation of brochures.

The Identity Team is funded mostly by project work within the company, for example the production of forms, literature, providing project managers and dealing with internal and external staff. Typically, the Identity Team offers expert project management skills in branding, identity management, reports, brochures, manuals, forms and customer literature that involves visual and graphic work. The team sources suppliers and can manage the whole design process from concept development to implementation.

## WORKING WITH OTHERS

As well as having a mandate to maintain the corporate identity, the Identity Team has 'customers' within the company that 'buy in' the Identity Team's expertise in design and project management. The marketing function is the main customer base for the Identity Team. As David Griffiths explains, 'We have no budget and start each year with a zero base, so we have to get the clients and projects. We are a self-contained business within RM Consulting as part of Royal Mail.' The Identity Team does not have a monopoly on design management skills; its customers can carry out this work themselves, or find an external agency to do this for them. They choose to use the Identity Team because, David Griffiths claims, 'We are a strong team that is highly competent and we have the skills our customers need.'

The kind of problems that can arise with the projects the Identity Team deals with include inadequate planning, the failure to realize the complexities of producing copy and sorting out photography and visual material, the implications of leaving things too late, particularly the impact on print schedules and costs, and lay people trying to play at being a designer without appreciating the principles of good design and so on.

## THE GIFT DIRECTORY

The gift directory is an example of the design and project management skills delivered by the Identity Team, working closely with public relations and marketing staff.

The gift catalogue was first produced in 1990 and has been subsequently updated and enhanced by the Identity Team. The gift catalogue is a promotional tool that is mainly utilized by marketing and sales, public relations and community action areas of Royal Mail. It encompasses a wide range of products from T-shirts, to First Day Covers, to pens and diaries. These can be used for various activities, such as conferences, exhibitions, community action projects and retirement gifts, and as such form an integral part of the communication programme and public relations strategy.

The Gift Directory was redesigned in 1994 and key milestones in its management are presented here.

The objective of the 1994 gift directory was 'to create a catalogue that successfully communicates gifts and promotional material to a diverse audience and to ensure ease of ordering and quality of products'.

A single supplier was sourced and appointed to provide the catalogue, gifts and promotional items. The centralisation of the ordering and promotion of Royal Mail gifts was advantageous in achieving economies of scale and a cost-effective service while maintaining the integrity of Royal Mail's corporate identity.

The Identity Team managed the project in three stages:

1  Content of gift catalogue.
2  Design, print and distribution of the catalogue.
3  Management of the catalogue.

One of the main tasks of the project manager was to source a supplier for the gifts and catalogue. A number of companies responded to the bid to tender and a supplier was selected. This supplier was asked to design and deliver the catalogue. A design brief was prepared by the project manager and a copy of the brief is presented in Figure 5.1.

*Figure 5.1* Design brief for the Royal Mail gift directory

# Design Brief for the Royal Mail Gift Directory

## Aim of brief

To create a visual style for the Royal Mail Gift Directory and implement to produce the Gift Directory and subsequent correspondence and marketing literature.

## Objectives for Royal Mail

To create a catalogue that successfully communicates gifts and promotional material to a diverse audience and to ensure ease of ordering and quality of products. Internal customers, as users of the catalogue, will have full streamlined guidance on purchasing Royal Mail branded items which maintain the integrity of Royal Mail's Identity;

## 1 Introduction

The current design of the Royal Mail Gift Directory is a glossy A4 booklet with three separate order forms. A number of problems have arisen from this type of communication tool, the number of order forms being one of the most prominent, and the listing of prices within the brochure. A methodical, customer-friendly document with a facility to store other printed matter such as order forms and updates is required to *advertise* and *order* Royal Mail branded products.

The directory will include the following product range;

- Writing instruments
- Clocks and calculators
- Conference selection and desk stationery
- Crystal and china
- Special promotions
- Recreation and travel
- Fine leather goods

- Children's range
- Flags and banners
- Other gift ideas

The directory will have an approximate shelf life of 12–18 months.

## 2 Project brief – consists of three stages

2.1 Design concepts for a visual style for all correspondence and compilation of the Gift Directory and order forms.

- recommendations for Gift Directory, updates, special offers, order forms, promotions, seasonal offers, etc.
- liaison with Royal Mail Managers who will be working on the project and supplying Royal Mail products for insertion in the catalogue to obtain input
- work with the purchasing team within Royal Mail to ensure ordering process is user-friendly and viable
- liaison with the Identity Team to ensure adherence to guidelines and quality monitoring

2.2 Print of the catalogue.

- 4,000 copies of the directory will be required

2.3 Ongoing design management of the catalogue, future updates and other correspondence.

## 3 Project deliverables and timing

| | | |
|---|---|---|
| 3.1 | Issue of brief to suppliers | 2 September |
| 3.2 | Recommendations for Gift Directory | 30 September |
| 3.3 | Compilation of Gift Directory | 14 October |
| 3.4 | Approval of final draft | 28 October |
| 3.4 | Delivery of Gift Directory | 25 November (Christmas prime time) |

## EPILOGUE

The project met its objectives and the gift catalogue is widely used by the target audiences. The project management skills used helped to achieve the completion of the project on time and within budget.

There was a time when the most aggressive thing about Royal Mail was the way its van drivers cut through the traffic at collection time. Now, billboards and a brace of zappy, prime-time television ad campaigns are currently driving Royal Mail forward as a successful brand in a competitive world. As hundreds of new postboxes and vending machines appear in supermarkets, shopping malls, airports and streets, Royal Mail is hoping that in the long term its business will increase accordingly.

## CONCLUSIONS

The main factors contributing to the success of the Identity Team are attributed to strong leadership and vision, pristine administrative systems, self-discipline of all team members and a sense of collective responsibility, a pre-emptive, positive and proactive attitude on the part of the staff and having the resources for the training that people need. As David Griffiths points out:

> a design manager is a good street-fighter; lots of things can go wrong in a large organization like this, so we have to keep up the momentum to keep on top of things and push ahead aggressively all the time.

# 6  *Stirling Cooper*

*Rachel Cooper*

## BACKGROUND

Stirling Cooper is one of the oldest names on the fashion high street, particularly in London, where the company was established twenty-five years ago. The company is a small chain of medium- to low-price women's clothes shops established in the 1960s. In 1992 Stirling Cooper were bought out by Bodybest, a small East End company owned by the Dass family, who had previously manufactured about 80 per cent of Stirling Cooper's merchandise.

Bodybest had recognized that Stirling Cooper were paying their bills late and probably had a problem with cash flow. They approached Stirling Cooper to buy the company (being their major supplier, they knew Stirling Cooper's market well) and spent a year negotiating the deal, which included doing research on how the company was structured, how the finances worked, and renegotiating the leases on some of the shops.

They effectively bought the company, initially retaining the managing director, who was also a shareholder. However, shortly after the buyout Bodybest also bought out the managing director, who subsequently left the company. Paul Dass then took over as managing director and replaced all Stirling Cooper's senior management with new people. The initial aim was to get the financial business of the company under tight control.

At this point they also began to examine the company image. Stirling Cooper had some very good central London locations. However, it was felt the image the shop interiors projected was 'a slightly tacky, glitzy, black and chrome late 1970s look'; despite this image they had still managed to retain fairly good business.

## BUSINESS STRATEGY

Stirling Cooper's main competitors are Top Shop, Miss Selfridge, Principles. They describe their merchandise as being for the East End girl who wishes to look fashionable on a limited budget.

The strategy for Stirling Cooper was to focus on this previously targeted market. However, they also recognized that they had existed for nearly two generations and therefore believed that both mothers and daughters could be targeted. In addition, in order to develop a slightly higher price point and promote a designer label to their customer, they negotiated a contract with Bella Freud to develop a range of Bella Freud merchandise and sell it through Stirling Cooper shops. This was to be launched in the Autumn of 1993.

In terms of benchmarking themselves, Stirling Cooper's managing director (Paul Dass) and senior management team looked towards another company called Jigsaw. Jigsaw had achieved success and expanded throughout the late 1980s, early 1990s recession, by carefully positioning themselves and choosing locations appropriate to their market. Jigsaw had focused on a mother and daughter market, selling high-quality, fashionable but simple merchandise, investing in quality, well-designed shops, good garments and well-made merchandise. Stirling Cooper used Jigsaw to benchmark where they wanted to be.

In order to achieve their goals they needed to revitalize their image and therefore their shops. David Quigley Architects were approached by Paul Dass, who had seen interiors for the Issue chain of middle-market womenswear, which David Quigley had designed. David Quigley subsequently accepted the contract to design the interior of Stirling Cooper shops.

## THE BRIEF

There was never any form of written brief, rather a series of meetings with Paul Dass, with the public relations company working for Stirling Cooper, with the senior management and the senior fashion designer. The aim was to establish how the company people thought, what they felt about the retail environment and what image they had of the company. Because, as David Quigley suggests, 'often clients tell designers what they think they need and miss out something vitally important'.

During these meetings they would walk down a high street with Paul Dass, look at images of garments, and also the manufacturing operations and the garments. All this was aimed at establishing the culture of the organization 'getting a feel' for Stirling Cooper, and particularly Paul Dass's values, because his management style meant he would want to be involved in the detail of all major design decisions. Therefore much of the company image would be a reflection of the managing director's values, views and business strategy. From the designers point of view, there is an analogy of the painter in this type of relationship, in that when you want to paint someone's portrait, you need to understand something of their character. In terms of designing the shops, it is necessary to thoroughly understand the character of the company, and of the people running it.

During discussions certain phrases were repeatedly used to describe the customer, 'East End, streetwise girls', 'gutsy girls' with a lot of confidence, looking for clothes for nightclubs, discos, weekend wear, possibly for going to work in but not specifically office clothes – very much all round fashionwear, street-clothes.

David Quigley, the designer, when shown the merchandise and the promotional photography, immediately noticed that all fashion photography of the clothes was located outside, in London. It was located in markets, in the East End, against the river, by Tower Bridge. This indicated not only that the clothes were aimed at urban life, but that they were set against an urban background. This became a catalyst for developing ideas.

Cost was considered a very important factor. David Quigley was told that Stirling Cooper had a very limited budget: £50 per square foot was the approximate budget to work to.

During these discussions, David Quigley also wanted to establish how Paul Dass and Stirling Cooper viewed the role of the designer and what criteria would be used to judge success. David Quigley suggested that his job was to encourage customers to come into the shop and to linger; it was the company's responsibility to sell the merchandise.

In summary, then, the briefing process was very interactive. Paul Dass had an open approach, the designers used persistence, and subtle questioning to pick up views and cues of what was wanted. During these early briefing meetings, the designers also explained how the work would be carried out, how contractors would be used and how the work would be charged to Stirling Cooper.

## THE DESIGN DEVELOPMENT

This partnership or teamwork between Stirling Cooper and David Quigley Architects continued through the design development. Initially the design team put together mood boards of urban imagery,

*Figure 6.1* An example of one of many mood boards

of textures and colours, of materials such as rock, stone, concrete, chains, metals, barbed wire, rusty cans. They considered the degeneration and the weathering of materials and the changes that result in their texture and colour. The mood boards (see Figure 6.1) were discussed, together with physical examples of found materials, to establish together with the Stirling Cooper management the visual and tactile quality required to support the marketing strategy.

Paul Dass and his team were led through the design experience, making design decisions with David Quigley, ensuring that Paul Dass understood that the designers were starting afresh and not mimicking work they had done for other retail chains.

## Planning the interior

Based on the role Quigley saw as his (i.e. bringing customers into the shop), the designers primary concern was to create a pleasant environment, an environment which enticed customers in and encouraged them to stay in the shop. In the first instance, therefore, Quigley concerned himself with the feel of the interior, rather than more mechanistic issues of merchandising space and routes to the cash desk. City road layouts were used as references for the floor plan, creating avenues or streets of texture and colour (see Figure 6.2), some with more curved patterns, other with more formal regular plans. These ideas were discussed with Paul Dass and his management team; the more formal designs were felt to be too tight while the others lent themselves to a relaxed/informal approach that they were looking for.

The designers then turned their attention to the shop front. The aim was to achieve an uncluttered window through which you could view deeply into the shop. The designer therefore had to create a minimalist effect using more glass and keeping all signage quite small (see Figure 6.3).

Using the most simple piece of metal that can be bought – the angle iron (used for everything from gates and fences to bed-frames) – the designers developed the basis of not only the shop frontage, but also a merchandising system, again discussing with their clients (by showing them samples) the treatment of the angle

*Figure 6.2* A floorplan idea

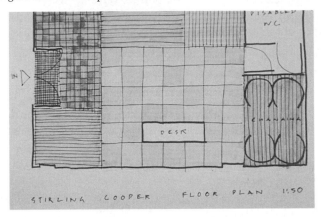

*Figure 6.3* The shop front elevation – one option

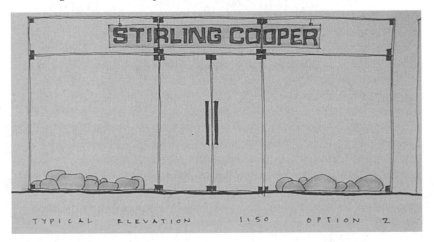

irons, deciding whether they should be stainless steel, mild steel, brass, etc. Through this process of finding materials and sharing them with their client, the designers assembled a palette of materials, textures and colours for use throughout the shops.

In order to develop the merchandising system, the designers spent some time analysing systems currently used by other retailers particularly Stirling Cooper's competitors. The aim in designing the merchandising system was not only to reflect urban life, but also to design it to enable factory manufacture and ease of assembly. Drawings were used to discuss with the client floor hanging, side and forward hanging and shelving, etc. Angle irons were used here too. Once decisions had been made, prototypes were built to consider usage, colour and texture. In this way the system was tested through drawings and prototypes, to examine all the various conditions for which it would need to be adapted. The changing rooms (see Figure 6.4) were developed from Parisian street cubicles, bringing elements of European culture into this urban environment.

## IMPLEMENTATION

Before introducing the design into the main flagship store in Oxford Street, London, a test site was chosen in Kingston-upon-

*Figure 6.4* Ideas for the changing rooms

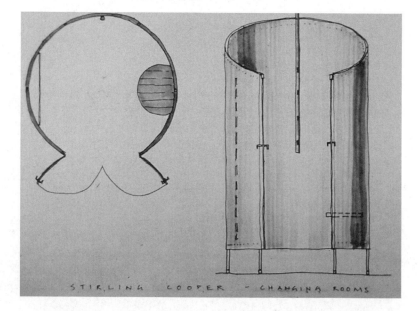

Thames. The designers commissioned and subcontracted the whole refitting project, managing and monitoring the work for Stirling Cooper. The finished shop (see Figure 6.5) was extremely successful; indeed the store doubled its turnover. The designers had

*Figure 6.5* The finished shop

achieved what they set out to do, which was to bring customers into the shop environment. Following on from Kingston, two more shops were opened in Watford and Lakeside, followed by the Oxford Street store in May 1993.

A rollout programme (i.e. every shop in treated the same way over a short timescale) was not planned; rather David Quigley Associates decided with Stirling Cooper to identify sites and, whilst retaining a coordinated look, treat each site slightly differently in accordance with its location, introducing six or seven new shops each year over a two- to three-year period.

This project is an example of good communication between designer and client. The designers actively encouraged collaboration throughout the development, and as a result they were able to correctly identify and interpret the client's marketing needs.

## ACKNOWLEDGEMENTS

This case study has been written with the help and cooperation of David Quigley of David Quigley Architects. Their help and permission to publish is gratefully acknowledged.

This chapter is reproduced with permission from *Marketing and Design: A Critical Relationship*, I. Wilson (ed); published by Pitman Publishing 1994.

# 7 *Developing a brand: Cafecream*

*Margaret Bruce*

## INTRODUCTION

This case is about the redesign and launch of a product designed for the indulgent countlines niche (that is, impulse purchase of chocolate at the checkout counter, mainly for self-consumption). Initial success of the product was short lived and market research revealed certain weaknesses with the product. However, there was felt to be sufficient strength in the product to warrant its redesign and relaunch. Whether the product was capable of becoming a brand in its own right or a variant of a family of related products was debated by the internal marketing team.

'The overall strategy is working well,' Jane Howe, Marketing Manager of Dairy's Chocolates, said with an air of confidence to John Starr, Senior Brand Manager, 'but there seems to be a problem with one of our products, Cafecream.' John had to agree. Dairy's Chocolates was one of the oldest confectioners in Britain and had just launched a new family of products for a new and growing market sector, that of indulgent countlines. Cafecream had enjoyed phenomenal success for the first six months of its launch and then sales had fallen sharply. Some people in the company were of the opinion that the product should be modified and introduced as part of another product line of indulgent countlines, known as Magic. John did not agree with this option. John turned to Jane and said, 'The concept for the product is good, but its taste and shape may not be the most appealing to the market. Using the market research data we have on the product, why don't we revitalize the product, change it in some way to give it a stronger consumer appeal?' Jane was sympathetic to this view, but cautious. If further investment were made and the product still failed to meet its sales targets, what then?

## DAIRY'S GROUP IN 1990

In 1990 Dairy's Group was the fourth largest confectionery producer in the UK, employing 1,000 people. It had steadily expanded throughout the 1980s and was a major force in the confectionery market, one of Britain's biggest food markets. It aimed to increase its market penetration, both in its existing markets and in new markets, by focusing on premium sectors where product quality and presentation were the key elements of the company's success. This was reflected in the company's approach to product development as well as acquisition of major brands.

Dairy's positioned itself in the 'top of mainstream' segment, in that it emphasized quality and supplied premium products at the top end of the volume market. However, its products were not as costly as those of specialist chocolate confectioners such as Godiva.

Dairy's had strengthened successfully and revitalized its flagship and core brands and had stepped up new product development, especially in the segment of indulgent countlines, such as Magic. This activity was based on a thorough reassessment of customers' needs, the market and Dairy's position within it.

Dairy's Group had established itself in international markets via joint ventures and acquisitions in France, Italy and Holland, and it aimed to achieve growth through geographical expansion in the single European market. In continental Europe, the intention was to take leading branded positions in carefully selected sectors of growing markets, mainly by a route of acquisitions and joint ventures.

## TRENDS IN THE UK CONFECTIONERY MARKET

The UK confectionery market in the early 1990s was dynamic and intensely competitive. In fact, only one in four new products succeeded commercially. In 1992 the market was valued at £3,724 million and 803,000 tonnes per annum, and it had experienced a growth rate of about 7 per cent per annum throughout the 1980s.

### Sectors

The confectionery market was segmented according to the following categories: boxed assortments, countlines, sugar confectionery, moulded chocolate bars and novelties. The rates of growth for these different segments varied. For example, boxed chocolates had a growth rate of less than 6 per cent compared with 14 per cent for the chocolate novelties market in 1988. Dairy's had a 28 per cent share of the market for boxed assortments, but this sector was in long-term decline. Between 1990 and 1992 actual sales of boxed assortments had dropped by one-fifth. Dairy's long-term strategy was to focus on the indulgent countlines sector, which was growing at a rate of 19 per cent.

## Indulgent countlines

Indulgent countlines are chocolate bars with indulgent ingredients bought as self-treats. This was a crowded market dominated by low-priced items, such as Cadbury's Flake, and more expensive choices, such as Suchard's Toblerone.

This market segment had certain distinguishing features. Unlike chocolate novelties bought as gifts, the indulgent countlines were bought largely for self-consumption, for example as a reward after a hard day's work.

Women of 15 to 40 years of age were the biggest consumers of indulgent countlines, constituting approximately 70 per cent of the market in 1991. They bought these products to eat themselves, rather than to give to someone else to eat.

# DAIRY'S MARKETING AND DESIGN STRATEGIES

## Market research

Dairy's countline brand group used extensive market research to identify the 'right' concept for a new type of chocolate product. Market research sources included use and attitude surveys, qualitative and quantitative research reports, Euromonitor reports, consumer discussions, and store surveys. The main thrust of research for product development was focus group discussions, where consumers provided insight into the motivations behind buying chocolate products, their feelings towards chocolate in general and towards coffee and other flavours in particular, attitudes to given examples of different products, frequency of purchase, reasons for purchase, and reasons for consumption. Focus groups helped the company to determine specific product features, such as the colour or name of a new brand.

In addition to extensive consumer research and product testing, Dairy's had undertaken extensive competitive analysis, both by asking consumers to compare Dairy's products with the competition and by monitoring their competitors' market positions and product impact. Such research was carried out on an ongoing basis. The review of the market position and packaging of competitors' products included identifying the impact of individual brands and the combination of all brands in a given category, identifying opportunities for development and so on. Both designers and marketers performed this task because it helped them to gain a fuller picture of what was happening and ensured that both design and marketing practitioners had a common understanding of the market potential.

For new products like Magic and Cafecream, qualitative research was used extensively to assist product design and development. John Starr supported this approach because, he reasoned:

> indulgent countlines are bought more for emotive reasons than to satisfy hunger. Brand managers need to tap into and understand the *motivations* people have for buying particular chocolates. Using qualitative research is also quicker, more immediate and cheaper than using quantitative market research.

## Dairy's strategy for indulgent countlines

Dairy's marketing carried out a usage and attitude survey in 1989 to discover time and frequency of purchase, awareness of brands, images of brands and so on. The market research was a nationwide survey. From this research, Dairy's identified a market gap at the premium end of indulgent countlines for special and imaginative chocolate bars.

Previous research had shown that consumers had particular favourites when selecting chocolates in a boxed assortment. As a result, Dairy's had the idea of taking people's favourite chocolates from boxed assortments and turning these into individual bars. Caramels and nuts and coffee chocolates were among the most popular choices.

John Starr stressed that 'indulgent countlines are all about emotional rewards. They are all about being indulgent and treating oneself. If people want to satisfy the physical need of hunger, then they eat a Mars bar, for example.' Hence the product has to be designed to appeal as an indulgent, impulsive buy.

## Rationale

Boxed assortments were Dairy's main business, but this was a declining market. Dairy's wanted to focus on a mainstream sector that was growing, but one that would enable Dairy's to develop premium products and maintain its reputation as a quality supplier. The company was looking for a market where its products would be sold throughout the year, rather than being seasonally dependent.

Another attraction of focusing on the premium end of indulgent countlines was that here the barriers to entry were lower than in lower-priced countline markets. The main chocolate suppliers did not dominate this sector. The higher-priced chocolate, coupled with its more infrequent purchase, did not appeal to the low-cost, high-volume suppliers. Mainstream countlines had a high barrier to entry. Exorbitantly high advertising costs were required to compete against established brands and to maintain a presence in this market.

Taking all of these factors into account, Dairy's chose to enter the premium end of indulgent countlines. New products based on the popular choices from boxed assortments were the cornerstone of its strategy. However, there was a risk involved. These individual chocolates were costly to make; would people pay more for them?

For the subsequent five years, the thrust of the company's effort was planned to be in this sector. Investment of £7 million was made in a new production plant to make innovative, indulgent products.

## Magic

An example of this strategy was Magic, a family or umbrella of products launched in 1990. Each chocolate bar had a different soft centre – such as a caramel and nut centre, or a hazelnut truffle – and was given a separate personality by its shape and packaging. Three had been launched by 1992.

The products within the Magic range were not developed to become major brands in their own right but were to contribute to building one substantial brand. They did not have sub-brand names but were called Magic. As the Magic Brand Manager pointed out, 'we wish Magics to be flexible and able to embrace a number of main flavour products within its umbrella.' The sales of each bar contributed to the total sales of the Magic brand, which was supported by a central core of advertising. This was a cost-effective approach to advertising.

## Design: a sense of 'Dairyness'

Dairy's had no formal written design policy; rather there was tacit understanding of what was being sought in terms of innovativeness. This could be summed up in the following underlying design objectives:

- innovativeness, a major factor giving a competitive edge;
- compatibility with the company image of 'Dairyness';
- packaging that communicates the product attributes to the target market and which must be distinctive when merchandised.

Design was particularly important in conveying a sense of 'Dairy-ness.' Market research showed that consumers viewed the elusive 'Dairyness' as embodying quality, expensive, special chocolates that one could give as presents. An important aspect of 'Dairyness' was the creation of an integrated design in terms of core product, packaging, promotions and advertising. All worked together to build up a coherent brand. Three dimensions – core product, formal product and augmented product – had to be integrated to do this (Figure 7.1).

To update its image the company chose to focus upon three elements. These were:

- imagination;
- indulgence;
- accessibility.

Each Dairy's brand had to have a distinctive identity and image that was in harmony with the overall strategy and identity the company wished to convey. Magic captured the elements of Dairy-

*Figure 7.1* Product dimensions

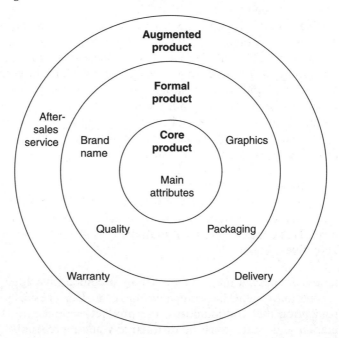

ness. Differentiated by shape and imagery, the soft centres had indulgent, extravagant, smooth textures and were easy to eat.

## Design and indulgent countlines

Dairy's identified a market gap for a chocolate product, for which they then considered the design in terms of both the core product and its packaging. The design had to help justify a given price point – in this case, a premium price – and the design also had to be distinctive, imaginative and indulgent. The design of the core product, first of all, entailed decisions about the shape of the chocolate bar, its taste, the thickness of the chocolate, the flavour and texture of the centre and its surface graphics. Packaging design involved decisions about the graphics and materials utilized for the packaging.

## Design management

Good communication was something the firm was proud of. Brand Managers were assigned by the Marketing Controller to work on a given product and were given a budget to do so. The Brand Managers were project managers and had to coordinate R&D and packaging development functions internally and the design consultancy externally. Formal monthly Product Development Team meetings, consisting of Brand Managers, Marketing Controllers and representatives from R&D and Production, were held to report on progress and to consider new ideas. Project team meetings for given projects were organized more frequently, as and when necessary to push the project along according to schedule. All of the Brand Managers reported ultimately to a Marketing Controller, who did not assume any day-to-day responsibility for product development. One issue that had to be resolved was the need to ensure that the product required by the Brand Manager was efficient to manufacture. For example, marketing might desire a dramatic visual effect, but the design of the packaging also had to be assessed in terms of the ease of construction. How easy was the packaging to make up? What were unit production costs? Could the packaging be altered so that the number of folds required to make up the packaging were minimized? These were constraints on design.

'Because there was a sensitivity to this issue and an overarching concern to capture a sense of quality inherent in the meaning of "Dairyness,"' explained John, 'these different perspectives do not cause problems.' He went on to say that 'the fostering of close relationships between the different people involved in the product development process with ongoing communication helps to resolve such issues'. The onus was on the Brand Manager to ensure that conflicts were resolved and that the tasks of each function dovetailed with that of the next.

## CREATING A NEW BRAND

Cafecream was one of the earliest products for the premium indulgent countlines sector. It was designed for the British market first and foremost. It was expected to become its own brand.

### Design process

#### The team

The design of the core product and the decisions about the shape, flavour and texture of chocolate were made within Dairy's new product development (NPD) team. This consisted of the Senior Brand Manager, John Starr, plus representatives from R&D, Production, and Logistics. The NPD process also had representation outside the company, including the design consultant, advertising agency, packaging supplier and market research agency which each had specific contributions to make to the process (see Table 7.1).

#### The Brand Manager's role

The Brand Manager, a marketing function, coordinated the different activities involved in devising chocolate products. The members of the team did not usually meet with each other. John argued that 'there is not necessarily a synergistic effect in having specialists meet together'. The Brand Manager builds up an intensive working relationship with each party to get the desired expertise and then moves onto the next and repeats

*Table 7.1* Inputs into new product development

| | |
|---|---|
| **Research & development** | generate and screen new product concepts |
| **Production** | test out moulds, feasibility tests |
| **Design consultant** | packaging |
| **Market research agency** | investigate market opportunities and consumer uses and attitudes |
| **Advertising agency** | strategic overview and product positioning |
| **Supplier** | specifications for packaging materials |
| **Brand manager** | coordinator, product champion |

this. It is the Brand Manager who is the at the centre and has the responsibility to get the project completed. Cafecream's Brand Manager worked 50 per cent of the time on Cafecream and the remainder on other brands.

## Product concept and design brief

Deciding on the product concept was critical too. Certain factors were fed into the decision-making process at this stage. These included the target market, consumer needs, product specification and packaging specification. The Brand Manager drew up a comprehensive brief for the product concept, which reflected these elements and articulated the rationale behind the product, its goals, the distinguishing features the product needed to offer, its target price and so on (see Table 7.2). The packaging had to exude a sense of luxury and quality. Cafecream's shape, name and imagery were to build up a strong identity for the brand.

The objectives underlying the development of Cafecream were stated thus, 'to create a brand that could be substantial, sustainable and valuable.' To build up a substantial brand, and one that would generate sales on a longer-term basis, required investment in advertising. To create a brand that was valuable, i.e. profitable, meant that the brand had to sell in sufficient volume per annum (in

*Table 7.2* The product brief

| | |
|---|---|
| **Background** | market information and Terry's position |
| **Objectives** | to create a brand that had to be substantial, sustainable and valuable. Volume, value, market share, gross profit, net profit, return on investment (ROI) |
| **Production costs** | unit production costs |
| **Product description** | size/weight/shape; taste/flavour; shelf life |
| **Visual representation** | individual |
| **Packaging** | distinctive and appealing |
| **Brand strategy** | positioning; test marker; usage; price |
| **Merchandising** | trade requirements |
| **Timetable & launch date** | |
| **Competitor information** | pricing policy; points of differentiation to be emphasized |

*Table 7.3* Product development process – stages

| Stage | Month |
| --- | --- |
| Market analysis and business analysis<br>Consumer research and forecasts | 1 |
| Concept generation, evaluation and market positioning<br>Focus groups, R&D, marketing, competitive analysis | 4 |
| Product development<br>Marketing brief given to R&D, graphics and packaging<br>Production feasibility and factory trials | 6 |
| Launch, national 'rollout' | 13 |
| Market feedback | Six months<br>after launch |

excess of 1,500 tonnes) to pay back the costs of a national advertising campaign (£1 million per annum) and overheads in excess of £150,000 per annum.

## Development of the product

The product development process for Cafecream was organized according to a number of stages (see Table 7.3) and took about thirteen months from market analysis and concept generation to national distribution of the new product.

Starting with R&D, chocolate bars of different flavours, shapes and textures were developed and tested. The Brand Manager, along with R&D and the taste panel, tried out the different products. Those selected underwent market research to appraise their popularity, and the most attractive candidate was chosen. An advertising agency was commissioned to work on a strategy for market positioning. Cafecream was distinguished by its soft centre and its imaginative nature, which differentiated it from other countline products. 'This was what made the product so appealing,' according to John. Production began devising moulds and carrying out feasibility tests for making the product. Last of all, a design firm was commissioned to devise the packaging, according to the specifications laid down by Dairy's. Packaging was the least costly element, at between £10,000 and £20,000 (per product line).

## The launch and its aftermath

The final Cafecream product was positioned as an indulgent count-line product. It was a dark chocolate with a fondant centre and had a distinctive shape. All aspects of the core, formal and augmented product were designed to harmonize with each other and to reinforce brand equity.

Cafecream was launched nationally as a dark chocolate with a coffee-flavoured fondant centre, similar in size to a small chocolate egg, in the summer of 1987, and had reached sales of 980 tonnes by the end of the year. In January 1988 sales began to decline. Market analysis was undertaken to find out what was going so wrong.

### Market analysis

Dairy's decided to review Cafecream, analyse the situation, and then potentially to recommend a revised marketing and design strategy for the chocolate product. The nature of the market research was qualitative. Focus groups were set up to elicit consumers' views and attitudes to Cafecream. After a general probing of attitudes to chocolate in general, the groups focused on countlines and then on Cafecream. Frequency of purchase and degree of specialness of the product was ascertained. Specialness was identified by such attributes as price, packaging, flavour and dark chocolate.

### Purchasing patterns

The pattern of purchase behaviour had been marked by people who enjoyed the novelty of the product, with fanatics eating as many as two a day and sending fan mail to Dairy's to praise the product. Then the novelty factor wore off. The product was felt to be 'too rich' and too messy to eat to find a permanent place in people's repertoires. Dairy's had determined that people have a portfolio of ten to twelve chocolate products they chose from, and that chocolate buying is impulsive and depended on, amongst other things, personal choice, feelings at the time, and what was uppermost in their minds. Unfortunately Cafecream disappeared from people's minds quickly.

### Weaknesses

From this type of market research, certain weaknesses in the core product were identified. Criticisms centered around its 'richness', its 'uncomfortable, awkward-to-eat shape' and the fact that it was made from primarily 'plain chocolate'.

## Strengths

Set against these factors, were Cafecream's strengths: the product had 'individuality and character', was 'highly imaginative'. Its integrated concept was its main strength, which could be built upon to make Cafecream successfully compete in the rapidly growing market sector of indulgent countlines. John Starr suggested that the market research showed that:

> we had struck on something that was valuable and had a high level of awareness. We felt confident that we could take the old product off the market before re-entering the market with something that was better suited to people's needs.

# RELAUNCH

The market research had yielded valuable insights into the strengths and weaknesses of the product. This information formed the basis for redeveloping Cafecream. Market research showed that the concept for Cafecream worked. It had a recognizable personality and the coffee taste was appealing. The main weaknesses were with the product itself. It was decided to change the product fundamentally: into a bar format, which made it easier to eat and yet still an indulgent eat.

Working with R&D and Production, John came up with a bar format made of milk chocolate and filled with a truffle centre. The bar was easy to eat, the truffle was a firm consistency and milk chocolate ensured a wide appeal for the product.

It was important that the strengths of the chocolate were emphasized in the packaging. The design objectives were to maximize the shelf impact and to communicate the personality of the product. For the packaging, John specified the use of high-grade metalized film with classic and imaginative imagery. Cafecream was relaunched nationally. It was well received and sales grew steadily. The market research showed that the product was highly appealing, people liked the product and it was regarded as a very special eat. This was attributed to its price, rich taste and glossy packaging.

# PART III
*Seminal papers*

# 8 *Silent design*

Peter Gorb and Angela Dumas

[First published in 1987, this paper by Gorb and Dumas coined the phrase 'silent design'. This refers to those non-designers, such as marketing managers, who make decisions that affect design, for example the choice of design supplies, the budget allocated to the suppliers and so on. Defining the role of 'silent designers' and recognizing their impact on design is an important outcome of this paper.]

## ABSTRACT

*This paper describes the outcomes of a one-year pilot research study and outlines the routes for the two-year wider study to follow.*

*The research was prompted by the growing interest in the UK in design and its contribution to business performance, and the need to replace anecdote about 'best practice' in organizing and utilizing design, with information about more 'general' practice.*

*After defining design as 'a course of action for the development of an artefact' and suggesting that design activity pervades organizations, the paper describes the methodology used to examine how design is organized. Using matrices to explore the interaction of design with other business functions the report suggests that 'silent design' (that is, design by people who are not designers and are not aware that they are participating in design activity) goes on in all the organizations examined, even those which have formal design policies and open design activities.*

*It is the scope and nature of 'silent design', and its conflict and/or cooperation with formal design activity, which will form the basis for the hypothesis on which the wider investigation will be built.*

*Keywords*: design activity, methodology, interaction with non-designers.

This is an interim report on a research investigation into the *organizational place of design*. The research, which is funded by the Leverhulme Trust, is expected to take three years to complete. For operating purposes it was divided into two parts: the first part, a pilot study over one year, was intended to develop propositions for examination in the wider part of the research. This interim report discusses the outcome of that study, which has just been completed. However, before discussing the pilot study, it is worth restating the overall objectives of the research, and describing the context in which it is taking place.

## DESIGN AND MANAGEMENT

In the last decade [1977–87], and particularly since 1982, there has been a growing interest in Britain in the contribution that design can make to business profitability. The government, through the Department of Trade and Industry, has given significant financial support to the promotion of this proposition. Through the Design Council it has funded a design consultancy scheme designed to help smaller industries to use design more effectively. It has asked the larger industries formally to commit themselves to supporting the importance of design, and is conducting a national advertising campaign. A Government Minister is charged with the national responsibility for design.

In the field of education the subject of design management has emerged as a new field of study in both design and business schools. The teaching of design at the MBA level was pioneered at London Business School in 1976 and is now firmly established [t]here. In 1985 the Council for National Academic Awards (CNAA) published a report on design management which has led to initial work at a postgraduate level in five polytechnic management studies departments (CNAA 1985). In-house training in the subject is beginning to happen in industry. In 1986 design appeared on the agenda of the conference of the European Foundation for Management Development, for the first time.

Britain's leadership in promoting the importance of design is being watched and emulated both in Europe and the USA. An outcome of this growing interest has been a key discussion on how best to organize and utilize the design activity.

## THE RESEARCH OBJECTIVES

It is perhaps a natural outcome of the interest shown in a new subject that what has been published so far about the organization of design has been largely anecdotal and almost exclusively concerned with best practice. This information has proved of great value in motivating others and as a starting-point for investigation. However, like all best practice it may be relevant only to the organization concerned and indeed may be only temporary.

Our research objective is to discover what constitutes *general* practice. We have set out to examine all those aspects of the business where design is utilized and to identify how the enterprise organizes itself to make best use of design. We are also concerned to identify strategies surrounding the implementation of design if and where they exist.

In order to achieve this, the general objectives of the research were to identify:

- the design understanding of managers; their view on the relevance and scope of design in their organizations;
- the operational role of design: how it relates to problem-solving and decision-making;
- the assignment of responsibility and accountability for the various aspects of design in organizations;
- resource commitments by way of people and funds, and the ways in which the performance of these resources is measured.

It was also hoped as an outcome of the research to establish a database which could be used by subsequent research into issues of design organization.

## THE SCOPE OF DESIGN

Design is a process. It is perhaps necessary to affirm this rather obvious fact in view of the common confusion between process and product which takes place when definitions of design are attempted. Furthermore, in defining design, we also need to recognize that external appearance, style, colour and other aesthetic and subjective considerations with which design is commonly associated constitute only part of the design process. Design is also concerned with use, with marketing and production considerations, and a wide range of technical and engineering resources and requirements. However, above all it is concerned with a methodology.

> Everyone who designs devises a course of action aimed at changing existing situations into preferred ones. The intellectual activity that produces material artefacts is no different fundamentally from the one that prescribes remedies for a sick patient or the one that devises a new sales plan for a company or a social welfare policy for a state. Design, so construed, is the core of all professional training: it is the principal mark that distinguishes the professions from the sciences.
>
> (Simon 1982)

This quotation proposes a methodology of design, which Herbert Simon differentiates from the methodology of science. He also points out the very wide-ranging nature of that methodology which has application well beyond his own concern with artefacts. His comment illuminates one main reason why confusion exists over the place of design in organizations, and why there is a need to identify and later specify some landmarks in the process that is design.

Simon limits his definition of design to artefacts, that is, man-made things; although he is also concerned with systems of artefacts, and how the individual artefacts within such a system relate to each other. We have adopted that limitation. However, we are also concerned with how people in organizations understand and make various contributions to the planning, strategies and goals surrounding those artefacts and systems of artefacts.

Our working definition of design is therefore:

> a course of action for the development of an artefact or a system of artefacts; including the series of organizational activities required to achieve that development.

It is important to point out that this definition is not so exclusive as to encompass merely the activities of the professional designer, a limitation which we abandoned at an early point in our investigation. If this definition seems narrow it is worth emphasizing that artefacts pervade industrial organizations. They comprise the products which a manufacturing organization makes and sells or a retailing organization buys in order to sell, or the products used by service business to provide its service. They also embrace those artefacts like buildings and equipment which go to make up the physical environment which constrains or enables the organization to achieve its purposes. In this context we include the work of the architects, engineers, interior designers and space and environmental planners. Finally, they also cover the artefacts which make up the information systems through which the organization communicates its purposes to its various audiences (e.g. employees, shareholders, customers); and include everything from annual reports to advertising material.

This means that although we begin with a simple definition, it has to span numerous activities usually planned and managed in different parts of the organization in different functional departments.

## THE PILOT STUDY

Because of the inevitable complexity of identifying an activity which cuts across traditional organizational lines we decided on a pilot study which would, we hope, not only throw up issues for wider study, but also alert us to any flaws in our method of enquiry. In addition we decided to cover a number of industry sectors to see if comparisons between sectors could be made.

Accordingly, the study was undertaken within four industry sectors: electronics and apparel in the manufacturing sector and retail and transport in the service sector. Sixteen firms in total were investigated, four in each sector. Unstructured interviews were conducted with a range of people involved (as the organization saw it) with the design process. In some organizations, more people were interviewed to add greater depth to the pilot study.

The method we used to undertake the investigation was the completion of a matrix. Along the horizontal axis of the matrix were placed the main areas of artefacts in which design operates and which have been outlined above. These are the 'products', the 'environments' and the 'information systems', each of them being subdivided into appropriate categories.

Down the vertical axis were shown seven levels of involvement in detail from 'shallow' to 'deep'. A description of each of these, together with the original matrix, is shown in Figure 8.1. Using this matrix it was hoped to plot resources for a commitment to design within each organization, and thereby identify and characterize the various organizations and business sectors in terms of their management of design.

## DEVELOPING THE MATRIX

From the information we received during our interview programme we realized that our original matrix could be expanded,
as an analytical tool. Our task was to examine the integration and
interaction of the design process, through the activities of individuals. However, we also began to see a need to identify separately contributions by professional designers. Accordingly we
developed two new matrices, each dedicated to producing a
clearer picture of one aspect of the data. The original matrix
was retained, with one main modification, the ability to record
'professional' design activity. Now known as Design Matrix 1, it
operates as a reference map for all design activity. Of the two
new matrices, Design Matrix 2 concentrates upon interaction
between functional areas and Design Matrix 3 on activity by
individuals. All these matrices are shown in the Appendix (Figures 8.1, 8.2, 8.3, and 8.4).

## OUTCOMES

As an outcome of our work with the matrices, we were able to
make the following two statements:

1   Design activity appears to be widely dispersed throughout the
    organization.
2   Design is very interactive, and cuts through many traditional
    functional areas.

Perhaps more significantly, we were able to make a third
statement.

3   Design activity is frequently not classified as such within
    organizations; nor does there appear to be any consistency of
    classification.

This statement was achieved in the course of the interview procedure, during which it became apparent that we needed to interpret
certain information in order to complete the matrices.

The matrix development had led us to the realization of a
'covert activity' in all the organizations we had investigated.
This covert activity was clearly an important element in all transactions affecting both individual goals and motivation and ultimately, therefore, the central goals of the organization. We could

also begin to see why organizations were experiencing difficulties implementing a design programme.

## SILENT DESIGN: THE ARGUMENTS

It can be argued that a great deal of design activity goes on in organizations which is not called design. It is carried out by individuals who are not called designers and who would not consider themselves to be designers. We have called this 'silent design'.

The aims and intentions behind the design activity of an individual cannot simply be subsumed under 'design' if his [or her] job description, title and his own intentions are not perceived by him and others as having design as a central activity. To assume that if the job entails design, it should be undertaken by a professional designer is to adopt an oversimplistic view. Indeed, within his particular business context his set of decisions might be more appropriate than those of the designers.

The degree to which the 'silent designer' is aware of his design role needs to be understood better. It is also of great significance in the interaction between the 'silent designers' and the 'professional designers'.

In our major investigation we plan to explore the 'silent' design issue. To develop a framework for this investigation we have posed the following questions:

1   How widespread is 'silent design'?
2   How does silent design relate to overt design where that function exists in an organization?

- Is it productive – are there conflicts and how are they resolved?

- Does the amount of each affect these issues?

3   Should silent design be made overt? Is this even possible?
4   If not, is there an optimum balance?

## THE MAJOR INVESTIGATION

With the establishment of a focus for the major investigation the authors plan to modify the form of the questionnaire as it was set out in their original research proposal. They plan to reduce slightly the number of organizations to be investigated on a broad front in order to make room for a few in-depth and more detailed studies.

These in-depth studies will deal with the problems involved in asking direct questions about 'silent design'. They also expect the in-depth studies to uncover some customs and habits of the silent designer and the wider questionnaire to provide an organizational context in which these customs and habits exist.

## CONCLUSION

The pilot study has indicated that design activity pervades organizations and that it is dispersed, interactive and frequently undertaken by people who would not recognize that their job involves design. For the time being we are naming this phenomenon 'silent design'. During the major investigation, the authors will look at organizations with and without formal design policies and resources.

Whilst most of the organizations already studied do have formal design policies, the initial study has found that 'silent design' exists in these organizations as well as those that do not. In the organizations that do have a formal and declared design policy, it is interesting to note words and phrases used to describe aspects of maintaining them. The words 'discipline' and 'control' and the phrases 'top management commitment is vital' and 'custodian of design' were all used by most of them more than once. This suggests a degree of unease, not surprising in a relationship as ambiguous and unclear as the design and management relationship appears to be. It is likely that the increasing promotion of design by government and other agencies will persuade more organizations to take on board a policy toward design.

In identifying the existence of 'silent design', the need for more knowledge on the interaction between 'covert' and 'overt' design activity is clearly vital. Without it one could postulate that a rush toward the introduction of design policies and practices might inadvertently demolish longstanding and successful 'silent design' activities. The need for caution is clear. One must be careful not to hamper success in utilizing design to increase profits.

## APPENDIX

The methodological approach for the pilot study originated from a working paper written for the general manager who had little background in design. Embodied in the paper is a conceptual framework with which to consider design activity within an organization. A simple matrix accompanied the paper and provided a device to explore the scope and depth of commitment to design

*Table 8.1* The original matrix

| A design implementation matrix | Products | | Environments | | | Information | | | |
|---|---|---|---|---|---|---|---|---|---|
| | Finished products | Components | Buildings | Machines | Equipment | Internal | External | Promotion | Advertising |
| Audit | | | | | | | | | |
| Advise | | | | | | | | | |
| Plan | | | | | | | | | |
| Specify | | | | | | | | | |
| Supervise | | | | | | | | | |
| Demonstrate | | | | | | | | | |
| Implement | | | | | | | | | |

within an organization. The matrix is illustrated in Table 8.1. Scope for design is allocated to the horizontal axis under three areas of activity: products, environments and information. Depth of commitment is on the vertical axis.

The working paper describes the vertical axis as 'a guide to establishing the level of involvement at all design stages'. Seven stages make up a scale which starts 'shallow' with an 'auditing' process where direct involvement is limited to evaluation, and finishing 'deep' where an organization directly implements design (probably by manufacturing). The stages are described from the paper as follows:

1   *To audit.* An attempt should be made to audit every product with the view to ensuring that it adheres as closely as possible to the design principles of the organization.
2   *To advise.* It will certainly be useful prior to or during an audit procedure to offer advice on design modifications which will help this happen.
3   *To plan.* Better still, as part of the general planning process for all products, attempts should be made to establish design planning guidelines.
4   *To specify.* As a more rigorous planning procedure for certain products it will be desirable to establish actual specifications for the design of those products.
5   *To demonstrate.* As a way of demonstrating the effectiveness of a specification, it is sometimes useful to design directly and make either a model of the product, or the first of a production run, or a fully completed detail. (An example might be the first of a chain of shops for which a specification has been established.)

6  *To implement.* The deepest level of involvement: actually undertaking the implementation yourself.

Employed as an analytical tool, the original matrix was our first formal step in developing a picture of the use of design in organizations. It also permitted those organizations who were considering developing the strategies for design to understand how broad the scope for design could be.

In dealing with the operational and organizational issues as they interact with the design process, the literature on complex and developing organizations has provided some useful definitions which have assisted in clarifying our task. One such is a working guideline of the roles of purposes of people within an organization, taken from Lawrence and Lorsch (1969). An organization is the coordination of different activities of individual contributors to carry out planned transactions with the environment.

Lawrence and Lorsch also describe an organization as 'a system of differentiated units which require integration and the view of the individual contributor as a complex problem solving system himself' (1969). This in particular is appropriate to the issues that emerged in the organizations that were talked to during the pilot study.

In all cases the authors asked the organizations to direct them to those people they considered to be the most active participants in design projects. This was to enable the authors to gain insight into the way the organization and the individual conceptualized their activity over design. On analysing the data received by using the original matrix, the authors discovered that the matrix itself needed development.

The two issues they found themselves unable to cover with the original matrix were, first, the activity of the individual as a contributor to the design process and, second, the integration of the various design activities.

This resulted in the development of three new matrices. In using these the authors did not attempt to alter significantly the terminology or the structure, merely to arrive at a working tool to record and analyse the two issues described above.

These three matrices are shown. The inclusion in Matrices 1 and 2 of a separate category for 'input by professional designer' was one of the final amendments and reflected the growing awareness of the need to differentiate between activity by 'professional designers' and all other design activity.

The word design can be, and often is, utilized legitimately in many different activities. Consequently, the word 'designer' cannot refer solely to those groups of individuals whose education and training overtly equips them to operate as professional designers. With a separate category one can record in Matrices 1 and 2 the activity of an individual who by education and training is qualified to produce design work. This differentiates between professional designers and all those individuals who are found to be active agents operationally in the design process irrespective of the degree of cognizance of their activity.

Design Matrix 1, 'Involvement of steps within artefacts' (Figure 8.1), is the closest to the original matrix. It allows activity to be recorded in the seven steps of involvement across the eleven artefact categories. It is important that it is not used to make comparisons and it operates as a map for the design activity recorded in the other matrices.

The second matrix was employed to record relationships at or between activity points. This is a very complex matrix, as its lengthy title implies, 'Interaction between artefacts – involvement of steps'. Each of the seven steps on the vertical axis of the first matrix uses one of these matrices. Taken together they can be used as a three–dimensional model on the contour map principle, with cumulatively high spots of end activity forming the peaks of the map. Figure 8.2 shows the basic matrix.

However, each of the seven steps of this matrix must first be considered separately. This allows design activity to be considered in relationship to the eleven artefact categories. Figure 8.3 shows an example of the step 'specify' in an apparel manufacturing organization. Each square on the matrix is subdivided into two triangles. In certain squares both sides of the square are filled in; others only on one side. This is done to suggest the likely direction of the activity. 'Research and development' have an activity with 'sourcing', since R&D will test a fabric that has been sourced and only if the test is successful will the source be utilized. The major responsibility in the (specify) activity resides in R&D. However, it can also been seen that there is an 'input by professional designer' activity which also has responsibility toward 'sourcing'. With 'process' (under the product category) and 'equipment' (under the environment category), the direction of activity is shown as more balanced. In this instance there is also activity *toward* the 'input by professional designer' column, suggesting that he would be affected by activity in the two categories rather more than he would directly affect them.

This matrix series allows us to look at the relationship of design activities. However, the activity of the *individual* as a contributor is only implied. The third matrix, 'Involvement of personnel

*Figure 8.1* Design matrix 1: involvement of steps within artefacts

| Steps | Artefacts | | | | | | | | | | |
|---|---|---|---|---|---|---|---|---|---|---|---|
| | | PRODUCTS | | | | ENVIRONMENTS | | | INFORMATION | | |
| | Input by designer | Research and development | Engineering | Process | Sourcing | Building | Space | Equipment | Operational | Product | Corporate |
| • EVALUATE – artefacts in relationship to principles and objectives | | | | | | | | | | | |
| • ADVISE – to provide professional advice following evaluation | | | | | | | | | | | |
| • PLAN – strategy for artefact development | | | | | | | | | | | |
| • SPECIFY – as part of development/production process | | | | | | | | | | | |
| • SUPERVISE – monitor and evaluate day-to-day decisions | | | | | | | | | | | |
| • DEMONSTRATE – to test and/or refine with a sample | | | | | | | | | | | |
| • IMPLEMENT – full or part production of artefact | | | | | | | | | | | |

Subject organization.......................................
Date .......................................

*Figure 8.2* Design matrix 2: involvement of steps within interaction between artefacts

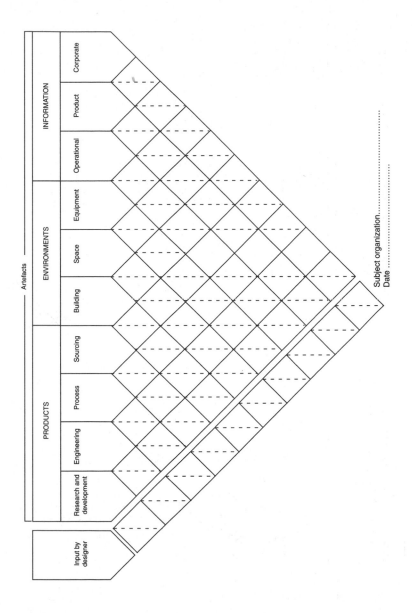

*Figure 8.3* Design matrix 2: involvement of steps within interaction between artefacts
*Note* specify shaded areas as part of the development process

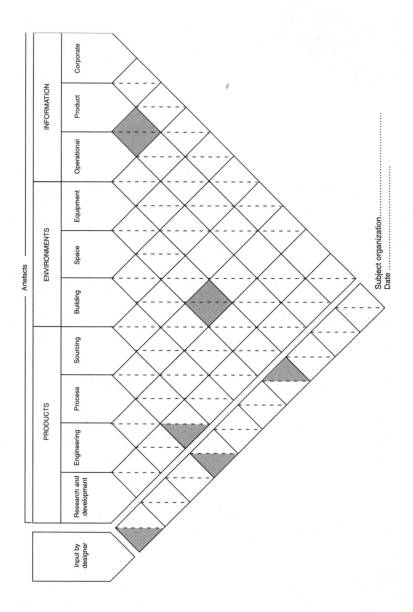

*Figure 8.4* Design matrix 3: involvement of personnel within steps

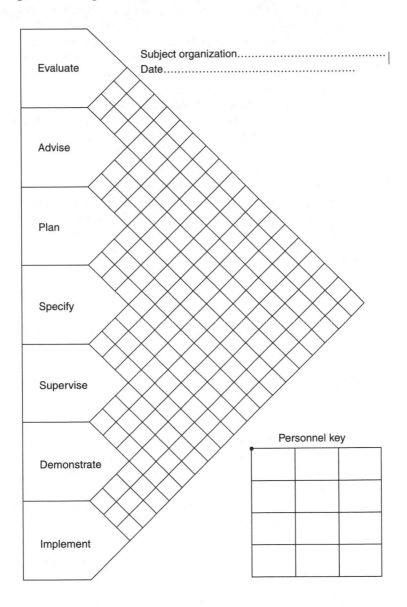

within steps' allows one to record an individual's activity and is illustrated in Figure 8.4. Here each of the seven steps is represented, while the eleven artefact areas are not. Each square on the grid is subdivided into twelve rectangles. By referring to the personnel key one has a layout of the people involved.

What the matrix does not in its present form illustrate is whether individuals operate as part of a team or singly, or whether the activity is constant or sporadic.

Further adaptations of the matrix would enable us to quantify this and much other information about the design activities of individuals and groups. For example, one may wish to know the rate at which they work, whether the design activity is continuous or intermittent.

However, before attempting to extend the matrix it would clearly be advisable to determine which kinds of design activities have priority in the eyes of the people participating in the design process. The questionnaire (to which the main text refers) is intended to provide priorities of this kind in our explanations of the place that design occupies in organizations.

## ACKNOWLEDGEMENTS

Reprinted with permission from *Design Studies*, 8(3), P. Gorb and A. Dumas, 'Silent Design', 1987, Butterworth Heinemann, Oxford.

## REFERENCES

CNAA (1985) Managing Design, an Initiative in Management Education, report of a project sponsored jointly by the Council for National Academic Awards, the Department of Trade and Industry and the Design Council, London: CNAA.

Lorsch, Lawrence (1969) *Developing Organizations: Diagnosis and Action*, Addison Wesley.

Simon, Herbert A. (1982) *The Sciences of the Artificial*, MIT Press.

# 9 The commercial impacts of investment in design

*Robin Roy and Stephen Potter*

[This article was first published in 1993. Measuring the commercial outcome of design investment is complex in terms of appropriate indicators of commercial outcome and the difficulty of separating design changes from other factors that may also impact upon an effective design outcome, such as advertising. Roy and Potter had the opportunity to assess the commercial outcome of design at a project level. They based their research on UK government-sponsored initiatives to support the use of design by British companies. Assessment of design investments and commercial outcomes from these were able to be made.

The results of this study are significant in that they provide evidence that investment in design is likely to yield positive commercial benefits. However, the design investment has to be managed work, for example by briefing designers effectively and keeping in regular communication with designers.]

## ABSTRACT

*A survey of 221 small and medium-sized UK manufacturers which received a government subsidy to employ a professional design consultant to help develop new or improved products or graphics showed that 60 per cent of all projects and 90 per cent of the implemented ones were commercially successful. Other benefits included the firms gaining design management skills and some impact on the UK trade balance. However, there is still a long way to go before industry makes full use of Britain's design expertise.*

*Keywords*: design, product development, government, investment, small firms.

In 1983 Britain became a net importer of manufactured goods for the first time since the Industrial Revolution. By 1989 the UK trade deficit in manufactures reached a peak of £17.2 billion, nearly half of which was due to the deficit in cars, textiles, clothing and consumer electronics – all products with a high technical and/or design content (Central Statistical Office 1991; NEDC 1989). This poor competitive performance of British manufacturing industry has been studied and discussed for over three decades [since the 1960s]. For much of this time attention has been focused on the issues of productivity, prices, exchange rates, etc. in determining economic performance. Over the past decade, however, there has been an understanding of the growing role of 'non-price factors', such as product quality, prompt delivery, marketing effort and, increasingly, environmental impact, both in the international competitiveness of nations and the business performance of companies. As we showed in our report, *Design and the Economy* (Roy et al. 1990), one of the most important non-price factors in competition and business performance is how well a company's products are designed.

The term 'design' is often misunderstood because it includes disciplines ranging from engineering, product and industrial design to fashion, textiles, graphics, interiors, exhibitions and architecture. What is common to all these types of design is that they involve the creation of concepts, plans and instructions, usually in response to a brief provided by a firm or client, that enables a two- or three-dimensional object to be made. The design of the object is the specific configuration of elements, materials and components that give it its particular attributes of function, shape, etc., and determine how it is to be made and used.

Design decisions therefore affect not only non-price factors, such as a product's performance, reliability, appearance, safety, ease of use, etc., but they also affect price factors, through their influence on how economic the product is to manufacture and its life-cycle cost to the users (Walsh et al. 1988).

In Britain there has been official recognition of the economic importance of design since the last century [nineteenth] and certainly since the establishment, in 1944, of the Council of Industrial Design, which in 1970 became the Design Council. However, over the past decade [since the mid-1980s] there has been significantly increased UK Government interest in the role of design in helping to arrest the declining competitiveness of British manufacturing industry. Following a seminar on 'Product Design and Market Success' in January 1982, chaired by the then Prime Minister, Margaret Thatcher, there have been several government initiatives to promote management awareness of the benefits of good design and to support design investment in British industry. The most important of these initiatives was the Department of Trade and Industry's Funded Consultancy Scheme/Support for Design programme administered by the Design Council.

This programme derives from the fact that the UK has perhaps the strongest design consultancy industry in the world (McAlhone 1987), yet UK industry, and especially smaller firms, is not making proper use of this national resource. The Funded Consultancy Scheme (FCS) therefore provided funds to enable small and medium-sized manufacturing firms to engage a professional design consultant for a limited period at zero cost or at a subsidized rate to help with the development of new or improved products, components, packaging, product graphics or technical literature. Support for Design (SFD), which succeeded the FCS, extended the scheme to the service sector with a reduced level of individual subsidy. The programme began in July 1982 and by April 1987 had involved nearly 5,000 projects and £22.5 million of government funding before being incorporated in 1988 into the Department of Trade and Industry's wider Enterprise Initiative (Shirley and Henn 1988). Under the 'Design Initiative', support for graphic design projects was later withdrawn.

## THE COMMERCIAL IMPACTS OF DESIGN STUDY

It is in this context that a team from the Design Innovation Group at the Open University and the University of Manchester Institute of Science and Technology (UMIST) conducted a three-year study of the benefits, costs and risks of investments in professional design expertise in small and medium-sized manufacturing firms in the UK. This study of the commercial impacts of design arose from previous work undertaken by the group (Walsh et al. 1988; Walsh et al. 1992) and others (Lorenz 1986; Pilditch 1987) together with an invitation from the Economic & Social Research Council and the Design Council to bid for funds to undertake research on how non-price factors, especially design, affect the international competitiveness of British industry.

This study surveyed a sample of firms that took part in the FCS and SFD programme with the aim of obtaining information on the commercial returns on investments in a variety of projects involving professional design expertise at the individual product level. One probable reason for scepticism in British industry about the value of design is that, prior to our work, there was no information available on the benefits, costs and risks of specific investments in design and product development at the product or project level. Such information is needed if industrial

*Table 9.1* Size of firms in sample

| Firm size (number of employees) | Number in sample | Proportion of sample (%) |
|---|---|---|
| <20 | 43 | 21 |
| 20–99 | 82 | 39 |
| 100–499 | 76 | 36 |
| 500 + | 8 | 4 |

*Source*: Potter et al. (1992)
*Sample*: 209 firms (12 'no answers' excluded)

managers are to assess the commercial value of design and decide how much to invest in research, design and development relative to other demands on funds. It is also needed by bodies such as the Design Council and the Department of Trade and Industry (DTI) who wish to promote the effective use of design in British industry. This paper summarizes the main findings of this research. A full report of the aims, methodology and results of the study is available from the Design Innovation Group (Potter et al. 1992).

## THE SURVEY SAMPLE

The sample was drawn mainly from the companies that took part in the FCS plus some from SFD. In total, 221 projects were surveyed either by face-to-face interview or via a postal/telephone survey. Since the study aimed to provide general information on the commercial impacts of design in manufacturing, the sample was designed to be representative of small and medium-sized firms across all UK manufacturing sectors rather than of firms participating in the FCS/SFD programme. As the FCS was restricted to firms with 30–1,000 employees and the SFD to firms with 1–500 employees, the majority (60 per cent) of the firms in the study were small, employing under 100 people, a third were medium-sized, with 100–500 employees, and only 4 per cent employed more than 500 people (see Table 9.1). A further study would therefore be needed to assess the commercial impacts of design in large firms.

### Who does design and development?

Prior to their subsidized project, in over half the firms (55 per cent), design and development was undertaken by full-time, in-house research, design and development (RD&D) staff, either alone or with some external assistance. In a third of firms (32 per cent), design was carried out by managers or other individuals whose main job was not RD&D and who often had no technical or design qualifications, either alone or with external assistance (what Gorb and Dumas (1987) term 'silent design'). In 10 per cent design was done externally by consultants, subcontractors or customers and 5 per cent had no prior design experience at all. However, the pattern varied with the type of design work, most engineering design projects were to be undertaken by in-house RD&D staff, while graphic design projects usually involved 'silent design' by managers and/or external inputs from consultants, suppliers, etc. Product design projects tended to involve a mixture of in-house RD&D, 'silent design' and external inputs. Comparison of the data with that from other surveys (Michael Neal and Associates 1988) indicates that the firms in our sample may be considered as typical of small and medium-sized UK manufacturers in their use of design/development staff. The results of this study should therefore be generally applicable.

For most firms, the FCS/SFD project was the first time they had employed a professional design consultant. Over two-thirds (68 per cent) of firms had not previously employed a design consultant in any capacity whatsoever. In addition, other firms were employing a design consultant in a new discipline for the first time (for example, several companies experienced in employing engineering design consultants used the scheme to employ an industrial designer). The experiences and results from this survey therefore very much represent firms in the early stages of the learning curve in using and managing external professional design expertise.

## Types of project

Each project was classified in terms of the inputs of design expertise involved and the type of design output that resulted (see Figure 9.1). On the *input* side most projects involved work by in-house RD&D and other staff as well as by the subsidized design consultants. Nearly half (47 per cent) of the projects mainly involved inputs of various product design skills (e.g. textile and furniture design); 29 per cent mainly involved either *engineering design* (e.g. electrical, mechanical) or combined *engineering* and *industrial design* work (e.g. electronics plus ergonomics); the remaining 24 per cent mainly involved *graphic design* skills. It is this classification by design input that is mainly used in the analysis of results given in this paper.

On the *output* side, three-quarters of the projects involved the

*Figure 9.1* Input of design expertise to and outputs from subsidized projects sampled

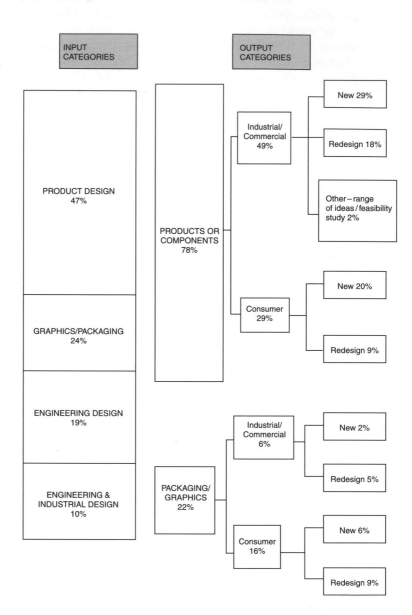

development of new (49 per cent) or redesigned (27 per cent) *products*, ranging from wind turbines, lasers and electronic components to kitchenware and shoes. About a quarter (22 per cent) were *packaging and graphics* projects, ranging from food packaging to the design of technical manuals. The remaining 2 per cent were feasibility studies and projects which produced a range of concepts rather than a specific design.

## Project costs

Information was gathered, for as many projects as possible, on the costs of design work (including any technical and market research) and of all the subsequent costs of developing that design and launching it on to the market. The mean total investment, including all research, design, development, plant, tooling, marketing and other costs, for projects that went into production, was £60,500. For non-implemented projects the average was about £4,500 (Shirley and Henn 1988). Clearly these were not projects with huge budgets, but typical of ordinary product development and other design work in small and medium-sized firms.

On average the engineering/engineering and industrial design projects cost nearly double the graphics ones, with product design projects in-between. This is not surprising, as the more technical a project becomes, usually the more investment is required to assess its feasibility and to put it into production. With the FCS/SFD contribution at between £2,000 and £5,000, non-implemented product and graphics projects lost little more than the government subsidy. For engineering projects, firms usually had to put in more of their own resources before deciding whether to proceed to production.

## PROJECT OUTCOMES

The outcomes of the projects were analysed at several levels:

- implementation (i.e. was the new or improved design put into production);
- financial returns on the total investment;
- indirect benefits.

Outcomes therefore ranged from complete successes, through various types of partial success and failure, to bad failures.

Overall, Table 9.2 shows that half of the projects could be considered completely successful: they were commercially successful and also produced indirect benefits, such as the firm's

*Table 9.2* Classification of successful and failed projects in sample

|  | *With indirect benefits* | *Without indirect benefits* |
| --- | --- | --- |
| Project commercially successful | Complete success 50% | Partial success 10% |
| Project made a loss | Partial success/failure 21% | Failure 19% |

*Source*: Potter et al. (1992)
*Sample*: 178 projects with quantitative or qualitative data

*Table 9.3* Implementation of subsidized projects according to design input

| *Design input* | *Implemented (%)* | *Not implemented (%)* |
| --- | --- | --- |
| Product design | 63 | 27 |
| Engineering/engineering and industrial design | 56 | 44 |
| Graphic design | 80 | 20 |
| All projects | 65 | 35 |

*Sample*: 221 projects

managers learning how to use designers more effectively. A small proportion (10 per cent) of projects were partially successful: they were successful commercially but produced no spin-off benefits. A further 21 per cent might be considered as part successes and part failures; they were projects which made a loss yet produced worthwhile indirect benefits. A fifth of the projects, however, were definitely failures; they both made a financial loss and produced no indirect benefits.

## Implementation

Two-thirds (65 per cent) of the subsidized designs were implemented by being put into production and marketed. This is similar to the figure of 68 per cent implemented projects from a parallel survey conducted by the DTI (Shirley and Henn 1988). Like the DTI, we found a higher rate of implementation of graphics projects than product or engineering/engineering and industrial design ones (see Table 9.3).

This statistically significant (chisquare $p < 0.03$) difference in implementation rates is not surprising given that the FCS provided only 15–30 days subsidized consultancy (and the SFD considerably less). This subsidy was insufficient for most product/engineering projects, which usually required much additional design/ development effort by the firm, but was often enough to complete design work for a packaging/graphics project. The issue of the amount of subsidy available is considered in our conclusions (pp. 199–201).

## Financial returns

Other studies have surveyed firms participating in the FCS/SFD programme and the Design Initiative (Shirley and Henn 1988; Michael Neal and Associates 1988; Department of Trade and Industry 1989). But this is the only research to have succeeded in producing data on the financial benefits, costs and risks of design and product development projects.

We obtained sufficient data on costs, sales and profit margins to calculate the payback or loss on ninety-one projects and partial or qualitative information for ninety others. If firms did not have, or were unwilling to release, financial data on their project, we used a number of qualitative indicators to assess its commercial success.

Overall, of the projects for which we had quantitative financial or qualitative data, 60 per cent could be considered 'commercially successful' while 40 per cent made a loss (see Table 9.2). Considering the different inputs of design expertise, fewer graphics projects (18 per cent) were loss-making than product design or engineering/engineering and industrial design ones (43 per cent and 57 per cent, respectively) and this difference was highly significant statistically (chisquare $p < 0.001$). However, it should be noted that most of the loss-making projects were not implemented, usually involving little more than the loss of the FCS/SFD subsidy. For the 120 implemented projects for which we had quantitative or qualitative data, 89 per cent were commercially successful and only 11 per cent were loss-making.

The subsample for which we had full quantitative financial data was analysed in more detail. In particular, we calculated the time it would take from the market launch of the new or redesigned product for profits from sales to recover the total investment (the payback period). This is the measure we found to be most widely used and understood by the type of firms we were dealing with. Some key results from this analysis are shown in Figures 9.2, 9.3 and 9.4.

*Figure 9.2* Profitable and loss-making projects according to design input, all projects

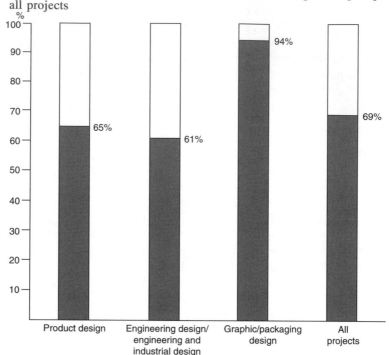

*Source*:  Potter et al. (1992)
*Sample*:  91 implemented and non-implemented projects with financial date
*Key*:

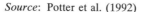

   ■  profitable projects
   □  loss-making projects

This subsample slightly overrepresents the proportion of commercially successful projects due to different response rates for the financial data in the face-to-face and the postal parts of the survey. The difference involved is not very large, although it needs to be noted.

Figure 9.2 confirms the finding mentioned above that graphic design projects are significantly more likely to be profitable (chisquare $p < 0.03$) than projects involving product design expertise or projects involving engineering or engineering plus industrial design. However, as Figure 9.3 shows, once the projects are put into production, the likelihood of product or engineering projects being profitable is almost as great as that for graphics projects. Indeed, the difference in risk is not statistically significant (Fisher $p = 0.33$). The main difference, as Figure 9.4 shows, is in the

*Figure 9.3* Profitable and loss-making projects according to design input, implemented projects

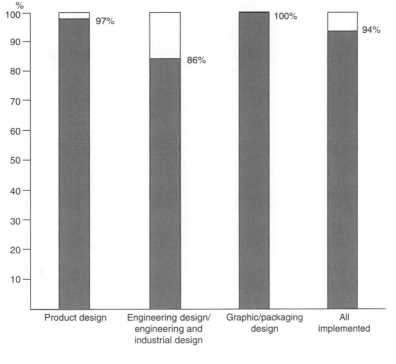

*Sample*: 67 projects with financial data
*Key*:
■    profitable projects
☐    loss-making projects

payback period, with graphics projects on average paying back somewhat faster than product or engineering projects.

Overall, in the quantitative sample, 69 per cent of all the projects and 94 per cent of those that were implemented paid back their total investment (i.e. were profitable) with a mean payback period of 14.5 months (see Figures 9.2, 9.3 and 9.4).

These figures indicate a very good case for investing in design projects. Graphics design projects appear to involve little technical uncertainty or financial risk. Although there is a relatively high risk of failure at the start of a product or engineering project, because most of the failed projects involved exploring ideas that were abandoned before being put into production, the financial loss (except for engineering projects requiring expensive feasibility studies) is likely to be quite small. And once a project has been

*Figure 9.4* Payback periods on profitable, implemented projects according to design input

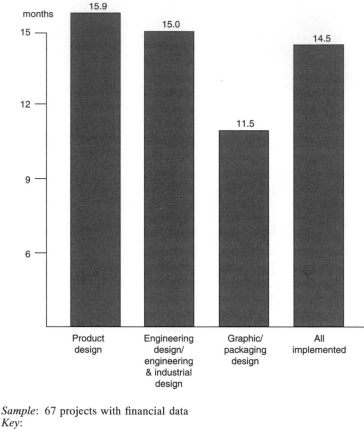

*Sample*: 67 projects with financial data
*Key*:
■    profitable projects
□    loss-making projects

implemented, the prospect of a rapid return on the investment becomes very good, and the risk of financial loss small, for all types of design.

## International trade

Investment in design is clearly worthwhile for the individual firm, but underlying government support for design is the desire to improve Britain's trade performance. The impact of these projects on international competitiveness is therefore of particular interest.

Of the firms for which export information was obtained, 70 per cent reported exporting their FCS/SFD product or design, the average amount exported being £151,000/year, representing a fifth (19 per cent) of total sales. This is encouragingly high. More detailed analysis provides some further interesting results (Potter and Roy 1991). Implemented engineering/engineering and industrial design projects on average produced much higher export ratios (41 per cent of annual sales) than product design (10 per cent of annual sales) and graphics projects (7 per cent of annual sales). The probable reason for this pattern of export performance is that engineering projects were for capital goods for both home and export, product design projects tended to be consumer goods aimed mainly at the UK market, while most packaging projects were for food and drink products also for the home market.

One of the main benefits of the subsidized projects was that they enabled firms to enter new markets. Over a quarter (28 per cent) of all projects resulted in firms entering a new market with their new or improved designs. For implemented projects, 15 per cent of projects led to new export markets and another 1 per cent of projects produced increased exports of products that before being redesigned were already selling overseas (see Table 9.4).

Entering an export market is only one of several international trade impacts. Import substitution, where domestic sales were captured from foreign competitors, was a major factor in 21 per cent of the implemented projects (see Table 9.4). One example was the development of a combination bicycle lock (see Figure 9.5) by an established UK lock manufacturer. The firm was convinced that a high-quality combination lock would find a market even though its price would be higher than Far East imports. In the first year of

*Table 9.4* Impacts of subsidized design projects on international trade

| Projects enabled firm to: | All projects (%) (n=91) | Implemented projects (%) (n=72) |
|---|---|---|
| Enter a new export market | 12 | 15 |
| Increase exports | 1 | 1 |
| Capture UK sales from foreign competitors | 16 | 21 |
| Maintain UK sales against high imports | 20 | 25 |
| No/unknown trade impact | 51 | 38 |
| Total | 100 | 100 |

*Figure 9.5* Combination bicycle lock designed with help from the FCS

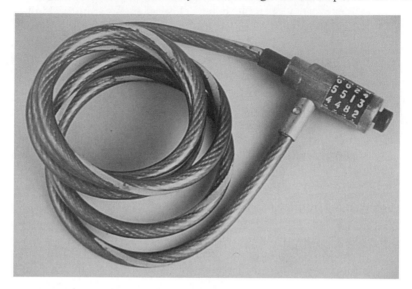

production they sold nearly 50,000 locks in a British market that had previously been supplied entirely by imported products.

Another area of international trade impact is where a new or improved product enabled the firm to hold its own against foreign competition in a sector of the home market already dominated by imports. This category involved 25 per cent of implemented projects (see Table 9.4). An example was a project to improve the engineering and industrial design of a shoe repairing machine. The company exported a third of its output, but in Britain the company's managing director noted that 'the project maintained the company's position in a market where there is intense international competition'.

## Other factors influencing project outcomes

Of course the objection might be made that the financial and trade effects outlined above are not necessarily due to better design, since many other factors might have been involved. To check this, firms were asked to rate the relative influence of design and other factors which might have affected the commercial outcome of the project. In only 15 per cent of projects were factors other than design considered to be the main influence on commercial outcomes. These other factors were mainly marketing effort, pricing,

*Figure 9.6* Motorcycle crash helmet redesigned with help from the FCS, to compete with imported Italian helmets (new design is on right-hand side)

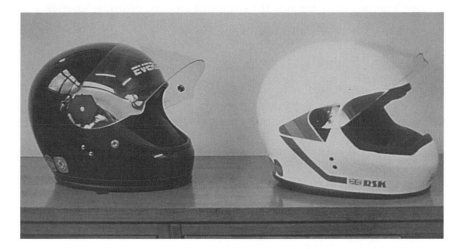

technical quality and market changes. So while one cannot attribute all the benefits to better design and development work alone, it is probable that design played the major part in the outcome of most of the projects studied.

## Indirect benefits and impacts

For many firms the indirect impacts of undertaking a project involving a professional design consultant were as important as the direct financial ones. Our analysis revealed a variety of learning effects, spinoff benefits, and changes in attitudes towards design.

### Attitudes towards design

A third (33 per cent) of firms said that their attitudes to design had improved as a result of the projects, including cases where the project had not been implemented. Of these, 20 per cent became generally aware of the commercial importance of professional design. In 6 per cent of cases manufacturers of engineering or other products became aware of the contribution that industrial design could make to their commercial success. For example, the chairman of a firm that used an industrial design consultancy to help redesign its crash helmets (Figure 9.6) previously felt that design was 'a waste of money'. Now he admits 'the whole management team is aware of the contribution of visual design and packaging to sales'. A further 8 per cent of projects made the firm aware of new design possibilities and the importance of external design ideas. Even a firm whose main business was product design commented: 'wé remain confident of our ability to evolve new designs, but are now aware of how powerful an effect objective scrutiny from a professional design consultant can have.'

## Employment of designers

Perhaps more important than changed attitudes are changes in the resources devoted to design. The results are encouraging. As noted earlier, only about half (55 per cent) of the firms employed in-house RD&D staff prior to the FCS project and two-thirds (68 per cent) had no previous experience of using design consultants. Following the subsidized projects nearly half (47 per cent) of all firms increased their use of professional design: 19 per cent use design consultants more; another 20 per cent either introduced in-house designers for the first time or increased their in-house design capacity, and 8 per cent increased use of both in-house and consultant designers. The effect was that by the time of the interview nearly two-thirds of firms had in-house RD&D staff compared to about half before their FCS/SFD project. In addition there was greater reliance on design consultants relative to other external sources such as suppliers and customers, plus an increased use of teamwork, for design/development work. A surprising result, meriting further investigation, was that few (8 per cent) of firms decided to use the FCS/SFD consultant again for subsequent projects.

## Managing design

Another important indirect benefit was that the projects helped firms to learn how to use professional design consultants. Three-quarters (75 per cent) of firms reported learning one or more design management lessons. Of these, 15 per cent learnt the importance of choosing an appropriate consultant; 33 per cent the importance of a clear and detailed brief ('results are only as good as the brief you give a consultant' was a typical comment); 10 per cent the importance of regular contact with the consultant during the project; and 16 per cent learnt other lessons, such as ensuring that consultants are aware of manufacturing constraints.

A variety of other indirect benefits resulted from the projects. Among those mentioned were that the project provided the ideas or technical basis for other products or designs (23 per cent); led to changes in the management of product development (9 per cent); improved the company's external image and credibility (8 per cent); taught in-house staff useful design skills (8 per cent); and improved confidence within the company (4 per cent). Some firms benefited in several ways. As the management director of a manufacturer of swimming aids said, 'The funding started a whole chain of developments in the company. Four products and their packaging have been designed since FCS plus a new logo. The project gave us impetus and confidence to move ahead.'

## Examples of successful projects

Below are examples of successful projects representing the four main categories of design input. All four projects were financially successful, as well as generating indirect benefits for the firms concerned.

---

### PRODUCT DESIGN

Company A, a small ceramic giftware manufacturer, used the FCS to employ a professional designer to redesign the shapes and surface patterns of its range of ceramic kitchenware which originally had been designed mainly by the firm's sales director. The total project cost was £14,000 and in the first year sales of the redesigned range reached £280,000, compared to maximum sales of £188,000 achieved by the old range. Although there were no savings in production costs or increased profit margins, payback on the project was just two months and the managing director believes that, without the FCS subsidy enabling them to produce the new range, the firm may not have survived in the highly competitive ceramics market.

---

### ENGINEERING DESIGN

Company B makes wire fencing and its managing director had the idea of providing customers with a wire-joining device in order to give the company's products a competitive edge. The SFD project was used to employ engineering design consultants to explore possibilities for joining devices, including a prototype device already developed by the firm, that could be made for about 5 pence. The SFD work only got the project started and considerable design and

*Figure 9.7* 'Gripple' wire-joining device

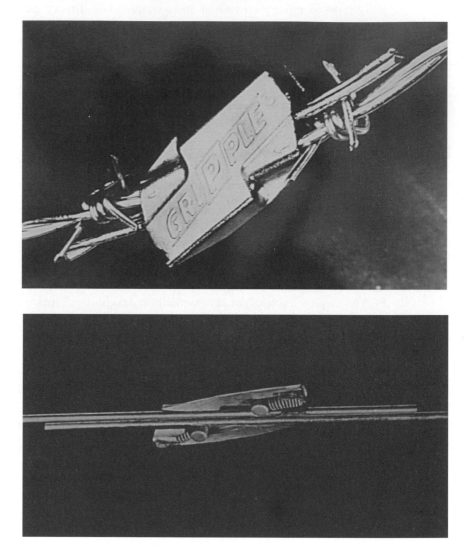

development were required before a practical product emerged. The 'Gripple' is a simple but ingenious device that grips wires using spring-loaded ball bearings, and in later versions toothed rollers, set in a die-cast zinc alloy tube (see Figure 9.7).

The company invested over £200,000 in developing and introducing the Gripple and a further £400,000, with help from several other grants, in getting it into mass production. The company also developed a special tool, the 'Gripper', again with help from design consultants, to tension wires joined by Gripples.

As well as adding value to the firm's fencing, the Gripple system has become a successful product in its own right, e.g. for joining wires in vineyards. By 1990 some 3.5 million Gripples were sold in over thirty countries and the company began to make money on its initial investment. In 1991 the Gripple won the Prince of Wales Award for Innovation.

## ENGINEERING AND INDUSTRIAL DESIGN

Company C is a major supplier of equipment used in professional sound recording studios. The FCS project involved the redesign of the existing desk and cladding of a sound mixing console with the aims of updating the appearance of the product to increase sales and of reducing costs to improve profits. The design consultant redesigned the desk and cladding, replacing the old wood and steel structure by large plastics mouldings (see Figure 9.8). The total cost of the project was £44,500, mainly in tooling.

Following the redesign, plus an electronics enhancement, sales of the product more than doubled, from £1.4 million to £3.4 million, the profit margin increased by 2 per cent and the company's already high world market share increased by 7 per cent. Payback on the investment works out at under two months. To date over 350 consoles have been sold at an average price of £250,000 each. There were also savings in stockholding costs as well as improved customer confidence in their products. Another sound mixer in the range was later redesigned along similar lines.

## GRAPHIC DESIGN

Company D produced a range of canned foods which had no identifiable packaging style. Retailers would therefore buy individual products rather than stocking the whole range. A design consultant was employed through the FCS to redesign the packaging in order to increase the firm's market share. The company's decision to invest in design came just in time, since their main customers, large supermarkets, were no longer buying from smaller suppliers unless they could offer a range of strong brands. The redesigned packaging, involving an investment of £43,000, created this clear brand identity and resulted in an increase in annual sales from £12.7 million to £13.9 million. Although this 10 per cent sales increase is relatively modest, payback was achieved in six months, and without the new packaging the firm considered that sales would have declined sharply. Following this project the company has significantly increased its use of in-house and consultant graphic designers and now views design as crucial to business growth.

## WHY SOME PROJECTS FAIL

The main aim of the research was to assess the commercial outcomes of design projects. A secondary aim was to identify some of the factors influencing those outcomes. We have analysed various factors which might have influenced the financial outcome, including firm size and previous experience in using design consultants. Surprisingly none of these factors seem to have significantly affected whether a project was profitable or made a loss. What was more important was the overall management of the project and in particular avoiding the problems, such as those outlined below, which afflicted less successful projects.

### Non-implemented projects

As mentioned in the previous section, a third of projects (34 per cent) were not implemented, while a further 6 per cent were implemented and made a loss. However, over half of this 40 per cent of loss-making projects were only partial failures in that they produced indirect benefits.

We analysed non-implementation, the main cause of financial loss, against several variables including firm size, prior experience of using design consultants and reasons for applying to the FCS/ FSD. Again, no statistically significant differences were found, although fewer firms with over 500 employees failed to implement their projects than the smaller firms, probably due to better access to finance. What is important in analysing non-implementation are the particular circumstances which affected each project (see the examples of partially successful and failed projects below).

Firms gave one or more reasons for non-implementation. The most common were commercial and/or technical. Non-implemen-

*Figure 9.8* Music recording console following redesign: the Neve 'V' series console with 'Flying Faders' automation

tation in 16 per cent of cases was due to changing market circumstances (e.g. a competitor launched a better design). In a quarter (27 per cent) of non-implemented cases the project was not considered commercially viable (e.g. the design was considered too expensive for market acceptance) and in another 27 per cent there were technical difficulties in development (e.g. the designer was unable to meet the specification). Not surprisingly, technical problems and questions of commercial viability affected engineering and product design projects more than graphics projects. More worrying was the fact that 14 per cent of firms simply could not afford to implement the design, even though it was judged to be commercially viable. This particularly affected product design projects: for example, a luggage manufacturer could not afford to implement designs for a new range even though the firm's management believed that a new range was 'desperately needed' to compete with French and US rivals. For such firms, subsidizing design was not sufficient; further help was needed for the development and implementation of new products.

## Managing design consultants

The above figures only partly reflect another important reason for non-implementation, namely problems experienced by the firms in managing design consultants. We have published another paper on this issue (Roy and Potter 1990) which showed two problem areas. First, nearly a quarter (22 per cent) of non-implemented projects were due to dissatisfaction with the consultant's proposals ('I get the designer's sketchbook out when I want a laugh,' said one manager). Sometimes this was due to inadequate technical skills on the part of the consultant, but often it was linked to the other problem area: deficiencies in the way in which the consultant was selected, briefed or managed. Some deficiencies usually delayed rather than prevented implementation, showing how vital it is for firms to persist with a design project if it is to succeed. But inadequate briefing of the design consultant (e.g. when the firm omitted key design parameters), poor design work by the consultant (in some cases due to the project being passed on to an inexperienced junior designer) and disagreements among management about the value of the project almost inevitably led to project failure (see the examples below[next section]). Nevertheless, only 10 per cent of firms experienced major consultant problems, which is encouraging given that most firms had not used design consultants before and a quarter had strong doubts about using them. These major problems occurred mainly in firms with under fifty employees, indicating that while small firms are most likely to lack specialist design expertise, they are most in need of advice to use external resources effectively.

## Examples of partially successful and failed projects

Below are some examples of projects displaying various degrees of partial success, partial or complete failure caused by one or more of the factors mentioned in the section above.

---

### PRODUCT DESIGN

This manufacturer had developed shatterproof laminated mirror panelling for the commercial sector and wanted to break into the retail market. A famous firm of design consultants was briefed, but the work was passed to a junior designer who was not present at the briefing. She treated the project as one of purely aesthetic design and ignored the innovative technical characteristics of the product. The firm considered the work as 'very expensive and unprofessional' and did not implement the design ideas. However, as a result of this experience the firm has learnt how to manage design consultants and has set up its own design team.

---

### ENGINEERING DESIGN

A supplier of motor vehicle components produced manual car-seat adjusters and wanted to develop a powered adjustment mechanism. The design produced by the consultant, a powered version of the manual system, was insufficiently robust because the brief failed to mention that powered seat mechanisms have to operate under load whereas manual ones do not. Developing robust new gearing for both powered and manual adjustors took the firm's in-house designers a further two years.

A general engineering company used the FCS to update the design and to reduce the manufacturing costs of its range of crane bucket grabs. The consultant's recommendations were not implemented because of management changes and a decision by the company to run down its design and development department.

## ENGINEERING AND INDUSTRIAL DESIGN

The company makes radio remote control units for industrial cranes and the FCS project involved the redesign of the casing and controls of a controller that was difficult to use and expensive to manufacture. The consultant industrial designer designed a vacuum-formed plastic casing and introduced joystick controls. Although the new design halved the production cost, the casing was inadequate and the firm had to glue extra bits of plastic into it in order to make it strong enough to sell. The cost savings from the total sales of the redesigned unit did not even cover the investment in tooling. However, this was the company's fault as, in retrospect, they realized that they had placed too much emphasis on cost saving in the brief and that more resources should have been committed to the project at the beginning. The inadequate design produced by the consultant also stimulated the firm's in-house engineers to redesign the controller with very satisfactory results.

## GRAPHIC DESIGN

This company had produced a telephone message book for in-house use and wanted help to develop a commercial range of message books. According to the company, the FCS-subsidized graphic designer was determined to be 'original and creative and completely ignored the brief'. The uniform black-bound books he designed were felt not to suit the market. The company's managing director, with the help of a printer, therefore designed a range of twenty message books himself, which in their first year sold nearly a quarter of a million copies.

A Scottish food manufacturer used the FCS to design the packaging for a chilled food product. Although the consultant designer's work was excellent the company could not afford to implement the design because of a financial crisis. However, when the company's fortunes improved its managers recognized the importance of packaging design and used the same consultant to design the packaging for a new range of frozen foods. The new range, which included batter-covered haggis, has been very successful.

# CONCLUSIONS

This study shows that the government's programmes of subsidized design consultants have encouraged a proportion of small and medium-sized UK manufacturers to make use of professional design expertise, many of whom would not have done so without help. Although before the subsidized design project over half of the firms employed full-time, qualified in-house RD&D staff, in nearly a third design/development was undertaken mainly by individuals with main jobs other than RD&D, and in most cases this was the first time the firms had used a design consultant or drawn on specialist expertise in areas such as industrial design.

The study shows that, even in typical small and medium-sized firms such as these, the development of new and improved products, components, packaging, etc. using professional design expertise can be an excellent commercial investment. Two-thirds of the projects were implemented and 60 per cent [of these] were commercially successful. Over 90 per cent of a subsample of implemented projects for which we obtained detailed financial data was profitable, with payback periods averaging under fifteen months, and almost all recovered the total project investment in under three years. This risk of financial loss at the start of the product/engineering/industrial design projects was significantly higher than for projects involving graphic design. But once the product or design had been put into production the risk of loss was low for all types of design project. This evidence on risks and returns should encourage UK firms and financial institutions to overcome their traditional reluctance to invest in design and product development.

Another important commercial benefit was that the projects enabled 28 per cent of all firms to enter a new market and a further 30 per cent to increase their market share. In terms of international trade the main benefit was import substitution. Nevertheless, 16 per cent of implemented projects led to new or increased exports and a fifth of all sales of FCS/SFD products were exported. Grossed up for the whole FCS/SFD programme this represents some £500 million worth of exports over six years, for a government investment of £22.5 million.

A majority (70 per cent) of the FCS/SFD projects produced indirect benefits for the firms which participated. The experience of undertaking a project involving a professional design consultant not only improved understanding of, and attitudes towards, design in many firms, it encouraged nearly half to employ consultant designers for subsequent projects at their own expense and/or to increase their in-house design staff. Thus by the time of our survey nearly two-thirds of firms had full-time RD&D staff compared with just over a half before the subsidized projects. Other important indirect benefits included helping firms to learn key design management skills, especially how to select, brief and manage professional designers. In many cases the indirect impacts are of greater long-term importance than the short-term financial returns. As a loudspeaker manufacturer observed, 'the project helped open the door to using design. Our experience was going through the learning curve rather than direct benefit.'

The study, however, shows that nearly a fifth of the design projects studied were failures, neither being implemented nor producing indirect benefits. Poor design work by the consultants, often linked to problems in managing the design consultants, in particular inadequate briefing and internal disagreements within the firm about the project, were important factors associated with such 'failed' projects. Although they suffered more from difficulties in managing consultants, small firms were no less likely to produce profitable projects than medium-sized and larger ones. Given the small amount of subsidy involved, successful projects (especially in product and engineering design, e.g. the Gripple) depended as much on the willingness of the firm to persevere and invest its own resources as on the skills of the design consultants. Indeed one of the few criticisms of the FCS/SFD programme was that the level of support was too low, especially for engineering design, and that differential subsidies should be available.

There were inevitably some projects which failed despite highly satisfactory design work. A few projects foundered for lack of finance, but other projects failed mainly due to factors such as the strength of the competition, market resistance and changes of ownership. While this reinforces previous research (Walsh et al. 1988; Walsh et al. 1992), which showed that 'good design' alone is not enough for commercial success, the main contribution of this study has been to demonstrate how important investment in professional design can be.

However, the wider economic and trade benefits can only be realized if a significant proportion of UK firms increase their investment in design and product development in the long term. Investment in design and development was one of the first things to suffer in the recession of the early 1990s. Lack of awareness of the potential commercial returns among small and medium-sized British firms seems to be a major barrier to this investment. Another is the fact that most of the firms surveyed viewed their projects as a once-off investment rather than as a way of incorporating design into their long-term strategy. This is one reason why the DTI's Enterprise Initiative provides subsidies to enable small and medium-sized firms to employ consultants to provide expert help not only with design but with the whole range of business activities, including business planning and marketing (Department of Trade and Industry 1989).

Unfortunately, such programmes only reach a small proportion of UK manufacturers which could benefit and the subsidies are low compared to those offered through similar schemes in other countries. In its 1991 report on manufacturing industry the House of Lords Select Committee on Science and Technology observed that 'DTI schemes such as . . . the Enterprise Initiative are worthwhile but are too small-scale to have appreciable impact' (House of Lords Select Committee). Finally, the fact that only very few of the projects subsidized under the Enterprise Initiative are in the field of design shows that there are still large numbers of firms that need to be made aware that design can be as essential to their business as marketing and manufacturing. Clearly much more can be done to utilize Britain's undoubted design talent to relieve the growing trade deficit in manufactured products.

## ACKNOWLEDGEMENTS

Reprinted with permission from *Design Studies*, 14(2), R. Roy and S. Potter, 'The commercial aspects of investment in design', 1993, Butterworth Heinemann, Oxford.

Most of the research reported in the paper was funded by the Economic & Social Research Council (Award WF20250021) as part of its Research Programme on the Competitiveness and Regeneration of British Industry, and conducted by a joint team from the Open University and the University of Manchester Institute of Science and Technology. The authors would like to acknowledge the contribution to the work of other members of the Design Innovation Group, especially Claire H. Capon, who conducted much of the data analysis for the project, Margaret Bruce, Jenny Lewis and Vivien Walsh. We also wish to thank Sally Boyle for graphic design support and all the individuals in the firms surveyed for their cooperation.

# REFERENCES

Central Statistical Office (1991) *The Pink Book 1991: UK Balance of Payments*, London HMSO.

Department of Trade and Industry (1989) *Evaluation of the Consultancy Initiatives: Report by Segal Quince Wicksteed*, London: HMSO.

Gorb, P. and Dumas, A. (1987) 'Silent design', *Design Studies* 8(3): 150–6.

House of Lords Select Committee on Science and Technology (1991) *First Report, Innovation in Manufacturing Industry*, vol. 1 (HL Paper 18–1), London: HMSO.

Lorenz, C. (1986) *The Design Dimension*, Oxford: Blackwell.

McAlhone, B. (1987) *British Design Consultancy: Anatomy of a Billion Pound Business*, London: Design Council.

Michael Neal and Associates (1988) *Attitudes of Industrial Managers to Promoting Design*, London: Design Council.

NEDC (1989) *UK Trade Performance*, paper attached to NEDC 89 (9) (March), London: National Economic Development Council.

Pilditch, J. (1987) *Winning Ways*, London: Harper & Row.

Potter, S. and Roy, R. (1991) 'The international trade impacts of investment in design and product development', in *Proceedings of the Fifth British Academy of Management Conference*, University of Bath, September.

Potter, S., Roy, R., Capon, C. H., Bruce, M., Walsh, V. and Lewis, J. (1992) *The Benefits and Costs of Investment in Design: Using Professional Design Expertise in Product, Engineering and Graphics Projects*, Report DIG-03, (September) Milton Keynes: Design Innovation Group, Open University and UMIST. (A revised edition is to be published by the Design Management Institute, Boston, Mass.).

Roy, R. and Potter, S. (1990) 'Managing design projects in small and medium-sized firms', *Technology Analysis and Strategic Management*, 2(3): 321–36.

Roy, R., Potter, S., Rothwell, R. and Gardiner, J. P., (1990) *The Design and the Economy*, London: Design Council.

Shirley, R. and Henn, D. (1988) *Support for Design: Final Evaluation Report*, London: Assessment Unit, Research and Technology Policy Division, Department of Trade and Industry.

Walsh, V., Roy, R. and Bruce, M. (1988) 'Competitive by design', *Journal of Marketing Management* 4(2): 201–16.

Walsh, V., Roy, R., Bruce, M. and Potter, P. (1992) *Winning by Design: Technology, Product Design and International Competitiveness*, Oxford: Blackwell.

# 10 *Design: a powerful but neglected strategic tool*

*Philip Kotler and G. Alexander Rath*

[First published in 1984, this paper by Kotler and Rath indicates the relationships between marketing and design. It is one of the few papers addressing design issues by a marketing 'guru', namely Philip Kotler.]

## ABSTRACT

*Design is a potent strategic tool that companies can use to gain a sustainable competitive advantage. Yet most companies neglect design as a strategy tool. What they don't realize is that good design can enhance products, environment, communications and corporate identity.*

In this era of intensifying global competition, companies are searching for ways to gain a sustainable competitive advantage in the hope of protecting or improving their market positions. A great many industries are characterized by intense service and/or price competition that only succeeds in driving down everyone's profits to an unhealthy level. One of the few hopes companies have to 'stand out from the crowd' is to produce superiorly designed products for their target markets.

A few companies stand out for their design distinctiveness, notably IBM in computers, Herman Miller in modern furniture, and Olivetti in office machines. But most companies lack a 'design touch'. Their products are prosaically styled, their packaging is unexciting, their information brochures are tedious. Their marketers pay considerable attention to product functioning, pricing, distribution, personal selling and advertising, and much less attention to product, environment, information and corporate identity design. Many companies have staff designers or buy design services, but the design often fails to achieve identity in the marketplace.

The following real (though disguised) example is typical of many managers' attitudes towards design:

Steven Grant, an entrepreneur, visited one of the authors and described a device he was developing called the Fuel Brain, which monitors room temperature and controls the heating and air circulation functions of oil furnaces. When asked whether he would use professional design services to assist in this venture, he said there was no need. His engineer was designing the product. His next-door neighbour was designing the logo. His marketing officer was designing a four-page brochure. The Fuel Brain would not need any fancy packaging, advertising, or general design work, becuase he felt that the product would sell itself. Grant believed that anyone with an oil burning furnace and a desire to save money would buy one. A year later, upon being recontacted, he sadly explained his disappointment in the sales of the Fuel Brain.

One only has to look at current US products in many product categories – kitchen appliances, office supplies, air conditioners, bicycles, automobiles, and so on – to acknowledge the lack of good design. Yet its potential rewards are great. Consider the dramatic breakthroughs that some companies have achieved with outstanding design.

- In the stereo equipment markets, where several hundred companies battle for market share, the small Danish company of Bang & Olufsen won an important niche in the high end of the market through designing a superbly handsome stereo system noted for its clean lines and heat-sensitive volume controls.
- In the sports car market, Datsun endeared itself by designing the handsome 240Z. For most buyers before 1976, the 240Z was a dream car at an affordable price, around $4,000–$6,000. The latest copy is by Mazda, which coupled innovative pricing with the 240Z design, capturing a large share of the sports car market with its first offering, the RX7.
- In the hosiery market, Hanes achieved a dramatic breakthrough in a mature market by using creative packaging design and modern packaged goods marketing techniques, catapulting the L' eggs division to the position of market leader. The L' eggs boutique (in-store display) used information design effectively, pulling consumers from other stores and brands. Design was a key component in the marketing strategy and created instant product recognition for the brand.
- In the kitchen furnishings market, Crate & Barrell selects products for its retail stores that meet good standards of material, finish, form and colour. Most of the products are Italian and Finnish. The

look has become so well entrenched that many consider it to be the standard in kitchen furnishings. Crate & Barrell also designed environments to promote traffic and used seconds of expensive products as loss leaders. Once again, good design is used as an element in a marketing strategy.

Well-managed, high-quality design offers the company several benefits. It can create corporate distinctiveness in an otherwise product- and image-surfeited marketplace. It can create a personality for a newly launched product so that it stands out from its more prosaic competitors. It can be used to reinvigorate product interest for products in the mature stage of their life-cycle. It communicates value to the consumer, makes selection easier, informs and entertains. Design management can lead to heightened visual impact, greater information efficiency, and considerable consumer satisfaction.

This article aims to help company strategists think more consciously and creatively about design leadership and to help company marketers work more effectively with designers. It addresses the following questions:

- What constitutes effective design?
- What keeps executives from becoming more effective design managers?
- How can a corporation's design sensitivity be measured (see Figure 10.1)?
- How can the interface between marketers and designers be improved?

## WHAT CONSTITUTES EFFECTIVE DESIGN?

The term 'design' has several usages. People talk about nuclear plant design and wallpaper design even though the two emphasize different design skills – those of functional versus visual design. Design also appears in the description of higher-priced products, such as designer jeans and designer furniture.

Certain countries – notably Italy, Finland, Denmark and Germany – are often described as being outstanding in design. These countries use design as a major marketing tool to compete in world markets. Even here, design connotes different qualities depending on the country: Italian design is artistic, Finnish design is elegant, Danish design is clean, and German design is functional.

'Design' is also used to describe a process. Pentagram, the noted

*Figure 10.1* How a corporations's design sensitivity and design management effectiveness can be measured

Companies need to review periodically the role that design plays in their marketing programme. At any point in time, company management will have a certain degree of design sensitivity. A design sensitivitiy audit (Exhibit 1) consists of five questions that will indicate the role design plays in the company's marketing decision-making. A design management audit (Exhibit 2) asks five more questions that rank how well management uses design. Each question is scored 0, 1 or 2. A corporation's design sensitivity will range from 0 to 10, and its design management will also range from 0 to 10. Companies with a combined design sensitivity and design management effectiveness rating of anywhere from 14 to 20 are in fairly good shape. Those scoring less than 8 should examine whether they are missing a major opportunity by not making more use of design thinking in their marketing strategy

| Exhibit 1<br>*Design sensitivity audit* | Exhibit 2<br>*Design management effectiveness audit* |
|---|---|
| 1  What role does the company assign to design in the marketing decision process?<br>(0) Design is almost completely neglected as a marketing tool.<br>(1) Design is viewed and used as a minor tactical tool.<br>(2) Design is used as a major strategic tool in the marketing mix. | 1  What orientation does the design staff follow?<br>(0) The design staff aims for high aesthetic ideals without any surveying of the needs and wants of the marketplace.<br>(1) The design staff designs what marketing or consumers ask for with little or no modification.<br>(2) The design staff aims for design solutions that start with awareness of consumer needs and preferences and adds a creative touch. |
| 2  To what extent is design thinking utilized in product development work?<br>(0) Little or no design thinking goes into product development work.<br>(1) Occasionally good design thinking goes into product development work.<br>(2) Consistently good design thinking goes into product development work. | 2  Does the design staff have an adequate budget to carry out design analysis, planning and implementation?<br>(0) The budget is insufficient even for production materials.<br>(1) The budget is adequate but typically cut back during hard times.<br>(2) The design staff is well budgeted, especially on new product development projects. |

| Exhibit 1<br>*Design sensitivity audit* | Exhibit 2<br>*Design management effectiveness audit* |
|---|---|
| 3  To what extent is design thinking utilized in environmental design work?<br>(0) Little or no design thinking goes into environmental design work.<br>(1) Occasionally good design thinking goes into environmental design work.<br>(2) Consistently good design thinking goes into environmental design work. | 3  Do managers encourage creative experimentation and design?<br>(0) Creative experimentation and design are discouraged.<br>(1) Designers are occasionally allowed creative freedom, but more typically they have to design within tight specifications.<br>(2) Designers have creative freedom within the limits of the project parameters. |
| 4  To what extent is design thinking utilized in information design work?<br>(0) Little or no design thinking goes into information design work.<br>(1) Occasionally good design thinking goes into information design work.<br>(2) Consistently good design thinking goes into information design work. | 4  Do designers have a close working relationship with people in marketing, sales, engineering and research?<br>(0) No.<br>(1) Somewhat.<br>(2) Yes. |
| 5  To what extent is design thinking utilized in corporate identity design work?<br>(0) Little or no design thinking goes into corporate identity design work.<br>(1) Occasionally good design thinking goes into corporate identity design work.<br>(2) Consistently good design thinking goes into corporate design work. | 5  Are designers held accountable for their work through post evaluation measurement and feedback?<br>(0) No.<br>(1) Designers are accountable for cost overruns in the production process.<br>(2) Design work is evaluated and full feedback is given to the designers. |

British design firm, sees design as a planning and decision-making process to determine the *functions* and *characteristics* of a finished product, which they define as something one 'can see, hold or walk into' (Gorb 1979). Our definition of design is as follows:

Design is the process of seeking to optimize consumer satisfaction and company profitability through the creative use of major design elements (performance, quality, durability, appearance and cost) in connection with products, environments, information and corporate identities.

Thus, the objective of design is to create high satisfaction for the target consumers and profits for the enterprise. In order to succeed, the designers seek to blend creatively the major elements of the design mix, namely performance, quality, durability, appearance and cost. These elements can be illustrated in the problem of designing, for example, a new toaster:

■ *Performance*: first, the designer must get a clear sense of the functions that the target consumers want in the new product. Here is where marketing research comes in. If target consumers want a toaster that heats up rapidly and cleans easily, then the designer's job is to arrange the features of the toaster in a way that facilitates the achievement of these customer objectives.
■ *Quality*: the designer faces many choices in the quality of materials and workmanship. The materials and workmanship will be visible to the consumers and communicate to them a certain quality level. The designer does not aim for optimal quality but affordable quality for that target market.
■ *Durability*: buyers will expect the toaster to perform well over a certain time period, with a minimum number of breakdowns. Durability will be affected by the product's performance and quality characteristics. Many buyers also want some degree of visual durability, in that the product doesn't start looking 'old hat' or 'out of date' long before its physical wearout.
■ *Appearance*: many buyers want the product to exhibit a distinctive or pleasing 'look'. Achieving distinctive style or form is a major way in which designed products, environment and information can stand out from competition. At the same time, design is much more than style. Some well-styled products fail to satisfy the owners because they are deficient in performance characteristics. Most designers honour the principle that 'form follows function'. They seek forms that facilitate and enhance the functioning of the object rather than form for its own sake.
■ *Cost*: designers must work within budget constraints. The final product must carry a price within a certain range (depending on whether it is aimed at the high or low end of the market) and designers must limit themselves to what is possible in this cost range.

Consumers will form an image of the product's design value in relation to its price and favour those products offering the highest value for money. Effective design calls for a creative banking of performance, quality, durability and appearance variables at a price that the target market can afford. Design work needs to be done by a company in connection with its products, environments, information and identity.

## WHAT KEEPS EXECUTIVES FROM BECOMING MORE EFFECTIVE DESIGN MANAGERS?

According to one estimate, over 5,000 US companies have internal design departments and many others use outside design consultants. There are eight industrial design consulting firms with over ten employees, as well as numerous smaller ones (Siegal 1982). In spite of the availability of design services, many companies neglect or mismanage their design capabilities. The reasons are design illiteracy, cost constraints, tradition-bound behaviour and politics.

### Design illiteracy

Some designers charge that US managers are largely illiterate when it comes to design. According to Rita Sue Siegal:

For the past 20 years American industry has been run by managers. They are trained in business schools to be numbers-oriented, to minimise risks and to use analytical, detached plans – not insights gained from hands-on experience. They are devoted to short-term technological competitiveness. They prefer servicing existing markets rather than taking risks and developing new ones.

(Siegal 1982: 24)

Although this is stereotyped thinking, it represents a widespread view that many designers have of the people who run America's corporations.

### Cost constraints

Many managers think that good design will cost a lot of money – more than they can afford. Using Skidmore, Owings & Merrill to design a new warehouse will be expensive. Many companies have found that having an internal designer or outside design consultant on retainer pays for itself many times, not only in avoiding costly errors but in creating a positive image for the company.

## Tradition-bound behaviour

Tradition-bound behaviour is also a barrier to effective design management. A catalogue format is very hard to change; and a product design or a company name is even harder to change. Salespeople will argue that their customers will be confused by name, product and catalogue changes. Managers prefer to stick with the original design instead of exposing their tastes to critical judgement. For example, after Pillsbury bought Green Giant Foods, several suggestions were made that a facelift was in order. Pillsbury asked Leo Burnett, the Green Giant's agency, to look into this, but after initial creative development, the agency gave up because no one would commit to backing the new designs.

## Politics

Company politics play a role in every firm. Some executives might oppose a proposed design simply because they want to block another group. Politics surface in creative reviews, budget meetings and strategy planning sessions.

## HOW CAN THE INTERFACE BETWEEN MARKETERS AND DESIGNERS BE IMPROVED?

If a company recognizes the need for more and better design work, then a two-way process of education must occur. Marketers must acquire a better understanding of the marketing process.

Marketers need to be aware of the split in the design community between the functionalists and the stylists. The orientation of the functionalists is based on putting good functional performance, quality, and durability into the design. The orientation of the stylists is to put good outer form into the design. Functional designers are normally responsive to marketing research and technical research, while stylists often resist a marketing orientation. The stylists prefer to work by inspiration and tend to pay less attention to cost. Fortunately, few designers are at the extremes, and most are willing to pay some attention to market data and feedback in developing their designs.

Marketers also often split into the same two camps. Some marketers, notably those in the salesforce, often plead with the designers to add 'bells and whistles' to the product to catch the buyers' attention and win the sale. They press for features and styling that are eye-catching, even though they might not contribute to good design and performance. Other marketers hold that the key to customer satisfaction and repeat sales is not simply attracting initial purchase but providing long-term product-use satisfaction. These marketers are more interested in supporting the incorporation of good performance, quality and durability characteristics into the product. They point to the success of Japanese automobiles as based not on style leadership so much as the consumer belief that Japanese automobiles offer better quality, durability and useful features. So marketers also need to get their act together when they work with designers and make recommendations as to what counts most in the consumers' minds.

A common management mistake is to bring designers into the new product development process too late or bring in the wrong type of designer. There are eight stages in the new product development process:

1   Idea-generation.
2   Screening.
3   Concept development and testing.
4   Marketing strategy.
5   Business analysis.
6   Product development.
7   Market testing.
8   Commercialization.

Typically, the designer is invited in at stage 6, product development, when the prototype product is to be developed. Designers, however, should be brought in earlier, preferably in the idea-generation stage or at least the concept development and testing stage. Designers are capable of producing ideas that no customers would come up with in the normal course of researching customers for ideas. And, during the concept development and testing stage, designers might propose intriguing features that deserve investigation before the final concept is chosen.

## Design philosophy

Each company has to decide on how to incorporate design into the marketing planning process. There are three alternative philosophies. At one extreme are design-dominated companies which allow their designers to design out of their heads without any marketing data. The company looks for great designers who have an instinct for what will turn on customers. This philosophy is usually found in such industries as apparel, furniture, perfumes, tableware, and so on.

At the other extreme are marketer-dominated companies which require their designers to adhere closely to market research reports describing what customers want in the product. These companies believe designs should be market-sourced and market-tested. This philosophy is usually found in such industries as packaged foods, small appliances, and so on.

An intermediate philosophy holds that designs need not be market-sourced but at least should be market-tested. Consumers should be asked to react to any proposed design because often consumers have ways of seeing that are not apparent to designers and marketers. Most companies espouse the philosophy that designs should be market-tested even if not market-sourced.

---

### ATMOSPHERES

Here is how one firm, Atmospheres, develops its designs for bank retail environments.

The designers at Atmospheres construct settings of bank interiors and test them on small focus groups of bank customers. Customer responses to different layout arrangements, textures, furniture, etc. help Atmospheres gain insight into customer perceptions and preferences. Based on customer responses, the designers then develop a design proposal for the bank. The design package is tested with another focus group to refine and verify the effectiveness of the design. The final version is presented to management with evidence of the degree of interest and satisfaction of the bank's customers in the proposed design.

This rhythm between the visual conceptions of the designer and the consumers' reactions to proposed designs represents the essence of market-oriented design thinking. It neither inhibits the designer from coming up with great ideas nor allows bad design ideas to be accepted without testing.

---

## CONCLUSIONS

While every corporation buys and uses product, environmental, information and identity design, very few have developed a sophisticated understanding of how to manage design as a strategic marketing tool. Design has been defined as a process that seeks to optimize consumer satisfaction and company profitability through creating performance, form, durability and value in connection with products, environments, information and identities. Strong design can help a company stand out from its competitors. The best results can be achieved by training general managers, marketers, salespeople and engineers to understand design and designers to be aware of and understand the functions of these people. Design ideas should at least be market-tested, and preferably be market-sourced or stimulated by market survey data. As other strategic marketing tools become increasingly expensive, design is likely to play a growing role in the firm's unending search for a sustainable competitive advantage in the marketplace.

## ACKNOWLEDGEMENTS

Reproduced with permission from P. Kotler and A. G. Rath, 'Design: a powerful but neglected strategic tool', *Journal of Business Strategy*; published by Faulkner & Gray, 1984.

## REFERENCES

'Architecture as a corporate asset' (1982) *Business Week* (4 October): 124–6.

Gorb, P. (ed.) (1979) *Living by Design*.

King, J. P. (1982) 'Robots will never be practical unless products are designed for them', *Industrial Design* (January–February): 24–9.

Kotler, P. (1973–74) 'Atmospheres as a marketing tool', *Journal of Retailing* (winter): 48–64.

Siegal, R. S. (1982) 'The USA: free to choose', *Design* (January): 24.

# 11 *Managing relations between R&D and marketing in new product development projects*

*William E. Souder*

[This article was first published in 1988. Marketing and design may have interface problems, as do R&D and marketing. Considerable effort has been taken to research the R&D marketing interface for new product development projects and Souder is an expert in this area. Some of the problems with the R&D–marketing interface are shared by design and marketing, particularly lack of appreciation, poor communication and feelings of distrust.]

## ABSTRACT

*This article examines the R&D – marketing interface conditions found within an extensive data base of new product development innovation projects. The incidence of different types of problems between these two important functions are analysed and the effects of these observations on project outcomes are discussed. The article contains a number of recommendations for increasing the success rates of innovation projects by using a model that improves conditions at the R&D–marketing interface.*

## INTRODUCTION

Research and development (R&D) and marketing personnel depend on each other for the creation of new product innovations. Yet R&D and marketing departments have frequent misunderstandings and conflicts.

Many managers have first-hand experience of R&D–marketing interface problems and behaviours between R&D and marketing groups have been carefully studied (Gupta et al. 1985; Shanklin and Ryans 1984; Souder 1987a, 1987b; Souder et al. 1977, 1983; Moung 1973). However, much more information is needed about this complex and important topic. This paper examines the R&D–

marketing interface conditions found in 289 new product development innovation projects. Based on these findings, strategies and
guidelines are presented for improving the relationships between
R&D and marketing groups.

## METHODOLOGY OF THIS STUDY

This study was carried out on a comprehensive data base of life-
cycle information on 289 new product development innovation
projects. The data were collected through ten years of intensive
field research at fifty-six consumer and industrial product firms
(Souder 1987a, 1987b; Souder et al. 1977, 1983). Exhibit 1 and
Table 11.1 present the methodology and the project outcome
measurement scales used in collecting that data base. The 289-
project data base contains numerous detailed descriptions and
ratings of key events, activities, attitudes and behaviours of the
R&D and marketing personnel who worked on each project. As
part of the content analyses, statistical reduction and factor ana-
lyses of this large data base (Berelson 1952; Crollier 1986;
Kerlinger 1973), these items were reduced to forty-two attitudinal
and behavioural descriptors of the R&D–marketing interface.
Some examples of these descriptors are 'Frequency of Joint
Meetings', 'Frequency of Joint Customer Visits', 'Degree of
Perceived Need to Interact' and 'Degree of Regard for the Other
Party's Competency'.

Each of the 289 projects was rated on each of these descriptors.
Some of these ratings came directly from the instruments, while
others were developed through content analyses of the interviews
(Berelson 1952; Crollier 1986; Souder 1987a, 1987b; Souder et al.
1977, 1983). Redundancies were built in at several points. For
example, the 'Frequency of Joint Meetings' was primarily measured by questionnaire items that asked for the number of times per
year that joint meetings were held. Details about these joint meetings were solicited during the interviews. Differences greater than
10 per cent in the questionnaire responses of the marketing, R&D
and other personnel on the same project were reconciled during the
interviews. As another example, the 'Degree of Perceived Need to
Interact' was primarily measured by asking pointed questions of
the respondents during interviews. The information from the interviews was then checked against the Likert-type scale ratings supplied on the questionnaires. Apparent disparities were resolved by
returning to the subjects to clarify their responses and ratings. This
type of multi-method, multi-trait measurement approach is com-

**Exhibit 1** *About the data base*

*Data*: life-cycle data were collected on 289 new product development innovation projects at fifty-three consumer and industrial product firms (Souder 1987a, 1987b; Souder et al. 1977, 1983). The data collection focused on project events, with detailed attention given to organization structures, environments, climates, behavioural processes and project success/failure factors. The ultimate objective was to understand development processes for new product innovations.

*Sample of firms*: using published statistics, an industry-by-industry compilation was made of firms with significant new product activities in either consumer or industrial goods. Target firms were then randomly selected from this list, based on a compromise design that carefully considered the cost of travelling to distant sites and the need to maintain representativeness on several important dimensions (Souder 1987a, 1987b; Souder et al. 1977, 1983). Approximately five firms were selected from each of the following ten industries: metals, glass, transportation (includes automotive and mass transit), plastics, machinery, electronics (includes computers and instruments), chemicals, food, aerospace and pharmaceuticals.

*Sample of projects*: using carefully specified definitions, the population of new product innovation projects initiated during the preceding five years was assembled at each firm. A random sampling of equal numbers of success and failure outcome projects was taken from these populations at each firm, while maintaining a range of types of technologics, types of innovations, degrees of difficulty of projects, central v. divisional R&D efforts, and several other important dimensions (Souder 1987a, 1987b; Souder et al. 1977, 1983). Several ongoing projects whose success or failure outcomes were unknown at that time were intentionally included in this sampling. Following these procedures, approximately 10 per cent of each firm's portfolio was selected into the 289 project sample studied here.

*Data collection*: a total of twenty-seven instruments, numerous telephone interviews and 584 in-depth face-to-face interviews were carried out on each project to record the life-cycle histories and extract the relevant data on each of the 289 projects (Souder 1987a, 1987b; Souder et al. 1977, 1983). A cascading interview procedure was used to cross-validate information collected from each marketing, R&D and other subject on each project (ibid.).

monly used to maximize the validity of social science measurements (Kerlinger 1973).

A profile of ratings was thus developed for each of the 289 projects. Some of these profiles appeared to be very similar; others appeared to be very dissimilar. Statistical cluster analyses techniques were then applied to the profiles in order to cluster the project exhaustively by the various types of profiles that were found (Crollier 1986; Kerlinger 1973).

*Table 11.1* Project outcome measurement scale

|  | Success outcomes Descriptors | |
| --- | --- | --- |
| *Degrees of success* | *Technical outcomes* | *Commercial outcomes* |
| High | Breakthrough | Blockbuster |
| Medium | Enhancement | Above expectations |
| Low | Met the specs | Met expectations |

|  | Failure outcomes Descriptors | |
| --- | --- | --- |
| *Degree of failure* | *Technical outcomes* | *Commercial outcomes* |
| Low | Learnt a lot | Below expectations |
| Medium | Gained some technology | Protected our position but lost money |
| High | Complete dud | Took a bath we won't forget |

*Other outcome*

SE = stopped the effort early due to poor progress

## SEVEN R&D–MARKETING INTERFACE STATES

Using a 95 per cent statistical significance level, seven different clusters were found from the cluster analysis. Each cluster was then labelled according to its observed items. For example, a review of the items in one cluster showed that it was characterized by a low frequency of meetings between the R&D and marketing personnel, highly specialized and organizationally separated R&D and marketing functions, and a low degree of perceived need to interact. Therefore, the label 'Lack of Interaction' was coined to describe this R&D–marketing interface state of affairs. Twenty-two of the 289 projects, or 7.6 per cent of the sample, exhibited this state. Similarly, the other states and percentages shown in Table 11.2 were found accordingly labelled.

Several firms that experienced the 'Lack of Interaction', 'Lack of Communication' and 'Too-Good Friends' problems on the projects studied here avoided these states on some subsequent projects. Follow-up studies with these firms showed that they

*Table 11.2* Incident of harmony and disharmony states

| States | Projects experiencing each state % |
|---|---|
| Mild Disharmony | |
|     Lack of interaction | 7.6 |
|     Lack of communication | 6.6 |
|     Too-good friends | 6.3 |
|     Subtotal | 20.5 |
| Severe Disharmony | |
|     Lack of appreciation | 26.9 |
|     Distrust | 11.8 |
|     Subtotal | 38.7 |
|     Disharmony total | 59.2 |
| Harmony | |
|     Equal partner | 11.7 |
|     Dominant partner | 29.1 |
|     Harmony Total | 40.8 |
|     Overall Total | 100% |

overcame these states through modest efforts. These efforts included more frequent joint meetings, joint involvements in planning proposed projects and increased sharing of information. Moreover, though these problems often lowered the organization's new product development effectiveness, they were not totally disruptive and they seldom led to major project failures. Therefore, as shown in Table 11.2, these problems were labelled 'mild'. By contrast, the 'Lack of Appreciation' and 'Distrust' problem states were labelled 'severe'. Follow-up studies showed that these types of problems were not easily overcome; they usually caused operating disruptions, consumed many hours of managerial talent in moderating disputes, delayed key actions and important decisions and led to project failures.

Many other projects were found that did not exhibit either mild or severe disharmonies. As shown in Table 11.2, these projects were considered to be in a 'harmony' state.

# CHARACTERISTICS OF THE MILD DISHARMONY STATES

## Lack of interaction

In this state of affairs, there were very few formal and informal meetings between the R&D and marketing personnel. Both parties were deeply concerned with their own narrow specialities and neither saw any reason to learn more about the other's work. Neither party saw the need for close interaction. R&D expected marketing to use whatever they gave them, and marketing expected R&D to create useful products.

This state resulted more from simple neglect than from any strong animosities between the parties. For example, one subject noted: 'You get busy and you don't stop to think about whether or not they should know about this or that . . . when you have to get your part of the job done.' Another subject said: 'If you don't get used to seeing each other you don't miss each other, and if you don't think about each other your don't make any effort to get together. And you always have to make an effort.' It may be noted that several projects experiencing the 'Lack of Interaction' state were in older, commodity-product firms that were attempting to develop new product lines. Most of these firms had no histories of close R&D–marketing interactions.

## Lack of communication

In this state, the two parties purposely maintained verbal, attitudinal and physical distances from each other. R&D purposely did not inform marketing about their new technologies until very late in the development cycle. Marketing purposely did not keep R&D informed about market needs. This occurred because neither party felt the other had much information of significant value. And neither felt it was important to inform the other of the details of their own work. This state was aptly summed up in the comments of one respondent: 'If we told them all this . . . We know more about it than they do. Our best source of information comes from right here, from ourselves.' Note how this state of affairs is different from the above 'Lack of Integration' syndrome, where the perceived urgency of pursuing their own activities caused the parties to neglect each other. Here, both parties harboured negative feelings about the worth of the other that stood in the way of interaction.

Though various causes of the 'Lack of Communication' state were observed within the data base, two experiences repeatedly led directly to this problem. One was the perceived theft of credit. When either party took what the other thought was undue credit for meritorious project achievements, this inevitably led to a 'Lack of Communication' problem. The impression that the other party had taken unfair advantage was long remembered. Another experience that frequently led to the 'Lack of Communication' state was top management's uneven use of accolades. If top management praised one party and did not praise the other, rivalry invariably developed that shut off some future communication. As one subject noted: 'If we don't tell them anything, they can't go to management and take credit for it.'

## Too-good friends

In this state of affairs, the R&D and marketing personnel were too friendly and maintained too high a regard for each other. They enjoyed each other's company so much that they frequently met socially, outside the work environment. These social affairs often included the individual's families, e.g. family picnics and Sunday afternoon socials were common. In most of the 'Too-Good Friends' cases, work and social aspects were commingled, e.g. joint visits to customer facilities might also involve a round of golf and the Sunday afternoon socials always included some informal discussions of business. Each party felt that the other had their own area of exclusive expertise, and that the other was beyond reproach. This inhibited each party from challenging the other's assumptions and judgements. Consequently, important information and subtle observations were overlooked that were significant for the project.

What factors led to this type of problem? Surprisingly, past successes sometimes led the team members to become too-good friends. Teams of R&D and marketing personnel who had worked together successfully for long periods of time often became complacent. Their potency appeared to decline once they had achieved complete harmony. Apparently, they needed some conflicts or the challenge of building harmonious relationships to maintain their alertness. A related factor was a kind of blind faith in the correctness of the counterpart person. As one respondent observed: 'You are always sort of reluctant to challenge and question what your colleague tells you. He's the expert in that area. And you don't expect that he'll play politics with you, so there's no reason to question his integrity. And you figure he's the best man you've got, so he probably won't steer you wrong.'

A detailed examination of the other clusters of projects showed that past successes and great faith in each other also characterized effective R&D–marketing interfaces, i.e. the 'Equal Partner Harmony' state in Table 11.2. What were the distinguishing factors?

The answer appears to be a matter of interpersonal dynamics. The parties to an effective interface always challenged and penetratingly questioned each other. They appeared to enjoy and thrive on this aspect, sometimes with impish good humour. When one partner found a gap in the other's logic, both partners were suddenly energized to close that gap. Such experiences further strengthened their relationship. The partner who committed the logic gap never seemed to suffer any loss of prestige in the other's eyes. Rather, the ambience was described by one partner as 'a climate where we look for flaws, and it's not important who committed the flaw. We just want to find it and work together to fix it.' This is clearly a different climate from the above 'Too-Good Friends' state.

It should be noted that such professional disagreements and challenging behaviours, which often characterize effective R&D–marketing interfaces, may give the outside observer the mistaken impression of disharmony and strife. Professional disagreement appears to be a very healthy and enlightening climate for its members. At times, such disagreements may seem to become very heated and destructive. Yet if these discussions are confined to the issues and do not become personally threatening to the participants, they can actually strengthen the R&D–marketing interface. Thus, it is the lack of professional disagreement ('Too-Good Friends') that constitutes disharmony, and not its presence.

## CHARACTERISTICS OF THE SEVERE DISHARMONY STATES

### Lack of appreciation

This state was characterized by strong feelings that the other party was relatively useless. Marketing felt that R&D was too sophisticated, while R&D felt that marketing was too simplistic. Marketing felt that R&D should be prohibited from visiting customers because they would talk over their heads. R&D felt that marketing did not have a good grasp of the market needs. In this state, the marketing groups often purchased their R&D work outside the firm rather than use the in-house R&D group. R&D often independently moved ahead with its own ideas, bypassing marketing and attempting to launch their own new products. These efforts seldom succeeded, and the failures were usually rationalized by the R&D personnel as marketing's fault for failing to assist them!

What caused the 'Lack of Appreciation'? No single cause was identified. Some cases had long remembered histories of ineffectiveness by one party, e.g. R&D failed to develop the promised product or marketing failed to identify the market correctly. Sometimes, the organizational climates fostered a lack of appreciation.

For example, several respondents indicated that they 'never see any signals from management that collaboration is desired'. Other respondents noted that management has not indicated that we are expected to cooperate with them'. It is interesting that management must make a special effort to encourage cooperation: it does not seem to be automatic.

The organization of R&D and marketing into separate departments with separate budgets and operations often fostered a lack of appreciation. As evidence, consider the following sampling of statements from personnel at five firms in the 'Lack of Appreciation' state:

- 'We don't have any inputs into their plans and budgets.'
- 'They have their own operations and so do we.'
- 'We get our rewards from doing our thing and they get theirs from something else.'
- 'No one is responsible for how it all comes together.'
- 'We just go our separate ways.'

## Distrust

Distrust is the extreme case of deep-seated jealousies, negative attitudes, fears and hostile behaviours. In this state of affairs, marketing felt that R&D could not be trusted to follow instructions. R&D felt they were blamed for failures, but marketing was credited for successes. Several R&D groups in this state feared that marketing wanted to liquidate them. R&D lamented that marketing often attempted to dictate exactly what, where, when and how to do the project, allowing no room for rebuttal and no tolerance for their suggestions. Marketing lamented that when R&D got involved the project disappeared and they never saw it before it was completed, at which point it was seldom what they wanted. Several cases were found where R&D initiated many projects and kept them secret from marketing 'so marketing wouldn't kill them before they gained enough strength to move along on their own'. Cases were found where marketing brought R&D into the picture only after the product specifications had been finalized 'in order to avoid any arguments from R&D about how to do it'.

What caused the 'Distrust' state? Though no single cause was found, several important contributing factors were isolated. All the 'Distrust' cases began as either a 'Lack of Appreciation' or a 'Lack of Communication' problem that evolved into 'Distrust'. Many of the 'Distrust' cases were characterized by personality conflicts that top management had allowed to exist for a long time. In some cases, these conflicts had become so institutionalized that even personnel who had not been involved harboured feelings of 'Distrust'. As an example, take the following quote from one respondent, referring to his counterpart in another department: 'He once did some things to us. I'm not sure what they were. It all happened before I came into this group. So, you see, you really have to watch out for him.' This type of institutionalized 'Distrust' was found surprisingly often.

## CHARACTERISTICS OF THE HARMONY STATES

### Equal partner harmony

In this state, each party appeared to share equally in the workloads, activities and rewards. Each party felt free to call joint meetings on almost any issue. These meetings were characterized by an open give and take of facts, opinions and feelings. No issues were left unresolved and consensus was sought by everyone. Study committees and taskforces with joint memberships were common, with the taskforce chairmanships rotated between the R&D and marketing personnel. Moreover, it was part of the 'Equal Partner' culture to involve R&D and marketing personnel jointly in all customer visits, customer follow-ups, customer service, new product planning and forecasting, project selection and product strategy formulation activities.

Three features were common to all the 'Equal Partner' cases. First, the marketing personnel were technically trained. They all had undergraduate degrees in science or engineering. Second, the marketing personnel had prior careers in R&D. Thus, personnel were often successfully exchanged or rotated between the R&D and marketing functions. Third, the R&D and marketing personnel had a strong sense of joint partnership. As evidence, note the following sampling of quotes collected from R&D and marketing personnel in 'Equal Partner' states:

- 'We couldn't get along without them.'
- 'We're on the phone with each other constantly.'
- 'I feel like I've known them a long time.'
- 'We've been through "thick and thin" together.'

### Dominant partner harmony

In this state, one of the parties was content to let the other lead. Both R&D-dominant and marketing-dominant cases were found. For example, one R&D subject in a marketing-dominant case noted: 'We have no idea at all what the market needs are. But if they'll tell us what they want and supply the specs we can sure make it for them.' A marketing respondent in an R&D-dominant case said: 'We can usually sell what R&D gives us. We don't really know what they are able to come up with. They know what it takes to make a good performing product better than we do.'

It may be noted that the dominant partner cases seldom involved complex technologies, exacting customer needs or large R&D efforts. Most of these cases involved developmental efforts as opposed to research efforts. This reinforces the notion that problems at the R&D–marketing interface escalate as the technology or the user's environment become more complex.

## INCIDENCE, SEVERITY AND CONSEQUENCES OF DISHARMONY

As the percentages in Table 11.2 show, a surprisingly high incidence of R&D–marketing disharmony was found. Nearly two-thirds (59.2 per cent) of the projects studied here experienced some type of R&D–marketing interface disharmony. Moreover, it is especially disconcerting that over one-third (38.7 per cent) of the projects studied here experienced severe disharmonies. These results are statistically significant at the 99.9 per cent level of confidence (using the biomial statistical test; Siegal 1956). That is, a statistically significant number of projects were found to be experiencing disharmonies. And a statistically significant number of these projects had severe disharmonies.

But is disharmony disruptive to project success? Table 11.3 responds to this question. Most of the 'Harmony' projects succeeded. Partial success characterized the 'Mild Disharmony' projects. And most of the 'Severe Disharmony' projects failed. As noted in Table 11.3, these results evidence a statistically significant relationship between the degree of harmony/disharmony and the degree of project success/failure. This relationship is significant at greater than the 99.9 per cent confidence level. Thus, these results demonstrate that the quality of the R&D–marketing interface affects the degree of success of new product development efforts.

A case-by-case examination of the data base revealed many informative details underlying the results in Table 11.3. In many of the projects experiencing the 'Too-Good Friends' problem, important information was overlooked that severely diminished the effectiveness of the end products. In many of the projects experiencing the 'Lack of Communication' problem, the new products either did not match the market needs or failed to meet some

*Table 11.3*: Distribution of project outcomes by harmony/disharmony states

| States | Projects in each state exhibiting each outcome[a] (%) | | |
|---|---|---|---|
| | *Success* | *Partial Success* | *Failure* |
| Harmony | 52% | 35% | 13% |
| Mild Disharmony | 32% | 45% | 23% |
| Severe Disharmony | 11% | 21% | 68% |

$X^2$ statistic = 88.84, $C^a$ = 0.61, significant at <.001[b]

[a] The following definitions are used, based on Table 11.3:
  Success =    High plus Medium Degrees of Commercial Success (Blockbuster plus above Expectations)
  Partial Success =   Low Degree of Commercial Success plus low Degree of Commercial Failure (Met Expectations plus Below Expectations)
  Failure =    Medium plus High Degrees of Commercial Failure (Protected Our Position But Lost Money, plus Took a Bath We won't Forget)
[b] For details on the $\chi^2$ and contingency correlation statistics see, Sidney Siegel, *Nonparametric Statistics for the Behavioral Sciences*. McGraw-Hill: New York, 1956. pp. 196–202. Note that the statistical tests were run on the absolute numbers and not on the percentages.

important customer specification. In about half of the projects with 'Lack of Interaction' problems, the end products either did not perform as originally planned or arrived too late to capture a rapidly changing market. Thus, 'Mild Disharmonies' generally depreciated the degree of success of the end products. But they seldom resulted in dismal product failures.

By contrast, a majority of the projects experiencing 'Lack of Appreciation' problems either failed to perform or they were not cost-effective. In many of the projects where 'Distrust' occurred, the products did not perform at all. Thus, 'Severe Disharmonies' resulted in a high frequency of rather dramatic failures. Moreover, it should be noted that 'Severe Disharmonies' were very difficult to overcome. Attempts by management to ameliorate them through negotiation, reorganization, bargaining or personnel transfers often left deep scars and sowed the seeds for a renewed outbreak of similar problems elsewhere. Thus, the prognosis for firms experiencing 'Severe Disharmonies' is unusually pessimistic. Once they appear, their persistence can doom the firm's new product success rate for a long time.

Thus, these results show that the incidence and seriousness of R&D–marketing interface problems are distressingly high. Moreover, many of these problems are chronic, persistent, difficult to correct and seriously detrimental to new product success. These results are both surprising and disappointing. In spite of previous awareness and study of these problems (Gupta et al. 1985; Shanklin and Ryans 1984; Sonder 1987a, 1987b; Sonder et al. 1977, 1983), they still persist.

The reader is cautioned to use some care in interpreting these results. As mentioned above in connection with the discussion of the characteristics of the various R&D–marketing interface states [see pp. 218–19], disharmony is a complex facet of human behaviour. Professional disagreements, which may appear disharmonious to a casual observer, are often a sign of a very healthy and harmonious interface. The strong statistical relationships found here between disharmony and success do not mean that every disagreement and all apparent disharmonies are bad. One must be very careful in defining what constitutes real disharmony. In fact, the results show that a lack of professional disagreements ('Too-Good Friends') may indicate disharmony. Thus, the reader is cautioned to use these results in the context of definitions of the R&D–marketing states set forth here.

## EIGHT GUIDELINES FOR OVERCOMING DISHARMONY

An analysis of the projects in the data base revealed eight practices that alleviated R&D–marketing interface problems. These practices are summarized in Exhibit 2.

Each of these eight practices reflects an actual experience of one or more firms in the data base. The users contended that the practice significantly increased the harmony of their R&D–marketing interface. In every case, these contentions were borne out by the data. The firm's interface became more harmonious after the practice was implemented.

Each guideline in Exhibit 2 is effective for managing innovations because it pushes the R&D and marketing parties into a more collaborative, partnership role. The guidelines create conditions in which disharmonies are discouraged and harmonious behaviours are encouraged. Unfortunately, the guidelines do not provide much information about where and when they should be used. For example, when is it best to use guideline 8 (decision authority clarification)? Should guideline 8 always be used, on every project?

**Exhibit 2** *Guidelines for improving relations between R&D and marketing*

1 *Break large projects into smaller ones*: three-quarters of the projects with nine or more persons assigned to them experienced interface problems. By contrast, projects with five or fewer persons assigned to them seldom experienced problems. The smaller number of individuals and organizational layers on the small projects permitted increased face-to-face contacts, increased empathies and easier coordination.

2 *Take a proactive stance toward interface problems*: in those cases where potential interface problems were avoided and actual problems were overcome, the parties maintained a posture of aggressively seeking out and facing such problems head-on. They openly criticized and examined their behaviours. As one individual noted: 'We don't treat it like a social disease and sweep it under the rug. If we got it, we want to know about it so we can get rid of it.'

3 *Eliminate mild problems before they grow into severe problems*: all the cases of severe ('Lack of Appreciation' and 'Distrust') problems studied here began as mild problems at some earlier point in time. As noted elsewhere in this paper, severe disharmonies were extremely difficult to eliminate. Mild disharmonies were much easier to overcome. Thus, it is wise to eliminate mild problems while they are still mild.

4 *Involve both parties early in the life of the problem*: much has been said and written about the benefits from participation and early involvement of the R&D and marketing parties in decision processes (Gupta et al. 1985; Shanklin and Ryans 1984, Souder 1987a; Young 1973). The results here reinforce the conclusion that when R&D and marketing are joint participants in all the decisions, from the start of the project to its completion, 'Lack of Appreciation' and 'Distrust' are lessened.

5 *Promote and maintain dyadic relationships*: a dyad is very powerful symbiotic, interpersonal alliance between two individuals who become intensely committed to each other and to the joint pursuit of a new product idea (Souder 1987a; Young 1973). Dyads are fostered any time persons with complementary skills and personalities are assigned to work together and given significant autonomy. Dyads are worth promoting not only because they encourage innovation in particular cases, but because they can become the kernel of a much wider circle of interrelationships between R&D and marketing. A successful dyad composed of an R&D person and a marketing person will draw the R&D and marketing personnel on to their bandwagon.

6 *Make open communication an explicit responsibility of everyone*: this was dramatically illustrated by the open-door policy at one of the firms in the data base that had a history of poor R&D–marketing interfaces. This policy consisted of quarterly information meetings between R&D and marketing, day-long and week-long exchanges of personnel, periodic gripe sessions, and the constant encouragement of personnel to visit their counterparts. Every employee was formally charged with the responsibility of playing a role in this open-door policy. Moreover, each employee's success in meeting this responsibility was formally evaluated at the end of each quarter. The open-door policy survived the initial scepticism that surrounded it, and the examples set by a few diligent individuals eventually spread.

7 *Use interlocking taskforces*: a vivid illustration of the use of interlocking taskforces was provided by one firm in the data base. The top-level taskforce or steering committee consisted of the company president, the vice presidents of R&D, marketing and finance, the project coordinator, the R&D taskforce leader and the marketing taskforce leader. The marketing and R&D taskforce memberships changed as the project metamorphosed over its life-cycle in the early stages of the project, phenomenological research work was carried out by PhD scientists. Application-oriented scientists gradually replaced them as the project aged. Finally, engineering personnel replaced them. This interlocking taskforce structure was repeatedly successfully used by this firm to foster R&D–marketing harmony and new product development success.

8 *Clarify the decision authorities*: the decision authority is a kind of charter between R&D and marketing. It governs and guides the R&D–marketing venture by detailing who has the right to make what decisions, under which circumstances. For example, at one firm the policy specified that marketing had the sole authority and responsibility for defining the user's needs. R&D had the ultimate authority and responsibility for selecting the technical means to meet those needs. R&D and marketing were given the joint responsibility for deciding when an adequate product had been defined. Complaints and appeals to top management could not be made unilaterally by either party. Top management only entertained an audience composed of both parties. A decision authority policy, as well as the group process of developing such a policy, can contribute enormously to clarifying the roles of R&D and marketing. Well-developed decision authority policies were observed at several firms. They fostered a sound foundation for the avoidance of many time-consuming conflicts.

In order for managers to apply the guidelines intelligently, a framework is needed for analysing the role needs of the situation and for selecting the guidelines that best meet that need. The customer–developer conditions (CDC) model depicted in Table 11.4 is such a framework.

## FRAMEWORK FOR INTEGRATION: THE CDC MODEL

A detailed examination of the data base revealed some new product customers with little awareness of their own needs. Other customers understood their needs but were unable to translate them into product specifications. Still other customers were highly sophisticated: they could specify precisely what they needed and they could write a complete set of exact product specifications that met those needs. Analogously, the data base revealed some R&D groups that possessed a detailed understanding of the forms and specifications of most types of new products and the technical means to create them. Other R&D groups were found that did not have these high levels of sophistication. They possessed extensive knowledge of product forms, but they lacked the technical means to create them. Still other R&D groups were found that were technically astute, but lacked the know-how to convert their knowledge into successful new products.

The customer–developer conditions (CDC) model depicted in Table 11.4 evolved from an awareness of these facets. Two variables describe the customer's level of sophistication: need awareness (the customer's awareness of their own needs) and translation abilities (the customer's ability to communicate their needs). Two variables describe R&D's level of sophistication: product know-how (R&D's understanding of products) and means know-how (R&D's technical sophistication). Each of these variables can be scaled on a continuum from low to high, as indicated in Table 11.4. Taken together, these variables create various conditions or cells. Each cell dictates the roles that must be played for success under those cell conditions. Though many cells are possible, only twelve characteristic cells are shown here for illustration in Table 11.4. This version of the CDC model depicts R&D and the customer. Other versions can depict other parties within the new product development process (Souder 1987a).

### Twelve cells and their implications

Customers who reside in cell A are highly sophisticated. They know exactly what they want and can state precisely what will

*Table 11.4:* Customer–developer conditions (CDC) model

|  | Customer's level of sophistication | | |
|---|---|---|---|
|  | | Need awareness and translating abilities | |
|  | High | Understands own needs but can't translate them into product specifications | Low |
|  | Understands own needs and can translate them into product specification | | Does not understand own needs |
| **R&D's level of sophistication** — Product know-how and means knowledge — High: Understands the product specification and the technical means to develop new products | A | B | C |
| Understands the technical means but does not understand the product specification | D | E | F |
| Understands the product specification but not the technical means to develop it | G | H | I |
| Low: Does not understand either the technical means or the product specification | J | K | L |

satisfy their needs. R&D groups who reside in cell A are also sophisticated. Once the customer informs them of the needs, they can immediately use their superior knowledge to make the desired product. Thus, cell A is a case where R&D should lead marketing, e.g. a 'Dominant Partner Harmony' case.

Customers who reside in cell B fully understand their own needs, but are unable to translate them into product specifications. A translator is needed. Here is a role for the professional marketer. However, marketing personnel cannot perform this role without continuously interacting with R&D. The customer's needs will normally only be revealed through a series of repetitive activities: need translation, development of prototypes, translation of newly discovered needs from this trail, development of modified prototype based on these needs, trail of modified prototype, etc. Thus, cell B is a case where marketing should lead R&D, e.g. another 'Dominant Partner Harmony' case.

Based on the experiences of the firms in the data base that developed successful 'Dominant Partner' climates, guidelines 1–4 in Exhibit 2 should be used in cells A and B. These guidelines appear to be the most appropriate ones for evoking the required roles between R&D and marketing under the 'Dominant Partner' model. The information in the data base suggests that when management takes an active role in explaining the nature of the conditions in cells A and B, and when management consistently uses guidelines 1–4, 'Dominant Partner' climates can be maintained. Personnel at most of the 'Dominant Partner' field sites examined here quickly accepted and played the appropriate roles when the conditions in cells A and B were fully explained to them, and the rationales for the 'Dominant Partner' model became obvious to them. It may be noted that some dissatisfied personnel at one firm in the data base voluntarily left when the management dedicated that firm to a 'Dominant Partner' climate. However, dissensions between R&D and marketing diminished and product success rates rose at this firm after this change.

In cell C, the customers do not understand their needs and cannot therefore translate them into product specifications. Marketing professionals are needed to help the customer define needs and help the customer translate these needs into product specifications. Cell C thus places great demands on the joint R&D–marketing interface. Close collaboration between marketing and R&D is mandatory in order fully to understand the user's technical environments, define the user's needs and describe the user's motives. A strong willingness of the R&D and marketing parties to share information and generally act like a team is required for success in cell C. To achieve and maintain these roles, guidelines 1–5 in Exhibit 2 appear to be necessary. For example, one firm in the data base experienced repeated problems in transferring accurate information on customer requirements between its marketing and R&D departments. To correct this, it used a dyad (guideline 5). The firm appointed two counterpart project coordintors, one in the marketing department and one in the R&D department. These coordination jobs were staffed with two younger individuals who had worked together before and who had established a strong, longstanding interpersonal relationship (a dyad). Though neither person was a logical choice for these jobs on the basis of their technical knowledge, their personalities and their harmony in working together effectively eliminated the communication problems.

In cells D, E and F, R&D has lower product form sophistication than in the corresponding cells A, B and C. Here, R&D is technologically adept in the underlying sciences and skilled in the relevant engineering disciplines, but unsure about using these skills to achieve want-fulfilling products. Thus, marketing has a teaching function to perform in addition to their translation function. They must teach R&D the meaning of the product specifications that they translate from the customer. But they cannot do this alone. R&D must teach marketing enough about the world of R&D so that the two parties can build on this shared knowledge to develop the appropriate new product. To achieve this, the use of guidelines 1–6 from Exhibit 2 appear to be needed. Two firms in the data base found that open-door type policies (guideline 6) were important when it was necessary for the R&D and marketing parties to share openly and work very closely together.

Conditions in cells G, H and I are very different from any of those discussed above. Here, R&D needs to learn which particular means are associated with which particular end-performance specifications. Learning to match means with ends requires the joint efforts of both R&D and marketing. Typically, these joint efforts will take the following form. In response to marketing's presentation of the end specifications they think are needed, R&D will inquire what these specifications imply and whether or not they can be achieved in various ways. This dialogue will often stimulate whole new ways of looking at the problem, new technical processes and new product concepts. Thus, cells G, H and I will require very close team relationships between R&D and marketing, along with a patient mentality, and allow time for R&D to move up on their learning curve. Under these circumstances, guidelines 1–7 in Exhibit 2 may be needed. Guideline 6 (open-door policies) and guideline 7 (interlocking taskforces) were successfully used together by six firms in the data base under the conditions of cells H and I. The dual use of guidelines 6 and 7 appears to be especially important for large projects that cannot readily be broken up (e.g. where guideline 1 isn't feasible) or where the R&D and marketing groups have not previously worked together.

In cells J, K and L, R&D lacks both the depth of technical knowledge and the skills to convert this knowledge into want-satisfying products. These conditions demand the most effect R&D–marketing interface. Time, patience, experimentation, give and take, trial and error, and sharing are vital to success under these conditions. Thus, in cells J, K and L all the guidelines in Exhibit 2 should be used. Guideline 8 (decision authority clarification) may be especially important in these cells.

## Implications for managing the R&D–marketing interface

New product developers must take the time to study and assess their own levels of sophistication and the levels of sophistication of their customers for every new product they contemplate developing. This will provide them with the information to decide which cell of the CDC model they occupy in the case of that new product. The cell conditions define the roles that the R&D and marketing parties must play to succeed, and suggest which guidelines in Exhibit 2 to employ to evoke these roles. It must be noted that cell A is the only one where a highly developed R&D–marketing interface is not mandatory, and therefore where few guidelines are required. Since this is a relatively rare condition for new product innovations, developers who think they are in cell A are well advised to verify this impression.

Success in cell L demands great knowledge of the relevant sciences, applications know-how, user needs and user psychologies. Achieving this requires a very well-developed R&D–marketing interface, which may be attained through careful attention to the use of all the guidelines in Exhibit 2.

Success in the other cells requires varying degrees of R&D–marketing integration. As outlined above, various combinations of guidelines may be used to achieve the required levels of integration.

## CONCLUSION

Nearly two-thirds of the 289 projects in the data base examined here experienced one of five types of R&D–marketing disharmony. The severity of disharmony was found to be statistically significantly related to the degree of success of innovation projects. Eight guidelines and a customer-developer conditions (CDC) model framework for using them were empirically developed for success-fully overcoming disharmonies. Since the data base showed that severe disharmonies were extremely difficult to overcome, it is essential to prohibit their formation.

The results of this research indicate that R&D and marketing managers should jointly work together to help avoid disharmonies in seven ways. First, they should make all their personnel aware that R&D–marketing interface problems naturally occur. Second, they should encourage their personnel to be sensitive to the emer-gence of R&D–marketing interface problems by watching for the appearance of any characteristics of five types of disharmonies, as discussed above. Early detection is the key to their elimination. Third, managers should be especially careful to give equal credit and public praise to their R&D and marketing personnel in order to eliminate jealousies that might form a basis for severe disharmony. Fourth, R&D and marketing managers must make special efforts to reinforce in words and deeds their desire that the R&D and market-ing parties collaborate. They must constantly send signals to their personnel that cooperation is essential. Fifth, managers should use teams of R&D and marketing employees at every opportunity. This will help avoid the natural impression that R&D and market-ing are two separate organizational entities and cultures. Sixth, managers must not let personality clashes and other problems remain for so long that they become institutionalized into extremes of distrust. Finally, managers must also be aware that there is such a thing as too much harmony: R&D and marketing personnel cam become too complacent with each other.

Outdated role concepts appear to be a major obstacle to achiev-ing R&D–marketing harmony. This study encountered a surprising number of organization structures, organization behaviours, orga-nizational reward systems, product strategies and new product development processes that emphasized a clear separation of roles and specialization of functions between R&D and marketing. This separation was only effective for handling simple technologies, simple markets and well-defined customer needs, i.e. the 'Domi-nant Partner Harmony' case. To develop many types of new product innovations successfully, R&D and marketing must work closely together. In some cases, they must work jointly with the customer in a trial and error fashion, trying various prototypes as a means to discovering the customer's real needs and the appropriate product. In other types of innovations, a true creative process is required in which new information and concepts are generated on the basis of the information shared between members of the R&D–marketing team. In still other cases, it is essential that the parties feel a strong sense of joint responsibility for setting new product goals and priorities, generating and selecting new product ideas, researching and analysing customer wants, setting product performance requirements, and defining the new product's performance and cost trade-offs. The customer–developer conditions (CDC) model developed as a result of this research can be used to define the appropriate roles that the R&D and marketing parties must play to succeed with various types of innovations. Once the appropriate roles are defined, eight different guidelines may be implemented to eliminate disharmonies between the R&D and marketing parties.

It appears that the institutionalized roles between R&D and marketing must be radically changed before new product development success rates can significantly increase. The only effective means to avoid disharmonies permanently is for the R&D and marketing parties fully to understand and appreciate their reciprocal roles, and to play out these roles in a true team setting. Moreover, it is essential that the R&D and marketing parties establish a team relationship that permits them flexibly to swap roles in response to evolving technologies, markets and customer needs. Unfortunately, until the dynamics of harmony/disharmony states, the CDC model's cell conditions and movements between the cells in the CDC model are more fully understood, there is no recipe for such role swapping. Each R&D–marketing team must discover what works best for them. The point is that this discovery process can only unfold when the R&D and marketing parties act like a true team.

These conclusions and recommendations are all too familiar. Many firms are not implementing the team approaches and organizational techniques that this research has once again shown to be effective. Disharmonies between R&D and marketing continue to be surprisingly prevalent, chronic and disruptive to successful new product development. These findings are discouraging, in view of the obvious importance of the topic and an emerging awareness of it.

As noted above, the lack of detailed experimental knowledge of R&D–marketing interface problems remains a barrier to their prevention. Far too little is known about what constitutes real disharmony, the distinctions between professional disagreement and disharmony, how to alter the institutionalized roles between R&D and marketing and how to implement new team approaches between R&D and marketing personnel. It is hoped that this broad-based, ex-post exploratory field study may provide a convincing basis for more advanced experimental research. Perhaps these results can serve as a basis for deriving empirically based propositions and operational hypotheses, that can then be tested through interventions and administrative experiments in real organizations. The results from these experiments should eliminate the last barrier to informed actions for reducing R&D–marketing interface problems.

## ACKNOWLEDGEMENTS

Portions of this material are based on William E. Souder (1987) *Managing New Product Innovations*, Lexington, Mass.: Lexington Books by permission. The author is indebted to two anonymous referees for numerous thoughtful comments and suggestions that substantially improved the presentation of the material in this paper.

This chapter is reprinted by permission of the publisher from 'Managing relations between R&D and marketing in new product development projects', William E. Souder, *Journal of Product Innovation Management*, Vol. 5, pp. 6–19. Copyright 1988 by Elsevier Science Inc.

## REFERENCES

Berelson, B. (1952) *Content Analysis in Communication Research*, New York: Free Press.

Crollier, D. J. (1986) *Pattern Recognition Methods for the Social Sciences and Economics*, Cambridge: Cambridge Press.

Gupta, A. K., Raj, S. P. and Wileman, D. (1985) 'The R&D–marketing interface in high-technology firms', *Journal of Product Innovation Management* 2 (March): 12–24.

Kerlinger, F. N. (1973) *Foundations of Behavioural Research*, New York: Holt, Rinehart & Winston.

Shanklin, W. L. and Ryans, J. K. (1984) *Marketing High Technology*, Lexington, Mass.: Lexington Books.

Siegel, S. (1956) *Nonparametric Statistics for the Behavioral Sciences*, New York: McGraw-Hill.

Souder, W. E. (1987a) *Managing New Product Innovations*, Lexington, Mass.: Lexington Books.

Souder, W. E. (1987b) *Technology Management Studies Institute Field Instruments Package*, Pittsburgh, Penn.: Technology Management Studies Institute, University of Pittsburgh.

Souder, W. E. et al. (1977) *An Exploratory Study of the Co-ordinating Mechanisms Between R&D and Marketing as an*

*Influence on the Innovation Process*, Final Report, National Science Foundation Grant 75–17195 to the Technology Management Studies Institute 26 August.

Souder, W. E. et al. (1983) *A Comparative Analysis of Phase Transfer Methods for Managing New Product Developments*, Final Report, National Science Foundation Grant 79–12927 to the Technology Management Studies Institute, 15 August.

Young, H. C. (1973) 'Product development setting, information exchange, and marketing–R&D coupling', unpublished PhD dissertation, Evanston, Ill.: Northwestern University.

# Index